Data-Centric Systems and Applications

Intelligent data management is the backbone of all information processing and has hence been one of the core topics in computer science from its very start. This series is intended to offer an international platform for the timely publication of all topics relevant to the development of data-centric systems and applications. All books show a strong practical or application relevance as well as a thorough scientific basis. They are therefore of particular interest to both researchers and professionals wishing to acquire detailed knowledge about concepts of which they need to make intelligent use when designing advanced solutions for their own problems.

Special emphasis is laid upon:

- Scientifically solid and detailed explanations of practically relevant concepts and techniques
  (what does it do)
- Detailed explanations of the practical relevance and importance of concepts and techniques
  (why do we need it)
- Detailed explanation of gaps between theory and practice
  (why it does not work)

According to this focus of the series, submissions of advanced textbooks or books for advanced professional use are encouraged; these should preferably be authored books or monographs, but coherently edited, multi-author books are also envisaged (e.g. for emerging topics). On the other hand, overly technical topics (like physical data access, data compression etc.), latest research results that still need validation through the research community, or mostly product-related information for practitioners ("how to use Oracle 9i efficiently") are not encouraged.

George Katsogiannis-Meimarakis ·
Anna Mitsopoulou · Mike Xydas ·
Georgia Koutrika

Natural Language Interfaces for Databases with Deep Learning

The Never-Ending Quest for Data Accessibility

Springer

George Katsogiannis-Meimarakis
Athena Research Center
Marousi, Greece

Anna Mitsopoulou
Athena Research Center
Marousi, Greece

Mike Xydas
Athena Research Center
Marousi, Greece

Georgia Koutrika
Athena Research Center
Marousi, Greece

ISSN 2197-9723 ISSN 2197-974X (electronic)
Data-Centric Systems and Applications
ISBN 978-3-032-06904-7 ISBN 978-3-032-06905-4 (eBook)
https://doi.org/10.1007/978-3-032-06905-4

This Springer imprint is published by the registered company Springer Nature Switzerland AG
The registered company address is: Gewerbestrasse 11, 6330 Cham, Switzerland

Preface

Ever since the creation of the relational model, the idea of allowing users to interact with databases through natural language has intrigued both academia and industry. This is not something unexpected if we consider two key points. The first is the value of data – at the time, but even more so today – which is detrimental for the operation of most businesses and organizations. The second is the people who want or need to use data, who are not necessarily familiar with SQL and how databases work, or might not even be comfortable with using a computer beyond basic tasks. Thus, what quickly becomes clear is the opportunity (or even responsibility) to make this valuable data accessible to an increasing amount of potential users.

As in many other research domains, the field of Natural Language Interfaces to Databases (NLIDBs) has experienced a significant transformation driven by the advent of neural networks, and more profoundly, by the rapid advancement and widespread adoption of large language models (LLMs). As a result, researchers found themselves equipped with a powerful new set of tools, rendering many longstanding challenges seemingly obsolete—or, more accurately, reframing them into a new set of complex and intriguing problems. This is also the motivation behind this book, whose start can be traced to multiple tutorials that were given by the authors between 2021 and 2023. What initially began as a tutorial on neural Text-to-SQL systems gradually expanded to encompass the broader spectrum of research areas that constitute Natural Language Interfaces to Databases (NLIDBs). This work was met with considerable enthusiasm at conferences such as SIGMOD, VLDB, and TWC, and is now, at last, formally documented.

This book covers the main research areas that bridge the world of databases and SQL with the world of natural language. Our objective was to provide comprehensive coverage of the most influential works in the field. This book is intended for both researchers and practitioners interested in Natural Language Interfaces to Databases (NLIDBs), regardless of their prior familiarity with the topic. Readers with experience in this area will benefit from a structured overview and categorization of existing systems, along with an in-depth analysis of benchmarks, persistent challenges, and open research questions. Conversely, newcomers can explore the landscape of neural NLIDBs through an accessible presentation of the relevant subfields and key advancements, without requiring any prior background knowledge.

Starting of with how natural language is translated into SQL, Chapters 2, 3, 4 focus on the Text-to-SQL problem. More specifically, an overview of the problem is given, followed by a general architecture of Text-to-SQL systems and a deeper analysis of specific systems. Additionally, the reverse process of explaining an SQL query (i.e., SQL-to-Text) is examined in Chapter 5, along with open research problems and the currently available solutions. Chapter 6 provides an overview of the multi-turn Text-to-SQL problem, outlines the underlying system architectures, and introduces key representative systems. Chapter 7 takes a broader look on the more general areas of Code Understanding and Generation that encapsulate the problems discussed in the previous chapters. Moving on, Chapters 8 and 9 focus on generating NL explanations and summaries of data (i.e., the Data-to-Text problem), offering an overview of the problem and its challenges as well as an overall system architecture and specific Data-to-Text systems. Chapter 10 dives deeper into the Results-to-Text problem that focuses on how to express the result of a query in natural language (NL) in order to present it to the user in the context of a NLIDB. Finally, Chapter 11 concludes the book by offering insights on how all the discussed research areas and systems can be brought together in order to create a NLIDB, along with risk and challenges that must be considered in the process.

Last but not least, we would like to thank our colleagues at DARE Lab and Athena Research Center for their support during, but not limited to, the writing of this book.

Athens, Greece,
July 2025

George Katsogiannis-Meimarakis
Anna Mitsopoulou
Mike Xydas
Georgia Koutrika

Contents

Acronyms

AI	Artificial Intelligence
API	Application Programming Interface
AST	Abstract Syntax Tree
BPE	Byte Pair Encoding
BST	Binary Search Tree
CoT	Chain of Thought
CRF	Conditional Random Fields
CNN	Convolutional Neural Network
DB	Database
DPO	Direct Preference Optimization
EHR	Electronic Health Record
FCNN	Fully Connected Neural Networks
GNN	Graph Neural Network
GRU	Gated Recurrent Unit
ICL	In-Context Learning
LLM	Large Language Model
LoRa	Low-Rank Adaptation
LSTM	Long Short-Term Memory
MLM	Masked Language Modeling
MLP	Multi-Layer Perceptron
NER	Named Entity Recognition
NL	Natural Language
NLIDB	Natural Language Interface to Database
NLP	Natural Language Processing
NLQ	Natural Language Question
PEFT	Parameter-efficient fine-tuning
PL	Programming Language
PLM	Pre-trained Language Model
POS	Part-of-Speech
RGT	Relation-Aware Graph Transformer
RNN	Recurrent Neural Network

SQL	Structured Query Language
SFT	Supervised Fine-tuning
UI	User Interface
UX	User Experience
VES	Valid Efficiency Score

Chapter 1
Natural Language Interfaces to Databases

Abstract Enabling users to interact with databases using natural language is a problem as old as relational databases themselves. Through the years, a lot of interest has been shown in developing such systems both from academia and industry, showing the importance of the problem. However, the rapid advancements in deep learning are bringing a new wave of research, promising to open up data for more users. This chapter introduces Natural Language Interfaces to Databases and provides a brief history of the field. Additionally, a primer of neural networks mentioned throughout the book is given, along with an overview of related research fields on answering natural language questions over different types of data.

1.1 Introduction

Edgar Frank "Ted" Codd, the father of relational databases, first proposed the relational model of data [7, 10] in 1969, revolutionizing the way data was handled and paving the road for modern database systems. Only five years later he would go on to state that "*If we are to satisfy the needs of casual users of databases, we must break the barriers that presently prevent these users from freely employing their native language*" [8]. And thus, another research field was born, aiming to make databases accessible to the casual user, without the need for complex query languages or technical knowledge. Throughout the 1970s, he worked on a prototype of a natural language question and answer application that would sit on top of a relational database system, called Rendezvous. Rendezvous allowed a user with no knowledge of database systems — and even limited knowledge of a given database's content — to engage in a dialog with the system. More than 50 years later, natural language interfaces for databases (NLIDBs) are into the spotlight, this time in a new light, thanks to the rapid developments in deep learning.

Since the 70s, there was already an evident interest in developing NLIDBs, both from the industry and the academic sector. Systems such as *LUNAR* [33], CHAT-80 [32], Symantec's *Q&A* [11], and Microsoft's *English Query* [3] are only a few

G. Katsogiannis-Meimarakis et al., *Natural Language Interfaces for Databases with Deep Learning*, Data-Centric Systems and Applications,
https://doi.org/10.1007/978-3-032-06905-4_1

examples of the interest and commercial potential of NLIDBs at the time. Although these systems were relatively limited due to the state of the art in natural language understanding and processing at the time, the capabilities they would offer were already quite impressive. Users could pose questions in (almost) unrestricted natural language, the system would attempt to map the question to a logical form to retrieve the solicited data, and some would even ask for clarifications and offer alternatives for questions they couldn't understand.

The advancements in Deep Learning, Natural Language Processing (NLP), and eventually the widespread use of Transformers [28] brought a new era of rapid progress in NL Understanding and Generation. Combined with the increased needs for data access and exploration, recent years have witnessed a surge of work on NLIDBs that enable users to search and explore data using natural language. This is also evident in the research and commercial progress of NLIDBs. Multiple commercial databases are integrating Large Language Models (LLMs) to enable users to ask questions in NL such as IBM integrating IBM Watson in DB2 and Microsoft adding a "Q&A" feature to Power BI. This is also coupled with multiple scientific advancements through a large amount of published work that will be covered in this book.

The rest of this chapter contains a brief neural primer and an overview of research areas related to this book but not explicitly discussed in it. The former aims to provide an overview of the main building block of neural networks. Its purpose is to provide unfamiliar readers with the main ideas behind basic neural architectures, without going into technical details. The latter presents related research fields that also aim to help users obtain value from data through natural language. These areas focus on different data formats besides the relational model and might be of interest to readers of this book.

1.2 Neural Primer

The following section provides a brief primer on the main neural modules commonly used in the Deep Learning systems discussed throughout this book. It covers Fully Connected Neural Networks (FCNNs), Recurrent Neural Networks (RNNs), Convolutional Neural Networks (CNNs), and Transformers. However, it is important to note that (a) this list is not exhaustive and (b) the explanations are intended to convey a high-level intuition of how each module functions and is applied, rather than a detailed technical analysis.

1.2.1 Fully Connected Neural Networks (FCNNs)

A fully connected neural network (FCNN), also known as a dense neural network, is a type of artificial neural network where each neuron in one layer is connected to every neuron in the adjacent layers. This architecture was inspired by early attempts to mimic how biological neurons in the human brain communicate and process information.

In an FCNN, each neuron receives an input, either directly from the input data (for the first layer) or from the previous layer's outputs, applies a linear transformation using trainable parameters (weights and biases), and then passes the result through a non-linear activation function. This combination of linear transformation and non-linearity allows the network to model complex relationships in data. The parameters of the network are initially randomized and then optimized through training. Using a dataset with known inputs and outputs, a loss function measures the error between the model's predictions and the true values. Through backpropagation, the network adjusts its parameters to minimize this loss, gradually improving its performance over repeated iterations on the training data.

Theoretically, an FCNN can act as a universal function approximator [15], meaning that a network with a single hidden layer, sufficient neurons, and an appropriate activation function can approximate any continuous function to arbitrary precision. In practice, however, FCNNs face two significant limitations. First, they are prone to overfitting, where the model memorizes training data rather than learning how to generalize to unseen data. Second, due to every neuron being connected to all neurons in the previous layer, the number of trainable parameters grows rapidly as network size increases, leading to scalability challenges. To address these issues, more specialized neural architectures, such as RNNs, CNNs, and transformers, have been developed, as presented in the following sections.

1.2.2 Recurrent Neural Networks (RNNs)

RNNs are a type of neural network specifically designed to process sequential data, where the order of elements carries significant meaning. Such data includes text, speech, and various forms of time series. The key feature of RNNs is their ability to maintain a form of "memory" as they process inputs sequentially (e.g., token by token in the case of text) allowing them to capture contextual dependencies over the sequence.

The core idea behind RNNs is that, in sequential data, earlier inputs can influence the interpretation of later ones. For example, in the query *"Which car is the most expensive and what is its top speed?"*, when the model encounters the token *"its"*, it needs to recall that *"car"* was previously mentioned, so that *"its"* can be correctly linked back to it. RNNs achieve this by feeding the hidden state (the memory) from the previous step back into the network as part of the input at the next step, forming a loop that allows information to persist across the sequence.

Two wiidely used RNN variants are Long Short-Term Memory networks (LSTMs) [14] and Gated Recurrent Units (GRUs) [6]. LSTMs introduce three specialized gates: the *forget* gate, which removes irrelevant information from memory; the *input* gate, which adds new relevant information; and the *output* gate, which determines how the current memory state contributes to the next output. GRUs simplify this architecture by using only two gates, the *update* gate, which controls how much new information to incorporate, and the *reset* gate, which controls how much of the previous memory to retain. This simplification makes GRUs more computationally efficient while still retaining strong performance on many sequential tasks.

RNNs were considered the go-to solution for NLP tasks due to their ability to handle text sequences. However the introduction of the Transformer architecture in 2017 quickly changed this status, as we will also observe in multiple tasks discussed in this book.

1.2.3 Convolutional Neural Networks (CNNs)

Convolutional Neural Networks (CNNs) [20] are a class of neural networks primarily used in computer vision tasks, such as object recognition and image classification. They are called convolutional because they apply convolution operations, which act like sliding window functions, across a matrix of pixel values representing an image. These sliding windows, typically small grids such as 3×3 filters, scan over the image, extracting local features and producing numerical representations that describe the content within each window.

Multiple convolutional layers are typically stacked in a CNN. The early layers tend to capture low-level patterns such as edges, curves, and textures, while deeper layers abstract higher-level features like shapes or even complex objects (e.g., detecting *"has human eyes"*). This hierarchical feature extraction is inspired by the human visual cortex, which processes visual information in a similarly layered fashion.

Although CNNs are traditionally associated with image data, they can also be applied to textual inputs. In the context of NLIDBs, where the inputs are sequences of words rather than pixels, convolution operations can be used over token sequences instead. In this case, the sliding window moves across the text, extracting local n-gram patterns that help in modeling relationships between neighboring words, making CNNs useful for tasks such as text classification or sequence encoding.

Like RNNs, while CNNs are efficient in capturing short-range dependencies between words, they are not able to capture long-range dependencies, like the transformer architecture does introduced below.

1.2.4 Transformers

The introduction of the transformer architecture [28] marked a significant breakthrough in natural language processing, enabling efficient processing of sequential data and paving the way for powerful language models. A transformer is a Sequence-to-Sequence model. It takes an input sequence, typically a sequence of words or subword tokens in NLP, and generates a corresponding output sequence.

The core innovation of the transformer lies in its integrated attention mechanism. This mechanism allows every token in the input and output to attend to all other tokens simultaneously, regardless of their position in the sequence. As a result, transformers can effectively capture long-range dependencies without the sequential bottleneck of RNNs, which struggled with maintaining context over long distances.

The architecture itself consists of two primary components: the encoder and the decoder. The encoder processes the input sequence and produces a contextualized representation in the form of a matrix. The decoder then takes this encoded representation and generates the output sequence iteratively, one token at a time. Variations of the basic transformer architecture have been introduced, including encoder-only models such as BERT [9], and decoder-only models such as those in the GPT family [25].

Transformers form the foundation of modern Large Language Models (LLMs) and their earlier siblings Pre-trained Language Models (PLMs). These models are pre-trained on vast amounts of text from diverse sources, including web content, books, and other corpora. This pre-training equips PLMs and LLMs with a general understanding of how language works and allows them to excel in multiple NLP tasks. Following pre-training, they are often fine-tuned using simple Supervised Fine-tuning (SFT) or Reinforcement Learning from Human Feedback (RLHF) [22], a process where human evaluators assess model outputs, guiding the model to align its responses with human preferences and communicative goals. This alignment step is crucial for producing helpful, coherent, and safe outputs in real-world applications.

There is no formal distinction between PLMs and LLMs; what usually sets them apart is their size and the fact that LLMs can often be used without task-specific fine-tuning. More specifically, the number of parameters in PLMs is usually in the magnitude of hundreds of millions, while LLMs can have multiple billions of parameters. In this book we use the above criteria to differentiate PLMs and LLMs, although they are sometimes used interchangeably in the literature.

1.3 NL Interfaces over Different Data Types

While this book focuses primarily on relational databases, it is important to mention that there are other data types over which similar work has been done. Even though these works might not be as in-depth or as focused towards creating complete NL interfaces, they are also important given that useful data is not always found in a relational format.

1.3.1 Question Answering over Knowledge Graphs

Knowledge Graphs (KGs) a valuable source of information and can be very useful in specific use cases. However, querying KGs also requires technical knowledge and the use of querying languages such as SPARQL or Cypher. For this reason, there is interest in developing mechanisms that allow users to query KGs using NL.

On the one hand, there are systems that take advantage of the structure of the NL and attempt to map it to the KG using templates and grap matching. Some works [38] attempt to create a structural representation of the user's Natural Language Question (NLQ). This representation of the NLQ can then be matched with a sub-graph of the KG, thus reducing the problem into a sub-graph matching problem. Another approach [26, 27, 37] is based on query templates. In this case the NLQ is syntactically and semantically analyzed in order to extract entities that correspond to entities in the graph. These entities are then used to populate the slots of the query sketch, leading to the final query. A similar approach [34] is also based on mapping phrases and entities appearing in the NLQ to entities from the graph's ontology. However instead of using templates, it focuses on generating triplets using the extracted entities. These triplets can then be used as triple patterns in SPARQL queries.

On the other hand, there are systems [1, 2, 24] that rely on deep learning and leverage their power to translate NLQs to graph query languages. These approaches focus on either using specific architectures that allow the network to extract useful parts of the KG and use them in the generated query, or on using LLMs. Even when using LLMs, these works also focus on providing the most relevant parts of the KG to the model or finding similar examples that are related to the question at hand. What becomes clear in both cases is that the network needs information on how the graph is structured as well as examples about the subgraph related to the question.

1.3.2 Question Answering over Text and Tables

Answering NLQs based on unstructured data, such as text, and web tables are scientific fields that have also seen a lot of research efforts. These areas are usually referred to as Question Answering [23, 35] if the underlying data is text, Table Question Answering [18] if the used data are tables, and Hybrid Question Answering [29] if the data is a combination of text and tables. These research fields are also often combined with document and table retrieval, because a user will usually only ask a limited number of questions over a single (small) piece of data. For this reason it is more useful to be able to first identify relevant sources from a larger data corpus and then use them to answer it.

A first set of works focuses on retrieving relevant text passages or documents for a given question, and using them to answer it. To retrieve the needed text from a large corpus of texts, recent works usually rely on creating an index over the corpus using either sparse vectors such as TF-IDF [4] and BM25 [17], or dense vectors that can be generated from a trained model [16, 19, 21]. The NLQ from the user is then encoded into a query vector using a similar technique to how the index was created and it is queried for its nearest neighbors in the index.

Moving on to answering the question, there are two major categories: (i) extractive question answering which aims at extracting the answer from the given texts, and (ii) generative question answering which aims at generating a new piece of text that is the answer. While the answer might already exist in the retrieved texts, it is also possible that some reasoning or synthesis might be required, which means that it is not possible to simply extract the answer. For this reason, more recent approaches follow the second option. While some earlier works [4] used recurrent neural networks, later approaches [16, 17, 19, 21] rely on LLMs to process the question and retrieved texts and autoregressively generate the answer. Another interesting approach is training both stages (i.e., the retriever and the generator) jointly [21], which has shown increased performance.

A second set of works focuses on retrieving relevant tables for a given question, and using them to answer it. A difference to the previous works is that in this case the query and the retrieved items have heterogeneous formats (i.e., they are not both pieces of text). While it would be possible to consider every cell, column, or row of a table as an individual document and create an index similarly to before, this could lead to the loss of important structural information. For this reason, finding an effective table representation is not trivial. To tackle this, different approaches have been proposed such as table-specific encoders [13] that are trained to capture the peculiarities of tables, or creating a graph representation of the table and either processing it with a graph network [30] or performing walks to generate richer text documents [31].

Another challenge that arises due to the format differences between text and table is how to generate meaningful comparison scores between the representation of the query text and the table. To achieve this the retriever must be trained to provide high scores for relevant tables and low scores for tables that are not useful for answering a given question. This can be handled by using manually created data to train a relevance objective [5, 12, 30, 36], but this might lead to a loss in performance when applying the model to new data from a different domain. To tackle this, another approach [31] proposes to generate synthetic training data so that the model can be automatically re-trained when it needs to be applied on a new set of tables.

References

1. Caio Viktor S. Avila, Vânia M.P. Vidal, Wellington Franco, and Marco A. Casanova. Experiments with text-to-sparql based on chatgpt. In *2024 IEEE 18th International Conference on Semantic Computing (ICSC)*, pages 277–284, 2024.
2. Debayan Banerjee, Pranav Ajit Nair, Jivat Neet Kaur, Ricardo Usbeck, and Chris Biemann. Modern baselines for sparql semantic parsing. In *Proceedings of the 45th International ACM SIGIR Conference on Research and Development in Information Retrieval*, SIGIR '22, page 2260–2265, New York, NY, USA, 2022. Association for Computing Machinery.
3. Adam Blum. Microsoft english query 7.5: Automatic extraction of semantics from relational databases and olap cubes. In *Proceedings of the 25th International Conference on Very Large Data Bases*, VLDB '99, page 247–248, San Francisco, CA, USA, 1999. Morgan Kaufmann Publishers Inc.

4. Danqi Chen, Adam Fisch, Jason Weston, and Antoine Bordes. Reading Wikipedia to answer open-domain questions. In Regina Barzilay and Min-Yen Kan, editors, *Proceedings of the 55th Annual Meeting of the Association for Computational Linguistics (Volume 1: Long Papers)*, pages 1870–1879, Vancouver, Canada, July 2017. Association for Computational Linguistics.
5. Zhiyu Chen, Mohamed Trabelsi, Jeff Heflin, Yinan Xu, and Brian D. Davison. Table search using a deep contextualized language model. In *Proceedings of the 43rd International ACM SIGIR Conference on Research and Development in Information Retrieval*, SIGIR '20, page 589–598, New York, NY, USA, 2020. Association for Computing Machinery.
6. Junyoung Chung, Caglar Gulcehre, KyungHyun Cho, and Yoshua Bengio. Empirical evaluation of gated recurrent neural networks on sequence modeling. *arXiv preprint arXiv:1412.3555*, 2014.
7. E. F. Codd. A relational model of data for large shared data banks. *Commun. ACM*, 13(6):377–387, June 1970.
8. E. F. Codd. Seven steps to rendezvous with the casual user. In J. W. Klimbie and K. L. Koffeman, editors, *Data Base Management, Proceeding of the IFIP Working Conference Data Base Management, Cargèse, Corsica, France, April 1-5, 1974*, pages 179–200. North-Holland, January 1974.
9. Jacob Devlin, Ming-Wei Chang, Kenton Lee, and Kristina Toutanova. BERT: Pre-training of deep bidirectional transformers for language understanding, 2019.
10. E. F. E, F. Codd. Derivability, redundancy and consistency of relations stored in large data banks. *SIGMOD Rec.*, 38(1):17–36, June 2009.
11. Gary G Hendrix. Q&a: already a success? In *Coling 1986 Volume 1: The 11th International Conference on Computational Linguistics*, 1986.
12. Jonathan Herzig, Thomas Müller, Syrine Krichene, and Julian Eisenschlos. Open domain question answering over tables via dense retrieval. In Kristina Toutanova, Anna Rumshisky, Luke Zettlemoyer, Dilek Hakkani-Tur, Iz Beltagy, Steven Bethard, Ryan Cotterell, Tanmoy Chakraborty, and Yichao Zhou, editors, *Proceedings of the 2021 Conference of the North American Chapter of the Association for Computational Linguistics: Human Language Technologies*, pages 512–519, Online, June 2021. Association for Computational Linguistics.
13. Jonathan Herzig, Pawel Krzysztof Nowak, Thomas Müller, Francesco Piccinno, and Julian Eisenschlos. TaPas: Weakly supervised table parsing via pre-training. In Dan Jurafsky, Joyce Chai, Natalie Schluter, and Joel Tetreault, editors, *Proceedings of the 58th Annual Meeting of the Association for Computational Linguistics*, pages 4320–4333, Online, July 2020. Association for Computational Linguistics.
14. Sepp Hochreiter and Jürgen Schmidhuber. Long short-term memory. *Neural Comput.*, 9(8):1735–1780, November 1997.
15. Kurt Hornik, Maxwell Stinchcombe, and Halbert White. Multilayer feedforward networks are universal approximators. *Neural networks*, 2(5):359–366, 1989.
16. Gautier Izacard, Mathilde Caron, Lucas Hosseini, Sebastian Riedel, Piotr Bojanowski, Armand Joulin, and Edouard Grave. Unsupervised dense information retrieval with contrastive learning, 2022.
17. Gautier Izacard and Edouard Grave. Leveraging passage retrieval with generative models for open domain question answering. In Paola Merlo, Jorg Tiedemann, and Reut Tsarfaty, editors, *Proceedings of the 16th Conference of the European Chapter of the Association for Computational Linguistics: Main Volume*, pages 874–880, Online, April 2021. Association for Computational Linguistics.
18. Nengzheng Jin, Joanna Siebert, Dongfang Li, and Qingcai Chen. A survey on table question answering: Recent advances, 2022.
19. Vladimir Karpukhin, Barlas Oguz, Sewon Min, Patrick Lewis, Ledell Wu, Sergey Edunov, Danqi Chen, and Wen-tau Yih. Dense passage retrieval for open-domain question answering. In Bonnie Webber, Trevor Cohn, Yulan He, and Yang Liu, editors, *Proceedings of the 2020 Conference on Empirical Methods in Natural Language Processing (EMNLP)*, pages 6769–6781, Online, November 2020. Association for Computational Linguistics.
20. Alex Krizhevsky, Ilya Sutskever, and Geoffrey E Hinton. Imagenet classification with deep convolutional neural networks. *Advances in neural information processing systems*, 25, 2012.

21. Patrick Lewis, Ethan Perez, Aleksandra Piktus, Fabio Petroni, Vladimir Karpukhin, Naman Goyal, Heinrich Küttler, Mike Lewis, Wen-tau Yih, Tim Rocktäschel, Sebastian Riedel, and Douwe Kiela. Retrieval-augmented generation for knowledge-intensive nlp tasks. In *Proceedings of the 34th International Conference on Neural Information Processing Systems*, NIPS '20, Red Hook, NY, USA, 2020. Curran Associates Inc.
22. Long Ouyang, Jeffrey Wu, Xu Jiang, Diogo Almeida, Carroll Wainwright, Pamela Mishkin, Chong Zhang, Sandhini Agarwal, Katarina Slama, Alex Ray, et al. Training language models to follow instructions with human feedback. *Advances in neural information processing systems*, 35:27730–27744, 2022.
23. Hariom A. Pandya and Brijesh S. Bhatt. Question answering survey: Directions, challenges, datasets, evaluation matrices, 2021.
24. Dmitrii Pliukhin, Daniil Radyush, Liubov Kovriguina, and Dmitry Mouromtsev. Improving subgraph extraction algorihtms for one-shot sparql query generation with large language models. In *QALD/SemREC@ ISWC*, 2023.
25. Alec Radford. Improving language understanding by generative pre-training. 2018.
26. Nhuan D. To and Marek Reformat. Question-answering system with linguistic terms over rdf knowledge graphs. In *2020 IEEE International Conference on Systems, Man, and Cybernetics (SMC)*, pages 4236–4243, 2020.
27. Christina Unger, Lorenz Bühmann, Jens Lehmann, Axel-Cyrille Ngonga Ngomo, Daniel Gerber, and Philipp Cimiano. Template-based question answering over rdf data. In *Proceedings of the 21st International Conference on World Wide Web*, WWW '12, page 639–648, New York, NY, USA, 2012. Association for Computing Machinery.
28. Ashish Vaswani, Noam Shazeer, Niki Parmar, Jakob Uszkoreit, Llion Jones, Aidan N Gomez, L ukasz Kaiser, and Illia Polosukhin. Attention is all you need. In I. Guyon, U. Von Luxburg, S. Bengio, H. Wallach, R. Fergus, S. Vishwanathan, and R. Garnett, editors, *Advances in Neural Information Processing Systems*, volume 30. Curran Associates, Inc., 2017.
29. Dingzirui Wang, Longxu Dou, and Wanxiang Che. A survey on table-and-text hybridqa: Concepts, methods, challenges and future directions, 2023.
30. Fei Wang, Kexuan Sun, Muhao Chen, Jay Pujara, and Pedro Szekely. Retrieving complex tables with multi-granular graph representation learning. In *Proceedings of the 44th International ACM SIGIR Conference on Research and Development in Information Retrieval*, SIGIR '21, page 1472–1482, New York, NY, USA, 2021. Association for Computing Machinery.
31. Qiming Wang and Raul Castro Fernandez. Solo: Data discovery using natural language questions via a self-supervised approach. *Proc. ACM Manag. Data*, 1(4), dec 2023.
32. David H. D. Warren and Fernando C. N. Pereira. An efficient easily adaptable system for interpreting natural language queries. *Am. J. Comput. Linguistics*, 8(3-4):110–122, 1982.
33. William A. Woods. Procedural semantics for a question-answering machine. In *Proceedings of the AFIPS '68 Fall Joint Computer Conference, December 9-11, 1968, San Francisco, California, USA - Part I*, volume 33, pages 457–471, 1968.
34. Mohamed Yahya, Klaus Berberich, Shady Elbassuoni, Maya Ramanath, Volker Tresp, and Gerhard Weikum. Natural language questions for the web of data. In *Conference on Empirical Methods in Natural Language Processing*, 2012.
35. Qin Zhang, Shangsi Chen, Dongkuan Xu, Qingqing Cao, Xiaojun Chen, Trevor Cohn, and Meng Fang. A survey for efficient open domain question answering. In Anna Rogers, Jordan Boyd-Graber, and Naoaki Okazaki, editors, *Proceedings of the 61st Annual Meeting of the Association for Computational Linguistics (Volume 1: Long Papers)*, pages 14447–14465, Toronto, Canada, July 2023. Association for Computational Linguistics.
36. Shuo Zhang and Krisztian Balog. Ad hoc table retrieval using semantic similarity. In *Proceedings of the 2018 World Wide Web Conference*, WWW '18, page 1553–1562, Republic and Canton of Geneva, CHE, 2018. International World Wide Web Conferences Steering Committee.
37. Weiguo Zheng, Lei Zou, Xiang Lian, Jeffrey Xu Yu, Shaoxu Song, and Dongyan Zhao. How to build templates for rdf question/answering: An uncertain graph similarity join approach. In *Proceedings of the 2015 ACM SIGMOD International Conference on Management of Data*,

SIGMOD '15, page 1809–1824, New York, NY, USA, 2015. Association for Computing Machinery.
38. Lei Zou, Ruizhe Huang, Haixun Wang, Jeffrey Xu Yu, Wenqiang He, and Dongyan Zhao. Natural language question answering over rdf: a graph data driven approach. In *Proceedings of the 2014 ACM SIGMOD International Conference on Management of Data*, SIGMOD '14, page 313–324, New York, NY, USA, 2014. Association for Computing Machinery.

Chapter 2
Translating Natural Language Questions to SQL

Abstract Enabling users to query databases with natural language has been an active research area for many decades. This chapter presents the problem of translating natural language questions to SQL and the challenges it poses. It presents an overview of early efforts that did not rely on neural networks, their architecture, and the main techniques that they relied on. Finally, it focuses on setting the scene for the era of neural Text-to-SQL systems that has gathered significant research attention. To achieve this, an in-depth analysis of available datasets is presented, highlighting the main categories of datasets and analyzing the most important ones. Additionally, the metrics that are used to evaluate neural Text-to-SQL systems are presented, explaining the importance and the weaknesses of modern evaluation strategies.

2.1 Introduction

Data is integral to a wide array of tasks, from business operations and medical research to our daily activities. Data is typically stored in relational databases and can be accessed via programmatic interfaces like SQL or through graphical interfaces. However, programmatic interfaces are often cumbersome for anyone other than programmers and data scientists, as they require expertise in SQL and familiarity with the underlying database schema. Conversely, graphical interfaces simplify these complexities but often limit the ability to freely query and explore the data. These limitations present challenges for users such as business analysts, marketers, sales teams, and scientists who work with data.

The initial efforts to develop systems that allow users to query databases using natural language began in the 1960s. These early systems were designed for application-specific, non-SQL databases and were not adaptable to different data. Over the years, various approaches have emerged, focusing on translating natural language questions into SQL queries for relational databases. The advancement of deep learning techniques, and in particular Large Language Models (LLMs) later on, has given a great boost to the development of Natural Language Interfaces for

G. Katsogiannis-Meimarakis et al., *Natural Language Interfaces for Databases with Deep Learning*, Data-Centric Systems and Applications,
https://doi.org/10.1007/978-3-032-06905-4_2

Databases (NLIDBs). The term *Text-to-SQL* (or NL-to-SQL) has gained popularity to describe systems that specialize in translating natural language questions into SQL queries. This area falls under the wider research problems of Text-to-Query, where the goal is to translate NL into various query languages (e.g., SPARQL) and semantic parsing, where the goal is to translate Natural Language (NL) into a formal language (e.g., first order logic).

This chapter delves into the Text-to-SQL problem, examining its inherent challenges. It offers a comprehensive overview of earlier works that did not employ neural approaches. Additionally, it recasts the Text-to-SQL problem to a neural translation one and introduces benchmarks used for training and evaluating Text-to-SQL systems, along with the relevant evaluation metrics.

2.2 The Text-to-SQL Problem

A natural language question (NLQ) can be articulated in various forms. It may be expressed as a complete and fluent sentence, such as "*What movies has Spielberg directed since 2012?*" Alternatively, it can be conveyed through a few succinct keywords, such as "*Italian Food in Vienna.*" Both forms aim to retrieve specific information from a database, but they differ in their level of detail and structure.

Given a NLQ posed against a relational database with a defined schema, the objective of the Text-to-SQL problem is twofold: (a) to construct a SQL query that accurately captures the intent and meaning of the NLQ, and (b) to ensure that the generated SQL query is syntactically and semantically valid within the context of the specific database schema. To achieve objective (a), numerous challenges arise from understanding the input NLQ. These include interpreting the user's intent, resolving ambiguities, and mapping natural language expressions to database concepts. For objective (b), constructing a SQL query that is both syntactically and semantically correct involves overcoming obstacles related to SQL syntax and the intricacies of the underlying database schema. This includes ensuring the query adheres to the schema structure and constraints.

Early systems constrained their input to keyword queries to simplify understanding free-form natural language. However, this approach limited the expressiveness and flexibility of the queries, highlighting the need for more sophisticated solutions.

2.2.1 NL Challenges

Understanding natural language poses several challenges for systems, primarily due to the complexity and variability of human language. Here are some key challenges:

Ambiguity. Natural language is inherently ambiguous, allowing expressions to be open to multiple interpretations. There are several types of ambiguity [2, 42]. We describe the most common ones below.

Lexical ambiguity (or *polysemy*) occurs when a single word has multiple meanings. For example, "*Paris*" can refer to a city or a person.

Syntactic ambiguity arises when a sentence can be interpreted in different ways based on its syntactic structure. For example, the question *"Find all German movie directors"* can be parsed into *"directors that have directed German movies"* or *"directors from Germany that have directed a movie"*.

On the other hand, *semantic ambiguity* refers to a sentence with multiple semantic interpretations. For instance, *"Are Brad and Angelina married?"* may mean they are married to each other or separately.

As a result of ambiguity, a natural language question can yield multiple potential interpretations. Identifying the correct interpretation(s) can be challenging for the system and may impact its overall effectiveness. The system must not only discern the intended meaning but also efficiently generate and process various query interpretations. This requires sophisticated algorithms capable of handling the nuances of language, ensuring that the system remains both accurate and responsive.

Paraphrasing. In the simpler case, paraphrasing involves *synonymy* where multiple words have the same meaning (e.g. *"movies"* and *"films"*). More broadly, two sentences can convey the exact same meaning but be expressed in different ways. For instance, *"How many people live in Athens?"* vs. *"What is the population of Athens?"*. Paraphrasing presents a significant challenge because equivalent questions may require different handling to construct the correct SQL query. In the example above, the second natural language question (NLQ) might be easier to process if a "*population*" attribute exists in the database schema, allowing the system to infer the user intent with high confidence. However, the system must be adept at recognizing and handling various paraphrased expressions to ensure accurate query generation.

Context Sensitivity. It refers to a term having different meanings depending on the query context, the data domain, and the user goals. For example, based on the domain, the meaning of the term *"top"* may differ. For the query *"Return the top movie"* on a movie database, *"top"* may mean based on the number of ratings collected. On the other hand, for the query *"Return the top scorer"* on a football database, *"top"* may refer to the number of goals scored. Moreover, *"top"* may have different interpretations over the same data for different users. For example, for a business analyst, the query *"Return the top products"* should return the most profitable products, whereas for a consumer it should return the top-rated products.

Domain-Specific Knowledge. Different fields, such as medicine, finance, law, and technology, use specialized vocabulary and concepts unique to their domain. For instance, medical terminology includes words like "hypertension" and "tachycardia," while legal language might involve terms like "tort" and "jurisprudence." A system must be capable of adapting to these various domains to accurately understand and process language. This requires the system to have access to domain-specific knowledge bases and the ability to learn and recognize the specialized terms and concepts used within each field. Without this adaptability, the system may misinterpret queries or fail to provide relevant responses.

Inference. A natural language sentence may not contain all information needed for a system to fully understand it. In *elliptical queries*, one or more words are omitted but can still be understood in the context of the sentence. An example is *"Who was the president before Obama"*. The fact that the query refers to US presidents needs to be inferred. In *follow-up questions*, which are common in conversations between humans, missing information can be understood in the context of the dialog. We ask a question, receive an answer, and then ask a follow-up question assuming that the context of the first question is known. For example, *"Q: Which is the capital of Germany?"*, *"A: Berlin"*, *"Q: What about France?"*. The system has to infer that the user is asking for the capital of France.

Incomplete or Unstructured Input. Natural language input can often be incomplete, unstructured, or contain errors. For example, a user might input a query with missing information, such as "*population of Athens*" instead of "*What is the population of Athens?*" Alternatively, the input might be unstructured, like a stream of consciousness or a list of keywords without clear connections. Additionally, errors such as typos, grammatical mistakes, or incorrect word usage can further complicate the input. A robust system must be able to infer missing information, correct mistakes, and make sense of unstructured input to generate accurate and meaningful responses. It must also be able to determine when a NLQ does not map to a query over the underlying data. For example, if the user asks "*what is the weather today?*" over a database of products, the system should not try to generate a SQL query.

2.2.2 SQL Challenges

Even if a system could perfectly understand a NLQ, additional challenges stem from the nature of *SQL* and the *schema of the data*.

SQL syntax. SQL, developed by IBM, was designed as a human-friendly way to query relational data. However, SQL is a structured language with a strict grammar, which limits its expressivity compared to natural language or other programming languages. For instance, SQL lacks constructs for iteration and recursion, among other features. There are queries that are straightforward to express in natural language but become complex and less intuitive when translated into SQL. For example, the query "*Return the movie with the best rating*" might map to a nested SQL query, which may be more difficult for the system to automatically derive.

Natural language is inherently more expressive than single SQL queries. There are computationally reasonable queries that can be articulated in natural language but cannot be answered by a single SQL query. Additionally, while a sentence in natural language may contain errors and still be understood by a human, a SQL query must be syntactically correct to execute. This strict requirement for syntactical accuracy adds another layer of complexity for systems translating NLQs into SQL.

Database Schema. A SQL query must be semantically correct, meaning it should accurately reference the tables and columns in the underlying database. However, the user's conceptual model of the data – comprising entities, their attributes, and relationships – may not align with the database schema, presenting several challenges.

The *vocabulary gap* refers to the differences between the user vocabulary and the database vocabulary. For example, in the query *"Who was the best artist in 2011?"*, *"artist"* should map to the *Singer.name* attribute in the database. Users often use terms that are intuitive to them but may not directly correspond to the database schema, requiring the system to bridge this gap by understanding and mapping user terminology to the appropriate database elements.

Schema ambiguity occurs when a part of a query can map to multiple elements within the database schema. This ambiguity arises because the same term or phrase can be used in different contexts within the database. For example, *"model"* could refer to *car.model* or *engine.model*. Resolving schema ambiguity requires the system to understand the context in which the term is used and to disambiguate between the possible mappings. This often involves analyzing the surrounding words and phrases in the query, as well as considering the relationships and constraints defined in the database schema. For instance, if the query is "*Find the model of the car with the highest horsepower*", the system should infer that *"model"* refers to *car.model* rather than *engine.model* based on the context provided by *"car"* and *"horsepower"*.

Addressing the vocabulary gap and schema ambiguity is crucial for generating accurate SQL queries, as incorrect mappings can lead to erroneous or failed queries.

Entity modelling involves the problem where a set of entities may be represented differently in the database. As one instance, a question like *"Who is the director of "Beautiful Mind""* may hide implicit join operations due to database normalization. Moreover, similar NLQs may necessitate different processing depending on the database schema. For example, in a university database, every person is either a Student or a Faculty member, represented as two separate relations. Conversely, movies have multiple genres that cannot be stored as different tables. They are stored in a *Genre* relation and are connected with movies through a many-to-many relationship. As a result, similar queries, such as *"comedies released in 2018"* and *"students enrolled in 2018"* are handled differently. In the former case, the system maps *"comedies"* to a value in the *Genre* table and joins it with the *Movie* table whereas it just maps *"students"* to the *Student* relation in the latter case.

2.3 Early Non-Neural Approaches

Prototype NLIDBs appeared in the late sixties and early seventies [8, 53]. Some of these early systems relied on *pattern-matching* techniques to match user questions to actions the system would perform to answer the question (e.g., [28]).

Syntax-based systems used a grammar that described the possible syntactic structures of the user questions. A user question would be first parsed (i.e. analyzed syntactically). The resulting parse tree would be directly mapped to a query in some database query language. To perform this mapping, the system would use specific mapping rules that specified how each part of the tree would map to a part of the database query. These syntax-based NLIDBs usually interfaced to application-specific database systems that provided database query languages carefully designed to facilitate the mapping from the parse tree to the database query. For example, Lunar [58] was a natural language interface to a database with chemical analyses of moon rocks. At this stage, it was usually difficult to devise mapping rules to transform directly the parse tree into some expression in a database query language (e.g., SQL) [3].

Semantic-grammar systems (e.g., LADDER [23], EUFID [53]) also parsed the input and mapped the parse tree to a database query. However, the grammar categories (i.e., the non-leaf nodes that will appear in the parse tree) corresponded to semantic concepts (e.g., *Substance*, *Radiation*, or *Specimen*) instead of syntactic constituents (e.g., noun-phrase, noun, sentence). Semantic grammars contained hard-wired knowledge about a specific knowledge domain, and semantic grammar categories were usually chosen to enforce semantic constraints. Due to their domain-specific nature, these systems were difficult to port to other knowledge domains.

In early systems, the syntax and semantics rules were often based on rather ad hoc ideas and expressed in idiosyncratic formalisms. However, in the 1990s, systems began to adopt a more structured representation-based approach and integrate advances from the broader field of natural language processing. This shift allowed for improved syntactic and semantic parsing and interpretation.

These advanced systems would first transform the natural language question into an *intermediate logical query*. This logical query reflects the meaning of the user's question in terms of high-level world concepts, which are independent of the database structure. By abstracting the query in this way, the system could more accurately represent the user intent. The intermediate logical query would then be translated into an expression in the database query language. Examples of such systems include CLE [1] and TEAM [18]) as well as commercial ones including IBM's LanguageAccess [43] and Intellect [21] from Trinzic, reflecting the growing interest and investment in NLIDBs.

2.4 Text-to-SQL as a Database Mapping Problem

Database approaches view the Text-to-SQL problem as a *database mapping problem*, where the goal is to map query terms to database elements such as tables, columns, and values, and to identify the interconnections among these data elements that accurately capture the user intent. A query interpretation is a subgraph of the database schema graph that connects the relations containing the query terms through edges that represent the primary key-foreign key relationships between these relations. This subgraph aims to effectively capture the structure of the SQL query, ensuring that all query terms are correctly mapped to the corresponding database elements and that the relationships between these elements are accurately captured.

The concept of generating query interpretations as *subgraphs of the database schema graph* (also known as joining networks or trees), was introduced by Discover [25] and adopted by other systems, including DiscoverIR [24], Spark [39] and

SODA [5], since it provided a structured approach for generating SQL queries that are syntactically and semantically correct.

Précis [31, 51] provided a different approach to query interpretation, by extending the concept of joining networks and introducing the idea of a *logical database subset*. This logical database subset includes not only items directly related to the given query keywords but also items implicitly related to them. The goal is to provide users with a more comprehensive understanding of the data.

2.4.1 System Architecture

Systems that address Text-to-SQL as a database mapping problem adopt the general architecture shown in Figure 2.1 [17].

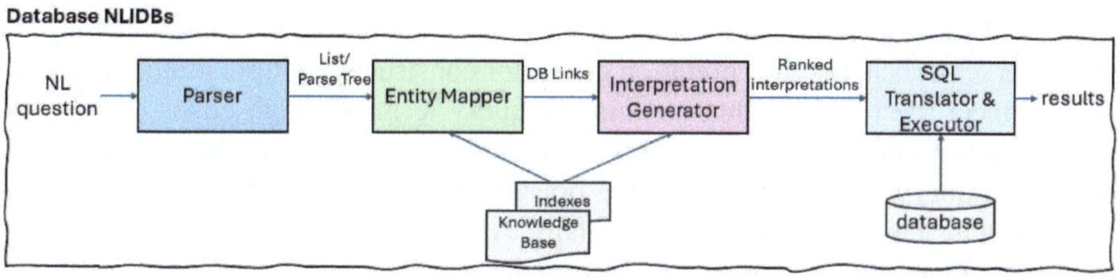

Fig. 2.1: Approaching Text-to-SQL as database mapping problem: system architecture

Parser. When a user submits a question, the parser's role is to gather linguistic information from the query. The complexity of the parser's output can vary significantly. In some systems, such as Discover [25], the parser may produce a simple set of keywords extracted from the query (e.g., "*movie*," "*Brad Pitt*"). These keywords are used to identify relevant database elements and construct the SQL query.

In more advanced systems, such as NaLIR [37], the parser generates a structured parse tree. This parse tree represents the syntactic structure of the user query, detailing the relationships between different parts of the sentence. The parse tree serves as a detailed blueprint for translating the natural language question into a precise SQL query. Additionally, query segments can be annotated with SQL-specific tags to further refine the translation process. These tags might include operators such as "count", "max", or "min", which indicate specific SQL functions to be applied. For example, if the user question involves finding the highest-rated movie, the parser might annotate the relevant segment with a "max" operator to ensure the SQL query correctly identifies the maximum rating.

Entity mapper. The entity mapper maps the terms identified by the parser to database elements. Some systems use inverted indexes to map the query terms to values in the database (e.g., Discover [25]). Others also search the database metadata, such as relation and attribute names (e.g., DiscoverIR [24]). NaLIR [37] also identifies the nodes in the parse tree that can be mapped to SQL elements (select, operator, function, quantifier and logic nodes) using a knowledge base of phrases.

The output of the entity mapper can be structurally the same as that of the parser, but with the terms annotated with the database elements (i.e.. metadata and values) they map to – one or more annotations per term. The entity mapper comes right after the parser as a crucial step towards understanding the NLQ from the perspective of the database. Together, they ensure that the final SQL will be *semantically correct.*

Interpretation Generator. The previous components mostly deal with parts of the query. The interpretation generator infers the semantics of the query as a whole. Dependencies between terms and phrases are analyzed in order to extract joins, aggregate functions, comparisons, etc., depending on the operations that the system supports. The output is an intermediate well-defined structured format that captures the meaning of the query and the order of the operations to be done. This intermediate representation is an *interpretation* of the query from the system's perspective.

Intermediate representations are useful because they are easier to modify, manipulate, and rank, as opposed to SQL queries. For example, in systems following the Discover approach, the interpretation generator constructs multiple joining networks that connect the relations that contain the query terms through edges that are the primary key-foreign key relationships between them. On the other hand, NaLIR [37] generated query trees that capture the operations dictated by the query semantics, while SODA generated patterns [5]. Finally, ATHENA [48] translated the NLQ into an intermediate query language over a domain ontology.

Ambiguity at the term level can be transferred from the output of the entity mapper, due to multiple mappings for a term. Ambiguity also exists in the linguistic dependencies between terms, in the extraction of joins, in the order of the operations, and so forth. As a result, the output of the interpretation generator may be *multiple candidate interpretations* ranked according to how well the system thinks an interpretation captures the user intent.

Indexes and knowledge bases. *Database inverted indexes* map input terms extracted by the parser to database values. These indexes function like lookup tables, efficiently linking terms to their locations within the database. In this way, the system can quickly retrieve relevant database values without scanning the entire database, making the translation of natural language questions into SQL queries more efficient. *Knowledge bases* enhance the system's ability to understand queries by providing context and definitions. These knowledge bases include dictionaries with word definitions, synonym lists, and grammar rules. They help the system grasp the precise meaning of terms and recognize different ways of expressing the same concept.

SQL translator and executor. These systems do not only translate NLQs into SQL but are responsible of generating the final response to the NLQ. The SQL translator and executor play a crucial role in this process by converting intermediate interpretations into syntactically correct SQL queries. Each system has its own set of rules for this conversion, ensuring that the SQL generated is both accurate and efficient. The quality of the highest-ranked interpretations is vital, as only a selected few are executed to produce the final result.

Significant effort has been invested in optimizing the execution algorithms of these systems. For example, Discover crafts an execution plan by pinpointing duplicate joining subnetworks and executing them only once. The results are then cached for reuse when necessary, significantly accelerating execution times. Précis [31] progressively populates the relations in a logical subset to reduce the number of database rows fetched to the ones needed in the answer.

Responses to a NLQ can be ranked. To expedite the retrieval of the top-k results, heuristics are employed to halt execution without materializing all potential joining trees. For instance, DiscoverIR [24] leverages *tuple monotonicity* to achieve this, while Spark [39] accesses fewer parts of the data to enhance efficiency.

2.4.2 Representative Text-to-SQL Systems

We delve into the important milestones marking the evolution of systems that address the Text-to-SQL as a database mapping problem, and discuss representative systems.

2.4.2.1 Query Interpretations as Database Subgraphs

Discover [25] generated query interpretations as subgraphs of the database schema graph. This method begins with a straightforward whitespace tokenization of the NLQ, where the input terms are searched against the database indexes to retrieve the tuples containing them, resulting in the *basic tuple sets*.

These basic tuple sets are then combined to generate, for each relation, one tuple set per combination of terms. The core component of Discover is the *Candidate Network Generator*, which is responsible for creating *connected graphs of tuple sets*. These connected graphs serve as the intermediate representations of the query. The process starts with an initial set of networks, each consisting of a single tuple set. These networks are iteratively expanded through a breadth-first traversal of the database schema graph. During this traversal, several pruning and acceptance conditions are applied to ensure efficiency and relevance. For a network to be accepted, its tuple sets must contain all the input keywords.

DiscoverIR [24] enhances the execution flow established by Discover. While Discover focuses on matching individual terms against the database indexes, DiscoverIR searches the entire query against the database indexes. This approach allows DiscoverIR to handle queries in a more integrated manner. Additionally, Discover generates multiple tuple sets for each relation, which can lead to a more fragmented and complex query processing. In contrast, DiscoverIR simplifies this process by associating each relation with a single tuple set that contains all tuples with any of the input keywords. This streamlined approach reduced the complexity of query processing and improved efficiency.

2.4.2.2 Query Disambiguation and Answer Ranking

Dealing with the ambiguity of natural language is important for these systems. Query disambiguation is performed at two distinct levels: interpreting a single term (entity mapper), and interpreting the whole query (interpretation generator).

A query term may have *multiple* potential mappings to database elements. The entity mapper may assign a score to each possible mapping in order to distinguish between likely and not likely mappings. For example, DiscoverIR [24] leverages *information retrieval-style ranking heuristics* to enhance the term disambiguation process. The tuples of each tuple set are sorted in descending order based on the score returned by the index.

On the other hand, terms may not map directly to any database element due to synonyms and non-exact matches. The system may attempt to find the closest mappings using a knowledge base with synonyms (e.g., SODA [5]), or a string similarity algorithm (e.g., NaLIR [37]).

To minimize the chances of ambiguity and properly interpret the query intent, some systems impose stricter syntactic constraints on their input (e.g., [5], [67]). The position of the keywords, functions and operators matters and minor changes can alter the semantics or even render the query incomprehensible. For example, a query could be "*count movies actor "Brad Pitt"*". Using this approach, ExpressQ [67] was the first system to accept keyword queries with aggregate functions and groupBy.

Query interpretations can be ranked using various schemes, ranging from simple to more sophisticated methods. Basic ranking schemes include evaluating the size of the joining network, as seen in Discover [25], or calculating the sum of term scores normalized by the tree size, as implemented in DiscoverIR [24]. Precis [51] is another approach that involves using a function of the edge weights.

More advanced formulas have also been employed to enhance the ranking process. For instance, Spark [39] treats a joining tree as a *virtual document* and computes its score based on several factors: an information retrieval score, a completeness factor that measures how many different query keywords are included in the tree, and the tree size. This multi-faceted approach ensures a more comprehensive evaluation of the query interpretation.

NaLIR [37] incorporates various factors into its ranking mechanism. It considers grammar violations and the mappings between parse tree nodes and database elements, which help infer the desired structure of the parse tree. By taking these elements into account, NaLIR aims at a more accurate and contextually relevant ranking of query interpretations.

2.4.2.3 From Keyword Queries to NLQs

Early systems have focused on keyword searches or queries with a restricted syntax and vocabulary, such as SODA [5]. These systems were limited in their ability to handle the full complexity of natural language questions (NLQs). NaLIR [37] represents a significant advancement as it is the first system to allow free-form NLQs.

To achieve this, NaLIR introduces natural language processing (NLP) techniques to capture the semantics of user queries. This approach divides the task of translating NLQs into SQL queries into two subproblems: understanding the query semantics and mapping the query to the underlying database.

NaLIR [37] utilizes the Stanford Parser [10] to generate a dependency parse tree, where nodes are the terms and edges represent the linguistic relationships between them. This parse tree serves as the foundation for mapping the nodes to SQL and database elements. To facilitate this mapping, NaLIR employs a knowledge base pre-filled with a set of phrases to identify select, operator, function, quantifier, and logic nodes. For example, the function node *COUNT* is mapped to phrases like "number of." This pre-filled knowledge base helps in accurately interpreting the user's intent.

To resolve ambiguities in node mappings, NaLIR performs similarity evaluations between the query terms and database elements. It combines the WUP similarity function [60], which assesses the semantic similarity between terms, with the square root of the Jaccard Coefficient, which evaluates the similarity in spelling. This dual approach ensures that the most relevant database elements are selected, enhancing the accuracy of the query translation.

NaLIR corrects any possible flaws in the structure of the parse tree to make it grammatically valid and generates intermediate representations of the query, called *query trees*. To rank candidate query trees, three factors are taken into account: (i) the number of parse tree nodes that violate the grammar, (ii) the mappings between the parse tree nodes and the database elements that can help to infer the desired structure of a parse tree, and (iii) the similarity of a resulting tree to the original linguistic parse tree. If the query tree does not contain function nodes or quantifier nodes, the translation is simple. Otherwise, the SQL statements will contain subqueries and NaLIR translates the tree one block at a time, starting from the innermost level.

2.5 Text-to-SQL as a Language Translation Problem

Neural Natural Language Interfaces to Databases (NLIDBs) approach the Text-to-SQL problem as a *language translation problem*. They train neural networks on extensive datasets of NLQ/SQL pairs [29], enabling the system to predict SQL queries for any given NLQ. The subsequent two chapters delve into these systems. This chapter will focus on the training and evaluation methodologies for such systems.

The development of neural NLIDBs was significantly propelled by the advent of Text-to-SQL benchmarks. A *Text-to-SQL benchmark* (or *dataset*) comprises pairs of NLQs and their corresponding SQL queries, defined over a single or different databases. These datasets are crucial for training and evaluating neural Text-to-SQL systems. They have become indispensable assets, providing a standardized reference for system development and performance evaluation.

Furthermore, to build an effective neural Text-to-SQL system, it is essential to have a robust evaluation methodology. This methodology is used to test the system's performance and compare it against other systems. Evaluation typically involves assessing the accuracy of the system in translating NLQs to SQL queries, ensuring that it meets the desired standards of performance.

The next sections focus on Text-to-SQL benchmarks and system evaluation.

2.5.1 Benchmarks

Text-to-SQL datasets can be categorized based on the number of databases they contain. *Single-domain* datasets only contain one database and *cross-domain* ones contain several databases. While single-domain datasets can be used to test a model's ability to specialize on a given database, cross-domain datasets can be used to test a model's performance on a dataset or domain that is hidden during training. Two additional categories must be considered for datasets that have been created based on previously available benchmarks. *Perturbed* datasets are created by manually modifying a dataset in order to cover desired features such as linguistic diversity. Finally, *augmented* datasets are created by a data augmentation pipeline that has been applied to a certain dataset. Besides the published augmented datasets, this section will also present approaches for synthetic data generation even if they don't publish a specific dataset.

2.5.1.1 Single-Domain Text-to-SQL Datasets

The first datasets in the Text-to-SQL research area focused on one domain and contained questions over a single database. They served for evaluating early systems, while their use in neural-based systems remained limited. *Geoquery* [27, 66] was created in the 1990s and focused on questions about US geography. Initially, the dataset contained queries in the Prolog format. Later on, its data were converted into a relational database and SQL queries were created for 700 of its natural language utterances [46]. Eventually, in 2017 the remaining 180 utterances were annotated with the corresponding SQL queries [27], resulting in the complete version of the Geoquery dataset for the Text-to-SQL problem. *Atis* [9, 47], also originating in the 1990s, is a dataset initially created for evaluating a spoken language system and contains questions related to air travel information. The questions were created by users, who were given a summary of the main database entities and a travel planning scenario. Then, the users were requested to ask questions related to the given travel plan. Finally, *Restaurants* [46, 52], a dataset created in the early 2000s, contains questions automatically generated from templates that can represent typical queries over a database with restaurant information.

With the advancements in natural language processing and the increasing interest in the field of Text-to-SQL, numerous new single-domain datasets emerged. *Academic* [37] is a dataset derived from the Microsoft Academic Search (MAS) database that was created in 2014. Its database, which is a subset of the MAS database, represents different entities in the academic domain, such as publications, authors, and

Dataset	NLQ-SQL	Databases	Domains	Category
Academic [37]	196	1	Microsoft Academic Search	Single domain
Advising [12]	4570	1	University courses	
Geoquery [27, 66]	880	1	US geographical facts	
IMDb [62]	131	1	Movies	
Yelp [62]	128	1	Business reviewing	
Scholar [27]	816	1	Academic database	
Atis [9, 47]	5418	1	Air travel information system	
Restaurants [46, 52]	250	1	Info about restaurants in N. California	
Fiben [49]	300	1	Financial	
MIMICSQL [56]	10000	1	Electronic medical records	
WikiSQL [70]	80654	24241	Wikipedia domains	Cross domain
Staqc [63]	119519	-	-	
Spider [65]	10181	200	Wikipedia, college courses, SQL tutorial websites	
KaggleDBQA [32]	272	8	Kaggle datasets in multiple domains	
EHRSQL [33]	24000	2	Electronic medical records	
SQUALL [50]	11276	1679	Wikipedia	
BIRD [38]	12751	95	Professional domains	
Spider 2.0 [34]	632	213	Finance, Education, Science, Social, Environment, Medicine, Biology, Engineering, Other	
Spider-Syn [15]	8034	200	Spider domains	Perturbed
Spider-realistic [11]	508	20	Spider domains	
Spider-DK [16]	535	10	Spider domains	
ADVETA [45]	-	-	Spider, WikiSQL, WDC domains	
DR Spider [7]	15269	-	Spider domains	
MT-TEQL [40]	62430	2273	Spider domains	
Spider-CG [14]	45599	-	Spider domains	Augmented
GRAPPA synthetic data [64]	475000	-	Spider domains	
PCFG-BART [55]	25977	-	Spider domains	
ScienceBenchmark [68]	4985	3	Scientific domains	

Table 2.1: An overview of Text-to-SQL Benchmarks and their size in queries and databases.

conferences. The queries are derived from user logs on the MAS website. *IMDb* and *Yelp* [62], both released in 2017, are based on well-established databases containing information about movies and business reviews, respectively. The natural language questions were created by a group of people who were provided with information about the data (e.g., business names or movie titles) but were not informed about the underlying database schema. *Scholar* [27] was created in the same year and it is a dataset over an academic database containing questions collected during a user study. Lastly, *Advising* [12], a dataset published in 2018, consists of questions from a course information database at the University of Michigan with fictional student records. The questions were collected from two sources: the department's Facebook page and computer science students. The students were instructed to generate questions they might ask during an academic advising session based on the existing database.

In the following years, several cross-domain datasets were created which as we will see in the following section dominated the evaluation process. Datasets focusing on specific domains continue to emerge, often addressing data scarcity in specialized domains. One of those datasets is *Fiben* [49] which contains analytical queries over a financial ontology created by BI experts. Additionally, *MIMICSQL* [56] contains retrieval and reasoning questions over a database with health records. The questions were generated from 4 natural language question templates that represent possibly asked questions in this domain. These questions were filtered and paraphrased by eight crowd workers with medical domain knowledge.

2.5.1.2 Cross-Domain Text-to-SQL Datasets

Player	No.	Nationality	Position	Years in Toronto	School/Club Team
Leandro Barbosa	20	Brazil	Guard	2010-2012	Tilibra
Muggsy Bogues	14	USA	Guard	1999-2001	Wake Forest
Jerryd Bayless	5	USA	Guard	2010-2012	Arizona
⋮	⋮	⋮	⋮	⋮	⋮

NLQ: What nationality is the player Muggsy Bogues?
SQL: SELECT nationality WHERE player = muggsy bogues

Fig. 2.2: An example from the WikiSQL dataset.

Cross-domain benchmarks contain multiple different databases, usually from diverse domains, allowing researchers to test their model's ability to generalize to previously unseen schemas and topics. *WikiSQL* [70] is a large crowd-sourced dataset for developing natural language interfaces for relational databases, released along with the Seq2SQL Text-to-SQL system. It contains over 25,000 Wikipedia tables and over 80,000 natural language and SQL question pairs created by crowd-sourcing. Each entry in the dataset consists of a table with its columns, a natural language question (NLQ) and a SQL query.

The complexity of the SQL queries found in WikiSQL is low because each query is directed to a single table and not to a relational database and they do not use any complex SQL clauses such as JOIN, GROUP BY, ORDER BY, UNION, and

INTERSECTION. Additionally, WikiSQL does not allow the selection of multiple columns in a single query or the use of the asterisk (*) operator. Consequently, the proposed task is much simpler than the ultimate goal of creating a natural language interface for relational databases. Figure 2.2 shows an example from the dataset, demonstrating the simplicity of both the SQL and NL queries. Finally, it should also be noted that WikiSQL contains multiple errors and ambiguities, which might hinder the performance of a model trained on it. Research even suggests that the state-of-the-art systems have reached the upper barrier of accuracy for this task [26].

Spider [65] is a large-scale cross-domain Text-to-SQL dataset annotated by 11 Yale students. It contains 200 relational databases from 138 different domains along with over 10,000 natural language questions and over 5,000 SQL queries. Its queries range from simple to hard, using all the common SQL elements, including nesting, and are of high-quality, since it was hand-crafted and re-checked. For these reasons, researchers have widely relied on it for building systems that generate more complex SQL queries. However, the Spider dataset also has limitations. Its databases were relatively simple, with a small number of tables and records. Consequently, Spider is not representative of the complexity and scale of real-world databases. Despite these limitations, Spider remained one of the most widely used datasets until 2024.

The *BIRD* [38] benchmark, introduced in 2023, rapidly gained traction within the research community, swiftly supplanting Spider as the preferred benchmark for evaluating state-of-the-art systems. BIRD distinguishes itself by featuring larger and more complex databases compared to its predecessors. These databases include dirty values and domain-specific knowledge, presenting a more realistic and challenging environment for system evaluation.

One of the key advancements of BIRD is the inclusion of questions that include mathematical operations, value formatting, and the application of external knowledge not explicitly found in the database schema. This complexity requires systems to possess a robust understanding of both natural language and database structure. Additionally, systems must be capable of leveraging supplementary information beyond the schema to accurately interpret and respond to queries. As a result, this benchmark proved to be a significant challenge even for very large language models.

While WikiSQL, Spider, and BIRD have been the main focus of many proposed systems, other cross-domain benchmarks have emerged. *SQUALL* [50] is based on the WikiTableQuestions dataset [44], consisting of NL Questions posed on Wikipedia tables along with the expected answers. In contrast to WikiSQL, there are no structured queries in the WikiTableQuestions dataset. The authors of SQUALL created the corresponding SQL queries for most of the examples in the WikiTableQuestions dataset, while also providing an alignment between words in the NLQ and the parts of the SQL query that they refer to. This additional feature could steer more thorough research on the schema linking and schema ambiguity problems.

KaggleDBQA [32] is another notable cross-domain dataset, albeit smaller in size compared to others. This dataset has been extracted from Kaggle and features real-world databases sourced from the Web. These databases exhibit all the peculiarities and complexities typical of real-world databases, which are often absent in datasets like Spider, whose databases were specifically created for benchmarking

Text-to-SQL systems. KaggleDBQA also includes comprehensive documentation and metadata for its databases. This additional information provides a rich context that can be leveraged to enhance system performance. The presence of documentation and metadata poses an intriguing research question of how this supplementary information could be effectively utilized to improve the accuracy and efficiency of Text-to-SQL systems.

Staqc [63] was developed by mining a vast number of SQL-related questions and their corresponding answers from Stack Overflow. Despite its considerable size, which surpasses many other benchmarks, its utility as a training or evaluation dataset is quite limited. This limitation arises primarily from two factors.

Firstly, Staqc lacks a defined database schema, which is a critical component for many Text-to-SQL systems. Without a schema, it becomes challenging to map natural language questions to specific database elements, thereby hindering the training and evaluation process. Secondly, many of the questions in Staqc do not conform to the typical format of other Text-to-SQL datasets. Instead of providing direct translations of natural language questions into SQL queries, many questions in Staqc are more about how to formulate specific information requests in SQL. This discrepancy means that the dataset does not align well with the structured format required for training Text-to-SQL models, which typically rely on clear and direct mappings between natural language questions and their SQL counterparts.

EHRSQL [33] contains questions over two databases related to health records. The natural language questions are based on a questionnaire to a university college that requested questions frequently asked on structured electronic health records (EHR). This ensures the variability and value of the questions, since they were not constructed for the task of Text-to-SQL and they were collected from domain experts. The dataset is augmented by filling natural language templates which contain database values as variables that need to be filled. It additionally contains unanswerable and time dependent questions posing several challenges to a Text-to-SQL system.

Finally, *Spider2.0* [34] is a benchmark introduced in 2025 to address the limitations of Spider and to provide a more challenging and realistic evaluation setting for Text-to-SQL systems. It consists of 632 real-world Text-to-SQL workflow problems covering a broad spectrum of tasks, from data transformation to analytics. These workflows derived from industrial applications, such as Google Analytics and Salesforce, and involve databases from cloud data warehouses that contain up to terabyte-scale data volumes and complex schemas.

2.5.1.3 Perturbed datasets

Creating a large Text-to-SQL dataset from scratch demands extensive manual effort. As an alternative, numerous initiatives focus on creating variations of existing datasets. These variations emphasize on specific challenges, such as robustness to synonym substitution or schema linking, which is the correlation of the natural language question with the database elements (tables, columns, values). They aim to

Dataset	NL perturbations Paraphrase	Alter	SQL perturbations	DB perturbations Rename	Add	Alter
Spider-Syn [15]	✓	✗	✗	✗	✗	✗
Spider realistic [11]	✓	✗	✗	✗	✗	✗
MT-TEQL [40]	✓	✗	✗	✓	✓	✓
ADVETA [45]	✗	✗	✓	✓	✓	✗
Spider-DK [16]	✓	✓	✓	✗	✗	✗
DR. Spider [7]	✓	✓	✓	✓	✗	✓

Table 2.2: Perturbations per dataset.

provide a more accurate assessment of the model capabilities and/or boost these capabilities by enriching the training dataset.

Spider-Syn [15] is created by replacing schema references in the NLQ with their synonyms in the train and development Spider dataset. More specifically, four graduate students majoring in computer science were tasked with manually generating synonym substitutions for each domain. After two rounds of reviews to assess the quality of the produced synonyms, 5672 questions were modified by replacing words or phrases with their annotated synonyms.

Similarly, for the creation of *Spider-Realistic* [11] a subset of the natural language questions existing in the Spider development set was manually modified, by removing or paraphrasing explicit mentions of column names.

MT-TEQL [40] uses Metamorphic Rules (MRs) to create equivalent alterations of NLQs and database schemas from given NL/SQL/DB-triplets. Even though this work mainly focuses on providing a more robust evaluation framework for Text-to-SQL systems, it also proposes a methodology for data perturbation that takes advantage of the MRs used for the evaluation. More specifically, a set of MRs is introduced that can be used to modify either the NLQ or the database schema, while keeping them semantically equivalent to the original. The transformation rules for the NLQs consist of (1) prefix insertion, (2) prefix removal, (3) prefix substitution, and (4) synonym substitution. Regarding the DB schema, the main transformations are: (1) normalization (removing a column from a table and using it to create a new table that is connected with a PK/FK relationship), (2) flattening (flatten a table if an explicit foreign key constraint exists), (3) opaque key (remove explicit FK constraints if their relation can be inferred from column/table names), and (4) column insertion (insert a related column taken from an external knowledge graph).

ADVETA (ADVErsarial Table perturbAtion) [45] is a dataset constructed by applying perturbations to the tables of three datasets, WikiSQL, Spider, and WTQ. Specifically, 5 vendors manually replaced column names with synonyms or added new columns in the provided tables and adapted SQL queries accordingly.

Spider-DK [16] is a dataset derived from Spider with the goal to investigate the domain knowledge that current Text-to-SQL models capture. The benchmark contains queries that require 5 different types of domain knowledge, (1) columns mentioned by omission, (2) simple inference, (3) synonyms substitution in cell value word, (4) cell-value word that generate a condition, (5) natural language words or phrases that are easy to conflict with other domains. The NL-SQL pairs derived from a sample of the Spider development set (265 NL-SQL pairs) that required domain knowledge (e.g., "*How many major cities are there*?") with modifications in the NLQs or both the NLQs and SQL questions to incorporate domain knowledge.

DR-Spider [7] was created by applying perturbations in NLQs, SQL queries, and database schemas, and simulates diverse task-specific robustness challenges. Regarding the databases, the authors define 3 types of perturbations: (1) Schema-synonym, (2) Schema abbreviation, and (3) Column equivalence. Regarding the NLQs they define 9 paraphrase categories consisting of synonym replacements (in columns, keywords, and values), keyword and column carriers that imply the keyword and column indicators by carrier phrases, respectively, column attribute and column value that imply the column indicators by aggregated attributes and values respectively. Additionally, they define the multitype perturbation which contains multiple of the above paraphrase categories. The final category is Others and contains sentence-level paraphrases. For the SQL perturbations, they consider (1) Comparison replacements, (2) Sort-order replacements, (3) NonDB-number, which changes a number in the SQL query, (4) DB-text that replaces the value of a column in a SQL query, and (5) DB-number that replaces a DB content number in a SQL query.

2.5.1.4 Augmented datasets

As previously mentioned, creating a dataset from scratch requires a significant amount of effort. For this reason, researchers are often looking for faster and less costly ways to create training and testing data for new use cases and domains. In contrast to dataset perturbation, this category includes datasets that are automatically created from scratch or from available examples, but go beyond from just making changes to the given examples. While data perturbation aims at modifying examples aimed towards a specific challenge (e.g., synonym understanding), data augmentation is mainly used to create new data or expand smaller datasets for underrepresented domains and use cases. As augmented datasets are automatically generated, their level of quality is not as high as manually created datasets. For this reason they are best suited for pre-training purposes or for fine-tuning, usually in combination with manually created datasets.

This section will first present Text-to-SQL datasets that were created using data augmentation techniques and made publicly available. It must be noted however that a significant amount of work focuses on proposing such techniques without releasing a dataset. These approaches will also be discussed shortly after but are not present in Table 2.1.

GRAPPA [64] contains augmented NL-SQL pairs over the WikiTables [4] dataset, and it was created by using a Synchronous Context-free grammar (SCFG) containing rules for the SQL queries and their corresponding questions induced from Spider examples.

PCFG-BART [55] describes a method for creating an augmented dataset using a database-specific probabilistic context-free grammar (PCFG) to generate new SQL queries and a SQL-to-Text system based on the BART [36] model to generate the equivalent NLQ. The method was used to create augmented datasets from the Geoquery [66] and Spider [65] databases and pre-train models in the downstream task.

Spider-CG [14] has been created by generating multiple variations of the NLQs and the SQL queries from the Spider dataset. This was achieved by adding new clauses or conditions, or substituting existing ones in the SQL queries, along with the corresponding changes in the NLQs.

ScienceBenchmark [68] is an augmented dataset containing NL/SQL pairs over databases from the scientific domain. Specifically, it focuses on domains that could greatly benefit from Text-to-SQL but have no dedicated datasets, such as astrophysics, cancer research, and EU research projects. It uses SQL query templates to generate new synthetic SQL queries and LLMs to create the corresponding NLQ for each SQL.

Furthermore, there are several proposed approaches for synthetic data generation that do not release a specific dataset. One such example is *DBPal* [57], a template-based approach for generating NL/SQL-pairs, which uses manually-crafted templates of NL/SQL-pairs, which can be filled with the names of tables and columns in order to create training instances. Additionally, DBPal uses NL augmentations such as paraphrasing, random deletions and synonym substitutions. However, this approach might create "robotic" NLQs whose quality might be reduced by the proposed augmentations, since designing rules that can consistently work across all possible questions is notoriously hard.

Finally, other approaches rely on using SQL templates for generating SQL queries and Recurrent Neural Networks (RNNs) to generate their equivalent NLQs. These templates can either by handcrafted and static, simply requiring a choice of table and column names to complete them [19], or they can be created using an abstract syntax tree grammar [59], leading to more diverse SQL queries.

2.5.1.5 Remarks

As Table 2.1 shows, a large number datasets are available for the task. However, not all datasets have seen the same level of adoption by researchers. In fact, there have been three benchmarks that have been almost exclusively used in most research works: (i) WikiSQL [71] was the first large-scale Text-to-SQL benchmark and was very popular in 2017 when the first neural systems started to appear, (ii) Spider [65] signaled the advancement to more complex models and databases, and was the first choice for researchers from 2018 onward, and (iii) BIRD [38] took over in 2023, addressing the drawbacks of Spider which contained relatively small and simple databases that systems of the time were already able to handle very well. One of the main reasons that these datasets became so popular is the large number of different databases that they offer and their online leaderboards that allowed researchers to effectively compare their solutions to the state of the art.

Besides the reasons mentioned above, another reason why single-domain benchmarks have seen relatively little use is that they do not test the model's generalization ability. Since they focus on a single domain, it is not possible to argue that a proposed system can be considered a "universal solution" even if it performs well on a specific domain. However, although the generalization capability of a Text-to-SQL model is an important challenge, a realistic application would most likely require a Text-to-SQL system to work with a single database of a specific domain, or with a few related databases. In such a scenario, a high performance on a single domain may be even more important than cross-domain generalization, and achieving this has been shown to be very challenging [22].

Finally, perturbed datasets can be a very important asset that is often overlooked when evaluating a Text-to-SQL system. Systems evaluated in both the original and the perturbed versions of datasets show a substantial performance drop in the latter highlighting the value of these datasets in the evaluation process. These datasets can highlight the limitations of Text-to-SQL models in handling new datasets and specific challenges, even with small differences from the originals.

2.5.2 Evaluation

Another important part in developing a neural Text-to-SQL system are the metrics that will be used to evaluate its performance. Having a ground truth SQL query for each NLQ enables us to train and evaluate a system on it, by comparing it to the system's prediction. In this section, we will present metrics used to evaluate a Text-to-SQL system's predictions, how Text-to-SQL data can be categorized to perform fine-grained evaluation on a system, and some insights on error analysis.

The metrics that have been used with Text-to-SQL systems can generally be split into two categories: accuracy metrics and efficiency metrics. *Accuracy metrics* measure how close the predicted SQL is to the ground truth SQL, while *efficiency metrics* measure the performance of the prediction. A complete evaluation must consider both types of metrics and, as we will see later on, can also greatly benefit from fine-grained data categorization that helps highlight weak points in a system.

2.5.2.1 Accuracy metrics

Accuracy metrics focus on comparing the predicted SQL to the ground truth and measuring if it retrieves the same data. This can often be a difficult task as the same logic can be expressed with different SQL queries. As such, an ideal metric must be robust to queries that appear dissimilar but ultimately return the expected results.

String Matching (introduced as Logical Form Accuracy [70]) is the simplest accuracy metric for Text-to-SQL. It considers the ground truth and predicted queries as simple strings and checks whether they are identical. A match is only found when the predicted query is written exactly as the ground truth, without taking into account that many parts of a SQL query can be written in a different order or even in a different but still equivalent way.

Execution Accuracy [65, 70] (or Query Accuracy [6]) is another simple approach for comparing SQL queries. For each NLQ, both the ground truth and the predicted queries are executed against the corresponding database (or table) and their results are compared. If the results are the same, then the prediction is considered correct. False positives can occur when both queries return the same results, but are different on a semantic level (e.g., when they return empty results or when an aggregation function is applied to different columns that happen to return the same result).

Test-suite execution accuracy [69] is an effort to minimize the false positive results of the execution accuracy. To accomplish this goal, the execution accuracy of two queries is calculated over multiple databases, creating more robust results. For each SQL, multiple databases are created, each containing uniformly sampling values from existing columns or from random distributions, and the constant values used in the SQL query. To determine the subset of the databases that will be included in the test suite of this SQL query, a set of neighbor queries are created by modifying the SQL query based on pre-defined rules (e.g., replace an integer). The databases that can distinguish the original query from their neighbors, based on the execution accuracy results, are selected.

Component Matching [65] is proposed in order to obtain a better understanding of which parts of the SQL query are predicted correctly. For example, we might consider the SELECT column accuracy, i.e., the percentage of the predicted queries that have the same columns in the SELECT clause as the corresponding ground truth queries. For some parts, a more sophisticated approach might be necessary to avoid incorrect classifications. For instance, when comparing the conditions of the WHERE clause, their order should not be taken into account.

Exact Set Matching [65] (or Query Match Accuracy [61]) considers all the possible component matches and classifies a prediction as correct if all component matches are correct (e.g., aggregation function, condition operators, SELECT columns, etc.).

Exact Set Match Without Values is a category in the Spider [65] benchmark, that works in the same way as exact set matching, but does not take into account if the values that appear in the predicted query are the same as the ones that appear in the gold query. The reason for this simplification is that predicting the correct values can be very challenging, especially when these values appear in the NLQ differently to the way they are stored in the DB (e.g., the word "Greek" might imply a condition such as country="Greece"). Although this metric might have been considered as common practice in the Spider benchmark, as research shows [12], disregarding values during evaluation removes an important challenge of the Text-to-SQL problem.

Sub-tree Elements Matching (or Partial Component Match F1 - PCMF1) [22] is a metric proposed to avoid a score of zero by the exact set match metric, when some parts of the predicted query are correct. It considers parts of the query such as the SELECT, WHERE, FROM, etc. clauses and it calculates the F1 score of each clause based on the precision and recall of the predicted attributes in the clause. The final PCMF1 score of a predicted query is the average F1 score of all the considered query parts. For example, in large queries, the system might predict a large part of the query correctly and make some errors in the WHERE clause. While the exact match metric would assign a score of zero even for a small mistake, the PCMF1 metric would assign a score relatively close to one, thus providing a better assessment of the system performance.

A **Multi-level Validation Framework** [30] has also been proposed, with a more thorough methodology for evaluating the semantic equivalence of two SQL queries. This approach starts by comparing the execution result of the two queries, as well as their results on additional generated data, in case the original database contains a small amount of data. Furthermore, a prover is used to provide a proof of equivalence between the queries or a counter example in the case of non-equivalence. If the prover cannot work for the given queries, then a query re-writer is applied on both queries and the re-written queries' parse trees are compared. If the re-written parse trees are structurally identical then the queries are semantically equivalent, otherwise the queries are manually evaluated by an expert. While this approach can detect matches even if queries are expressed in fundamentally different ways, the requirement of manual labor as well as the extra processing requirements it presents, are some of the reasons why it has been relatively less popular.

2.5.2.2 Efficiency metrics

The focus of efficiency metrics is measuring the time that a user must wait from asking a NLQ and receiving the data they are looking for. Unfortunately, only a few systems provide efficiency evaluations [13, 49], while most Text-to-SQL systems focus only on accuracy metrics.

Latency is the time that a system requires to generate the SQL query prediction.

Throughput is the number of SQL queries that a system can predict in a single unit of time. It is also the inverse metric of latency, i.e., $throughput = \frac{1}{latency}$.

Valid Efficiency Score (VES) [38] measures the efficiency of the valid predicted SQL queries, in comparison with the ground truth queries. A query is valid if its result set aligns with the result set of the ground-truth SQL query (i.e., if it returns the same results), which means that inaccurate queries are not taken into account when calculating VES. In the case of the BIRD [38] benchmark, efficiency refers to the query's execution time, but the metric could be adapted to use memory cost, throughput, etc.

2.5.2.3 Data Categorization

To achieve a more insightful evaluation, many research works categorize the SQL queries or NLQs in a dataset and report the accuracy results for each category. This approach enables a deeper understanding of the model's capabilities.

The most widely used categorization is the SQL query classification introduced in Spider, which divides the queries based on hardness criteria. More specifically, the queries are grouped into four difficulty levels: easy, medium, hard and extra hard. The difficulty is based on the number of SQL components, selections, and conditions existing in a query. While this method offers a deeper analysis than raw accuracy, it has limitations. The categorization is overly generic and fails to effectively highlight system challenges. For example, queries within the same category may vary significantly in structure, involving different clauses and operators, making it difficult to pinpoint specific strengths or weaknesses of a system.

Towards more extensive and complete categorization, there are efforts to divide the dataset based on criteria related with the SQL and the NLQs [17]. For example, categories like "GroupBy" and "Aggregates" group queries containing a group by clause or at least one aggregate function, respectively. Similarly, categories focusing on NLQ characteristics were introduced, such as the "Value synonyms" category, which includes queries where requested database values are not referenced the way they are stored in the database. A NL-SQL pair can belong to multiple categories. This categorization offered valuable insights into the effect of each category on system performance.

Other efforts focus solely on the natural language questions and divide the NLQs based on specific linguistic features to examine the effect of those features in the models' performance [57]. The 6 categories of questions defined are: (1) Naive, (2) Syntactic, (3) Morphological, (4) Lexical, (5) Semantic and(6) Missing information.

Despite their benefits, these categorizations face significant challenges. Many categories require manual data classification, limiting their scalability to new datasets. Additionally, the criteria underlying category definitions are often insufficiently justified, which restricts their generalizability. To address these issues, an automated approach has been introduced that creates categories based on a set of axes that can sufficiently describe the SQL queries, the NLQs and the underlying databases, enabling more consistent and scalable categorization [41].

In conclusion, while extensive and detailed categorizations enhance evaluation processes and provide valuable insights, they are not always capable of definitively identifying the sources of errors in a system.

2.5.2.4 Error analysis

Another approach toward a more comprehensive evaluation is error analysis. To gain insights into their system's weaknesses, many works [20, 30, 32, 35, 40, 54] manually examine a subset of incorrect predictions made by their models and categorize the underlying causes of errors. The categories vary across the works and can be of different granularity, from syntax errors to incorrect constraints or incorrect aggregates. While documenting these errors can significantly aid in identifying vulnerabilities, the process is labor-intensive and requires extensive, repetitive manual effort. An effort to automate this process divides the errors into structural, operation, and variable errors and detects them by automatically comparing the predicted and actual SQL query [41]. Even though they are general categories, they are able to identify if the main limitations of the system are attributed to its difficulty in understanding the correct structure of the requested SQL query, the struggle to recognize the operations needed or the incapability of understanding the required database schema elements or the database values. However, this framework remains overly generic, requiring further refinement to capture the diverse causes of errors.

Overall, reporting the sources of errors is critical for pinpointing specific challenges in semantic parsing tasks. By understanding these challenges, researchers can better guide the development of more robust and accurate systems.

References

1. Hiyan Alshawi, David M. Carter, Jan van Eijck, Robert C. Moore, Douglas B. Moran, and Stephen G. Pulman. Overview of the core language engine. In *Proceedings of the International Conference on Fifth Generation Computer Systems, FGCS 1988, Tokyo, Japan, November 28-December 2, 1988*, pages 1108–1115. OHMSHA Ltd. Tokyo and Springer-Verlag, 1988.
2. Ambiguity. https://stanford.io/2YXcECi.
3. Ion Androutsopoulos, Graeme D. Ritchie, and Peter Thanisch. Natural language interfaces to databases - an introduction. *Natural Language Engineering*, 1(1):29–81, 1995.
4. Chandra Sekhar Bhagavatula, Thanapon Noraset, and Doug Downey. Tabel: Entity linking in web tables. In *International Semantic Web Conference*, pages 425–441. Springer, 2015.
5. Lukas Blunschi, Claudio Jossen, Donald Kossmann, Magdalini Mori, and Kurt Stockinger. Soda: generating sql for business users. *Proc. VLDB Endow.*, 5(10):932–943, jun 2012.
6. Ruichu Cai, Boyan Xu, Zhenjie Zhang, Xiaoyan Yang, Zijian Li, and Zhihao Liang. An encoder-decoder framework translating natural language to database queries. In Jérôme Lang, editor, *Proceedings of the Twenty-Seventh International Joint Conference on Artificial Intelligence, IJCAI 2018, July 13-19, 2018, Stockholm, Sweden*, pages 3977–3983. ijcai.org, 2018.
7. Shuaichen Chang, Jun Wang, Mingwen Dong, Lin Pan, Henghui Zhu, Alexander Hanbo Li, Wuwei Lan, Sheng Zhang, Jiarong Jiang, Joseph Lilien, et al. Dr. spider: A diagnostic evaluation benchmark towards text-to-sql robustness. *arXiv preprint arXiv:2301.08881*, 2023.
8. Ann A. Copestake and Karen Sparck Jones. Natural language interfaces to databases. *Knowl. Eng. Rev.*, 5(4):225–249, 1990.
9. Deborah A. Dahl, Madeleine Bates, Michael Brown, William Fisher, Kate Hunicke-Smith, David Pallett, Christine Pao, Alexander Rudnicky, and Elizabeth Shriberg. Expanding the scope of the atis task: The atis-3 corpus. In *Proceedings of the Workshop on Human Language Technology*, HLT '94, page 43–48, USA, 1994. Association for Computational Linguistics.
10. Marie-Catherine de Marneffe, Bill MacCartney, and Christopher D. Manning. Generating typed dependency parses from phrase structure parses. *LREC*, pages 449–454, 2006.
11. Xiang Deng, Ahmed Hassan Awadallah, Christopher Meek, Oleksandr Polozov, Huan Sun, and Matthew Richardson. Structure-grounded pretraining for text-to-sql. *arXiv preprint arXiv:2010.12773*, 2020.
12. Catherine Finegan-Dollak, Jonathan K. Kummerfeld, Li Zhang, Karthik Ramanathan, Sesh Sadasivam, Rui Zhang, and Dragomir Radev. Improving text-to-SQL evaluation methodology. In *Proceedings of the 56th Annual Meeting of the Association for Computational Linguistics (Volume 1: Long Papers)*, pages 351–360, Melbourne, Australia, July 2018. Association for Computational Linguistics.
13. Han Fu, Chang Liu, Bin Wu, Feifei Li, Jian Tan, and Jianling Sun. Catsql: Towards real world natural language to sql applications. *Proc. VLDB Endow.*, 16(6):1534–1547, feb 2023.
14. Yujian Gan, Xinyun Chen, Qiuping Huang, and Matthew Purver. Measuring and improving compositional generalization in text-to-sql via component alignment. *arXiv preprint arXiv:2205.02054*, 2022.

15. Yujian Gan, Xinyun Chen, Qiuping Huang, Matthew Purver, John R. Woodward, Jinxia Xie, and Pengsheng Huang. Towards robustness of text-to-SQL models against synonym substitution. In *Proceedings of the 59th Annual Meeting of the Association for Computational Linguistics and the 11th International Joint Conference on Natural Language Processing (Volume 1: Long Papers)*, pages 2505–2515, Online, August 2021. Association for Computational Linguistics.
16. Yujian Gan, Xinyun Chen, and Matthew Purver. Exploring underexplored limitations of cross-domain text-to-SQL generalization. In *Proceedings of the 2021 Conference on Empirical Methods in Natural Language Processing*, pages 8926–8931, Online and Punta Cana, Dominican Republic, November 2021. Association for Computational Linguistics.
17. Orest Gkini, Theofilos Belmpas, Georgia Koutrika, and Yannis Ioannidis. An in-depth benchmarking of text-to-sql systems. In *Proceedings of the 2021 International Conference on Management of Data*, SIGMOD '21, page 632–644, New York, NY, USA, 2021. Association for Computing Machinery.
18. Barbara J. Grosz. TEAM: A transportable natural-language interface system. In *1st Applied Natural Language Processing Conference, ANLP 1983, Miramar-Sheraton Hotel, Santa Monica, California, USA, February 1-3, 1983*, pages 39–45. ACL, 1983.
19. Daya Guo, Yibo Sun, Duyu Tang, Nan Duan, Jian Yin, Hong Chi, James Cao, Peng Chen, and Ming Zhou. Question generation from SQL queries improves neural semantic parsing. In *Proceedings of the 2018 Conference on Empirical Methods in Natural Language Processing*, pages 1597–1607, Brussels, Belgium, October-November 2018. Association for Computational Linguistics.
20. Jiaqi Guo, Zecheng Zhan, Yan Gao, Yan Xiao, Jian-Guang Lou, Ting Liu, and Dongmei Zhang. Towards complex text-to-sql in cross-domain database with intermediate representation, 2019.
21. Larry R. Harris. Experience with INTELLECT: artificial intelligence technology transfer. *AI Mag.*, 5(2):43–50, 1984.
22. Moshe Hazoom, Vibhor Malik, and Ben Bogin. Text-to-SQL in the wild: A naturally-occurring dataset based on stack exchange data. In *Proceedings of the 1st Workshop on Natural Language Processing for Programming (NLP4Prog 2021)*, pages 77–87, Online, August 2021. Association for Computational Linguistics.
23. Gary G. Hendrix, Earl D. Sacerdoti, Daniel Sagalowicz, and Jonathan Slocum. Developing a natural language interface to complex data. *ACM Trans. Database Syst.*, 3(2):105–147, jun 1978.
24. Vagelis Hristidis, Luis Gravano, and Yannis Papakonstantinou. Efficient IR-style keyword search over relational databases. In *VLDB*, pages 850–861, 2003.
25. Vagelis Hristidis and Yannis Papakonstantinou. Discover: Keyword search in relational databases. In *VLDB*, pages 670–681, 2002.
26. Wonseok Hwang, Jinyeong Yim, Seunghyun Park, and Minjoon Seo. A comprehensive exploration on wikisql with table-aware word contextualization, 2019.
27. Srinivasan Iyer, Ioannis Konstas, Alvin Cheung, Jayant Krishnamurthy, and Luke Zettlemoyer. Learning a neural semantic parser from user feedback. In Regina Barzilay and Min-Yen Kan, editors, *Proceedings of the 55th Annual Meeting of the Association for Computational Linguistics, ACL 2017, Vancouver, Canada, July 30 - August 4, Volume 1: Long Papers*, pages 963–973. Association for Computational Linguistics, 2017.
28. Tim Johnson. Natural language computing: The commercial applications. *Knowl. Eng. Rev.*, 1(3):11–23, 1984.
29. George Katsogiannis-Meimarakis and Georgia Koutrika. A survey on deep learning approaches for text-to-sql. *The VLDB Journal*, 2023.
30. Hyeonji Kim, Byeong-Hoon So, Wook-Shin Han, and Hongrae Lee. Natural language to sql: Where are we today? *Proc. VLDB Endow.*, 13(10):1737–1750, June 2020.
31. Georgia Koutrika, Alkis Simitsis, and Yannis E. Ioannidis. Précis: The essence of a query answer. In Ling Liu, Andreas Reuter, Kyu-Young Whang, and Jianjun Zhang, editors, *Proceedings of the 22nd International Conference on Data Engineering, ICDE 2006, 3-8 April 2006, Atlanta, GA, USA*, pages 69–78. IEEE Computer Society, 2006.

32. Chia-Hsuan Lee, Oleksandr Polozov, and Matthew Richardson. KaggleDBQA: Realistic evaluation of text-to-SQL parsers. In *Proceedings of the 59th Annual Meeting of the Association for Computational Linguistics and the 11th International Joint Conference on Natural Language Processing (Volume 1: Long Papers)*, pages 2261–2273, Online, August 2021. Association for Computational Linguistics.
33. Gyubok Lee, Hyeonji Hwang, Seongsu Bae, Yeonsu Kwon, Woncheol Shin, Seongjun Yang, Minjoon Seo, Jong-Yeup Kim, and Edward Choi. Ehrsql: A practical text-to-sql benchmark for electronic health records. *Advances in Neural Information Processing Systems*, 35:15589–15601, 2022.
34. Fangyu Lei, Jixuan Chen, Yuxiao Ye, Ruisheng Cao, Dongchan Shin, Hongjin Su, Zhaoqing Suo, Hongcheng Gao, Wenjing Hu, Pengcheng Yin, Victor Zhong, Caiming Xiong, Ruoxi Sun, Qian Liu, Sida Wang, and Tao Yu. Spider 2.0: Evaluating language models on real-world enterprise text-to-sql workflows. In *The Thirteenth International Conference on Learning Representations, ICLR 2025, Singapore, April 24-28, 2025*. OpenReview.net, 2025.
35. Wenqiang Lei, Weixin Wang, Zhixin Ma, Tian Gan, Wei Lu, Min-Yen Kan, and Tat-Seng Chua. Re-examining the role of schema linking in text-to-SQL. In Bonnie Webber, Trevor Cohn, Yulan He, and Yang Liu, editors, *Proceedings of the 2020 Conference on Empirical Methods in Natural Language Processing (EMNLP)*, pages 6943–6954, Online, November 2020. Association for Computational Linguistics.
36. Mike Lewis, Yinhan Liu, Naman Goyal, Marjan Ghazvininejad, Abdelrahman Mohamed, Omer Levy, Ves Stoyanov, and Luke Zettlemoyer. BART: Denoising sequence-to-sequence pre-training for natural language generation, translation, and comprehension, 2019.
37. Fei Li and H. V. Jagadish. Constructing an interactive natural language interface for relational databases. *PVLDB*, 8(1):73–84, September 2014.
38. Jinyang Li, Binyuan Hui, Ge Qu, Jiaxi Yang, Binhua Li, Bowen Li, Bailin Wang, Bowen Qin, Ruiying Geng, Nan Huo, Xuanhe Zhou, Ma Chenhao, Guoliang Li, Kevin Chang, Fei Huang, Reynold Cheng, and Yongbin Li. Can llm already serve as a database interface? a big bench for large-scale database grounded text-to-sqls. In A. Oh, T. Naumann, A. Globerson, K. Saenko, M. Hardt, and S. Levine, editors, *Advances in Neural Information Processing Systems*, volume 36, pages 42330–42357. Curran Associates, Inc., 2023.
39. Yi Luo, Xuemin Lin, Wei Wang, and Xiaofang Zhou. Spark: Top-k keyword query in relational databases. In *ACM SIGMOD*, pages 115–126, 2007.
40. Pingchuan Ma and Shuai Wang. Mt-teql: evaluating and augmenting neural nlidb on real-world linguistic and schema variations. *Proc. VLDB Endow.*, 15(3):569–582, nov 2021.
41. Anna Mitsopoulou and Georgia Koutrika. Analysis of text-to-sql benchmarks: Limitations, challenges and opportunities. 2025.
42. Notes on ambiguity. http://bit.ly/2YTLFeR.
43. Nikolaus Ott. Aspects of the automatic generation of SQL statements in the natural language query interface. *Inf. Syst.*, 17(2):147–159, 1992.
44. Panupong Pasupat and Percy Liang. Compositional semantic parsing on semi-structured tables. In *Proceedings of the 53rd Annual Meeting of the Association for Computational Linguistics and the 7th International Joint Conference on Natural Language Processing (Volume 1: Long Papers)*, pages 1470–1480, Beijing, China, July 2015. Association for Computational Linguistics.
45. Xinyu Pi, Bing Wang, Yan Gao, Jiaqi Guo, Zhoujun Li, and Jian-Guang Lou. Towards robustness of text-to-sql models against natural and realistic adversarial table perturbation. *arXiv preprint arXiv:2212.09994*, 2022.
46. Ana-Maria Popescu, Oren Etzioni, and Henry Kautz. Towards a theory of natural language interfaces to databases. In *Proceedings of the 8th International Conference on Intelligent User Interfaces*, IUI '03, page 149–157, New York, NY, USA, 2003. Association for Computing Machinery.
47. P. J. Price. Evaluation of spoken language systems: The atis domain. In *Proceedings of the Workshop on Speech and Natural Language*, HLT '90, page 91–95, USA, 1990. Association for Computational Linguistics.

48. Diptikalyan Saha, Avrilia Floratou, Karthik Sankaranarayanan, Umar Farooq Minhas, Ashish R. Mittal, Fatma Özcan, IBM Research. Bangalore, and IBM Research. Almaden. *ATHENA: An Ontology-Driven System for Natural Language Querying over Relational Data Stores*. VLDB, 2016.
49. Jaydeep Sen, Chuan Lei, Abdul Quamar, Fatma Özcan, Vasilis Efthymiou, Ayushi Dalmia, Greg Stager, Ashish Mittal, Diptikalyan Saha, and Karthik Sankaranarayanan. Athena++: natural language querying for complex nested sql queries. *Proc. VLDB Endow.*, 13(12):2747–2759, jul 2020.
50. Tianze Shi, Chen Zhao, Jordan Boyd-Graber, Hal Daumé III, and Lillian Lee. On the potential of lexico-logical alignments for semantic parsing to SQL queries. In *Findings of the Association for Computational Linguistics: EMNLP 2020*, pages 1849–1864, Online, November 2020. Association for Computational Linguistics.
51. Alkis Simitsis, Georgia Koutrika, and Yannis Ioannidis. Précis: from unstructured keywords as queries to structured databases as answers. *The VLDB Journal*, 17(1):117–149, 2008.
52. Lappoon R. Tang and Raymond J. Mooney. Automated construction of database interfaces: Intergrating statistical and relational learning for semantic parsing. In *2000 Joint SIGDAT Conference on Empirical Methods in Natural Language Processing and Very Large Corpora*, pages 133–141, Hong Kong, China, October 2000. Association for Computational Linguistics.
53. Marjorie Templeton and John Burger. Problems in natural-language interface to DBMS with examples from EUFID. In *First Conference on Applied Natural Language Processing*, pages 3–16, Santa Monica, California, USA, February 1983. Association for Computational Linguistics.
54. Bailin Wang, Richard Shin, Xiaodong Liu, Oleksandr Polozov, and Matthew Richardson. RAT-SQL: Relation-aware schema encoding and linking for text-to-sql parsers, 2020.
55. Bailin Wang, Wenpeng Yin, Xi Victoria Lin, and Caiming Xiong. Learning to synthesize data for semantic parsing. In Kristina Toutanova, Anna Rumshisky, Luke Zettlemoyer, Dilek Hakkani-Tur, Iz Beltagy, Steven Bethard, Ryan Cotterell, Tanmoy Chakraborty, and Yichao Zhou, editors, *Proceedings of the 2021 Conference of the North American Chapter of the Association for Computational Linguistics: Human Language Technologies*, pages 2760–2766, Online, June 2021. Association for Computational Linguistics.
56. Ping Wang, Tian Shi, and Chandan K Reddy. Text-to-sql generation for question answering on electronic medical records. In *Proceedings of The Web Conference 2020*, pages 350–361, 2020.
57. Nathaniel Weir, Prasetya Utama, Alex Galakatos, Andrew Crotty, Amir Ilkhechi, Shekar Ramaswamy, Rohin Bhushan, Nadja Geisler, Benjamin Hättasch, Steffen Eger, Ugur Cetintemel, and Carsten Binnig. Dbpal: A fully pluggable NL2SQL training pipeline. In *Proceedings of the 2020 ACM SIGMOD International Conference on Management of Data*, SIGMOD '20, page 2347–2361, New York, NY, USA, 2020. Association for Computing Machinery.
58. William A. Woods. Procedural semantics for a question-answering machine. In *Proceedings of the AFIPS '68 Fall Joint Computer Conference, December 9-11, 1968, San Francisco, California, USA - Part I*, volume 33, pages 457–471, 1968.
59. Kun Wu, Lijie Wang, Zhenghua Li, Ao Zhang, Xinyan Xiao, Hua Wu, Min Zhang, and Haifeng Wang. Data augmentation with hierarchical SQL-to-question generation for cross-domain text-to-SQL parsing. In *Proceedings of the 2021 Conference on Empirical Methods in Natural Language Processing*, pages 8974–8983, Online and Punta Cana, Dominican Republic, November 2021. Association for Computational Linguistics.
60. Zhibiao Wu and Martha Palmer. Verbs semantics and lexical selection. In *Proceedings of the 32Nd Annual Meeting on Association for Computational Linguistics*, pages 133–138, 1994.
61. Xiaojun Xu, Chang Liu, and Dawn Song. Sqlnet: Generating structured queries from natural language without reinforcement learning, 2017.
62. Navid Yaghmazadeh, Yuepeng Wang, Isil Dillig, and Thomas Dillig. Sqlizer: query synthesis from natural language. *Proc. ACM Program. Lang.*, 1(OOPSLA), oct 2017.
63. Ziyu Yao, Daniel S Weld, Wei-Peng Chen, and Huan Sun. Staqc: A systematically mined question-code dataset from stack overflow. In *Proceedings of the 2018 World Wide Web Conference*, pages 1693–1703, 2018.

64. Tao Yu, Chien-Sheng Wu, Xi Victoria Lin, Bailin Wang, Yi Chern Tan, Xinyi Yang, Dragomir Radev, Richard Socher, and Caiming Xiong. Grappa: Grammar-augmented pre-training for table semantic parsing, 2020.
65. Tao Yu, Rui Zhang, Kai Yang, Michihiro Yasunaga, Dongxu Wang, Zifan Li, James Ma, Irene Li, Qingning Yao, Shanelle Roman, Zilin Zhang, and Dragomir Radev. Spider: A large-scale human-labeled dataset for complex and cross-domain semantic parsing and text-to-SQL task. In Ellen Riloff, David Chiang, Julia Hockenmaier, and Jun'ichi Tsujii, editors, *Proceedings of the 2018 Conference on Empirical Methods in Natural Language Processing*, pages 3911–3921, Brussels, Belgium, October-November 2018. Association for Computational Linguistics.
66. John M. Zelle and Raymond J. Mooney. Learning to parse database queries using inductive logic programming. In *Proceedings of the Thirteenth National Conference on Artificial Intelligence - Volume 2*, AAAI'96, page 1050–1055. AAAI Press, 1996.
67. Zhong Zeng, Mong Li Lee, and Tok Wang Ling. Answering keyword queries involving aggregates and groupby on relational databases. *EDBT*, pages 161–172, 2016.
68. Yi Zhang, Jan Deriu, George Katsogiannis-Meimarakis, Catherine Kosten, Georgia Koutrika, and Kurt Stockinger. Sciencebenchmark: A complex real-world benchmark for evaluating natural language to sql systems. *Proc. VLDB Endow.*, 17(4):685–698, mar 2024.
69. Ruiqi Zhong, Tao Yu, and Dan Klein. Semantic evaluation for text-to-sql with distilled test suites. In *Proceedings of the 2020 Conference on Empirical Methods in Natural Language Processing (EMNLP)*, pages 396–411, 2020.
70. Victor Zhong, Caiming Xiong, and Richard Socher. Seq2sql: Generating structured queries from natural language using reinforcement learning, 2017.
71. Victor Zhong, Caiming Xiong, and Richard Socher. Seq2sql: Generating structured queries from natural language using reinforcement learning. *CoRR*, abs/1709.00103, 2017.

Chapter 3
Text-to-SQL Architecture

Abstract Since the introduction of the first neural Text-to-SQL systems, a multitude of different approaches have been proposed, each trying to advance the state of the art in its own way. Understanding the trends and directions of this research area by looking at all the different systems can often be like looking for a needle in a haystack. However, when we systematically analyze all the different techniques that have been used, we start to observe the commonalities of different systems and the emerging trends. This analysis and categorization help us better understand the work that has been done and the possible design choices for a Text-to-SQL system. This chapter presents an architecture for neural Text-to-SQL systems that covers all the design choices that have been presented in the literature. We present all the parts of a system starting from the given inputs, until the generation of a SQL query and even possible refinements after a prediction has been made. For each step in the process we analyze the different possible choices, explaining their differences, advantages, and drawbacks, in an effort to provide a clearer picture of the research landscape.

3.1 Overview of a Neural Text-to-SQL System

Since the emergence of deep learning solutions for the Text-to-SQL problem, numerous systems have been proposed that bring a wide variety of novelties and employ different approaches. However, there are key parts that serve common purposes across almost all systems, which allow us to build a general model that can help us better understand them. The aim of this chapter is to present an overview of the most important parts of neural Text-to-SQL systems as well as a taxonomy of the possible choices in each part.

Figure 3.1 shows an overview of a neural Text-to-SQL system. The main input of a Text-to-SQL system is a natural language question (NLQ) and the database (DB) that the NLQ is posed on. The first step in the architecture is **Pre-processing**, which aims to enhance the input with useful information that is relevant to the user's NLQ. This includes specific database tables, columns and values that are closely related to

G. Katsogiannis-Meimarakis et al., *Natural Language Interfaces for Databases with Deep Learning*, Data-Centric Systems and Applications,
https://doi.org/10.1007/978-3-032-06905-4_3

the question and will be used in the SQL query. This additional information will be fed into the neural network, along with the rest of the inputs, improving the model performance.

Input Construction receives all the available information, such as the NLQ, DB schema, and all the additional information generated during pre-processing, and prepares it in a format that can be accepted by the neural network. This dimension is highly dependent on the type of neural model that is used and it examines various ways that the heterogeneous inputs of the problem can be given to the neural model.

SQL Generation focuses on the different possible methods for generating SQL queries with a neural network. There are multiple ways to formulate the generation of SQL query; for example, a SQL query can be viewed as a simple string, a structured program which follows a certain grammar, or a program sketch with missing parts that must be filled. These different ways to look at the problem can lead to different generation procedures, which are also directly related to the architecture of the neural network.

Additionally, the **Neural Learning** dimension looks into how the neural model learns to generate SQL queries. As we focus on deep learning techniques, it is necessary to use a dataset that contains examples of NLQ and SQL pairs. However, there are multiple ways that the model can learn how to perform Text-to-SQL, which can range from traditional training methods up to in-context learning approaches using powerful models such as large language models (LLMs). This dimension is clearly dependent on the underlying neural model and based on the chosen approach, will either provide a trained neural model, in-context examples to be used as part of the model's input, or may even rely on a strong model to perform the task in a zero-shot setting.

The last dimension of the taxonomy is **Post-processing**, which is applied to the generated SQL queries in order to reduce the possibility of errors and to achieve better results. It should be noted that this dimension is optional and it is applied to the predictions of the model. As such, most covered techniques are independent of the model and can be used interchangeably.

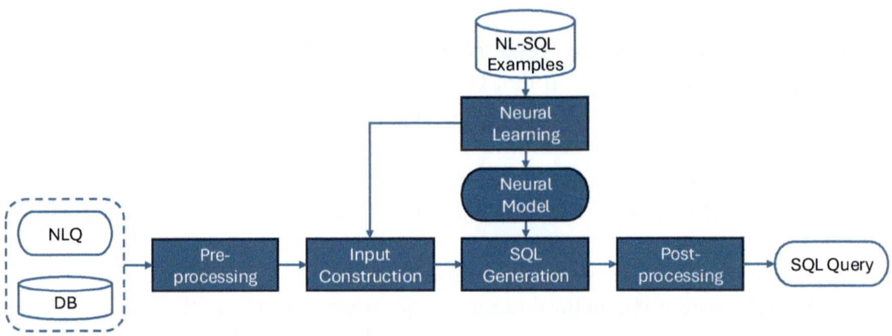

Fig. 3.1: Overview of a neural Text-to-SQL system

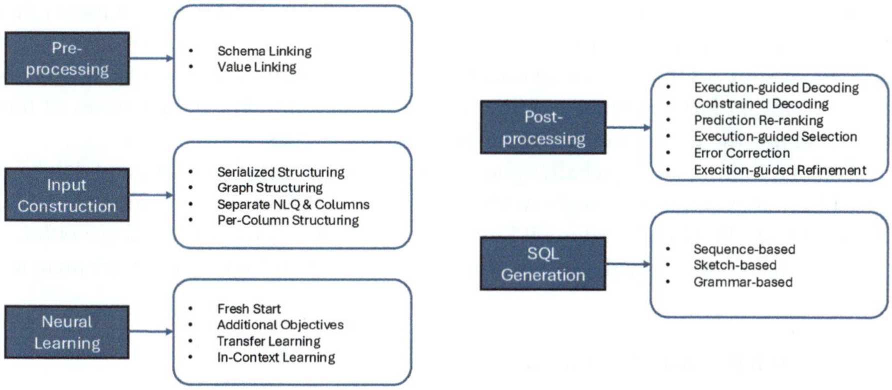

Fig. 3.2: Technique categorization based on the taxonomy dimensions

3.2 Input Pre-Processing

In order to make better and more informed predictions many systems employ pre-processing steps that create additional information related to the given NLQ. The two most important and commonly used pre-processing steps are schema linking and value linking. These two steps aim at retrieving database tables, columns, and values that are related to the user NLQ, facilitating its translation to SQL. While there is an overlap between these two procedures, the used techniques are quite different, thus requiring a different explanation of the two. It must also be noted that as the goal of these techniques is to enhance the input, systems can also operate without them. Hence, performing no input pre-processing is possible too.

3.2.1 Schema Linking

To better grasp the concept of schema linking, let us think of how a human, asked to write a SQL query from a NLQ, would start by looking at the underlying database and by trying to identify how the entities mentioned in the NLQ are stored in the database. In other words, they would attempt to *link* parts of the NLQ to the database elements they are referring to. Intuitively, a Text-to-SQL system could benefit by doing the same when translating a NLQ.

More formally, schema linking is the process of discovering which database elements (tables and columns) of the DB are referred to (directly or indirectly) by the NLQ. While earlier approaches [2, 21, 58] aimed to create specific links between words of the NLQ and DB elements, more recent works [32, 33, 46] consider a more relaxed version of the problem where they only search for DB elements that are relevant to the NLQ without finding the corresponding NLQ references. This second version is sometimes also referred to as *schema filtering*, because the goal is to find relevant DB elements and filter out irrelevant ones. For the purposes of this book, we use the term schema linking for both approaches.

Schema linking is very challenging for a variety of reasons. Query and database candidates may not use the same vocabulary nor appear in the exact same phrasing. For example, the phrase *"sang by"* in the NLQ might refer to the database column *"singer"* (same word stem, phrased differently) or *"artist"* (vocabulary mismatch).

3.2.1.1 Match-based Schema Linking

Early schema linking approaches attempt to establish hard matches between parts of the NLQ and DB elements. This means that a part of the NLQ must be written exactly or almost exactly as the name of a table or column to achieve a match. While this is a straight-forward approach, it is not able to recognize schema links when synonyms and paraphrases are used.

More specifically, these approaches start by considering specific parts of the NLQ. Usually this will either be each word separately or phrases of multiple words, called n-grams. Considering each token of the NLQ separately is the simplest approach, but it is also prone to errors as it is likely that a reference spans over multiple tokens (e.g., *"New York"*, *"Iggy Pop and the Stooges"*). To find multi-word references, it is necessary to consider n-grams of varying length. For example, IRNet [21] uses all n-grams of length from 1 to 6 in the user question as possible schema links. It processes them in descending order of length and if a n-gram is marked as a schema link, the system discards all the smaller n-grams that are contained in it, to avoid generating duplicate links.

As a next step, each of the aforementioned parts of the NLQ are compared to the table and column names of the database to decide if there is a match or not. This leads to multiple comparisons and requires the use of a metric to perform these comparisons.

Exact and Partial Matching. The simplest approach is to look for exact and partial matches, as it is done by IRNet [21]. An exact match requires that the candidates are identical, while a partial match occurs when one candidate is a substring of the other. Admittedly, this approach is bare-bone and while it can discover more obvious links, it can also result in false positive matches when candidates share the same words (e.g., *"residence"* would be considered a partial match with *"former residence"*).

Fuzzy/Approximate String Matching. Another useful technique for identifying matches when the reference in the NLQ is not written exactly as it appears in the DB, is approximate string matching. An example of such an approach is the Damerau-Levenshtein distance [8], used by ValueNet [3]. While such techniques aid at identifying matches with different spelling or spelling mistakes (e.g., *"color"*-

"colour"), they cannot handle synonyms and thus are not robust to the use of different vocabulary.

Learned Embeddings. To calculate the similarity between words of the NLQ and schema entities, an earlier work in the area of semantic parsing [28] proposes the use of learned word embeddings. The system learns word embeddings using the words of the Text-to-SQL training corpus and combines them with additional features that are calculated using NER, edit distance and indicators for exact token and lemma match. These embeddings are then used to calculate the similarity of query candidates to DB candidates. While this approach is more expensive than previous matching techniques, it allows for much more flexible and intelligent matching. This approach had also been adopted by Text-to-SQL systems [1, 2].

Classifiers. Given the complexity of schema linking, it may be possible to achieve better results by training a model to perform schema linking.

A Conditional Random Field (CRF) model [29] can be trained on a small group of hand-labeled samples to recognize schema links for numerical and textual values [4]. The predictions of this model can then be passed to the main neural network of the Text-to-SQL system along with the rest of the inputs. DBTagger [55] uses a similar approach to solve the schema linking problem as a sequence tagging problem. It employs CRFs on every token of the NLQ to identify: (*a*) its Part of Speech (POS), (*b*) schema link type (e.g., table link, value link, etc.), and (*c*) the specific schema element that it refers to. The authors argue that learning these three tasks in a multi-learning paradigm helps the system achieve better performance than it would if it only learned to identify the schema element each token refers to.

The SDSQL [25] system is simultaneously trained on two tasks: (*a*) the Text-to-SQL task, similarly to all systems, and (*b*) the *Schema Dependency Learning* task. For this additional learning task, the system is essentially trained to discover schema links in the form of dependencies between the words of the NLQ and the parts of the SQL query. Namely, the possible dependencies are: select-column (S-Col), select-aggregation (S-Agg), where-column (W-Col), where-operator (W-Op) and where-value (W-Val). For example, a select-column (S-Col) label is assigned to the dependency between the column appearing in the SELECT clause and the word of the NLQ that refers to it. A deep biaffine network [15, 16] is trained along the rest of the system to detect the existence and type of these dependencies. Training data for this task is created from the already available NLQ and SQL pairs, by assigning dependency labels between the NLQ tokens and table columns. Although the schema links discovered by the system are not directly used for predicting the SQL query, training for both tasks simultaneously has a positive effect on the system performance. This task goes beyond the schema linking task, as some of the aforementioned dependencies include query candidates that might refer to query parts (e.g., aggregation functions and condition operations). It should also be noted that this approach has only been applied to WikiSQL [76] and extending it to more complex DBs is not a trivial task.

3.2.1.2 Ranking-based Schema Linking

Schema linking can also be viewed as a ranking problem where, given an NLQ, the goal is to assign the highest scores to DB elements that are needed to translate it to SQL. This approach was adopted by RESDSQL [32] which proposed to fine-tune an encoder-only PLM such as RoBERTA [37] to generate relevance scores for each DB element, given a NLQ. One advantage of this approach is that it allows for some explainability, since it is possible to examine the relevance scores to understand the model performance. However, it is also necessary to fine-tune this ranking model on a Text-to-SQL dataset and the use of ranking scores also necessitates the definition of a score threshold in order to decide which DB elements to keep. It is also possible to avoid setting thresholds following the approach of RESDSQL [32] where the top-m ranked tables and the top-n columns are kept. Nevertheless, this approach also has its drawbacks as it will lead to having a constant pre-defined number of tables and columns predicted for each question regardless of how relevant they might be, often leading to keeping more DB elements than necessary.

3.2.1.3 Schema Linking via SQL Generation

Another way to perform schema linking consists of generating a preliminary SQL query with a Text-to-SQL model and extracting the used columns and tables as schema linking predictions [67]. On one hand, this approach can perform schema linking without the need for an additional model, because it uses the already available Text-to-SQL model. On the other hand, it is very likely that a preliminary SQL will contain a smaller amount of schema elements than the predictions of other systems, because they must all appear in a single query. As such it is more likely that such an approach might miss tables and columns that could have otherwise been predicted, leading to a lower recall which can lead to a degradation of Text-to-SQL performance. Additionally, if a Text-to-SQL model was able to generate a query that uses all the right schema elements, then it might already good enough that it does not need schema linking.

3.2.1.4 LLM-based Schema Linking

Finally, there are approaches that perform schema linking by prompting LLMs to generate the needed tables and columns. These approaches [14, 19, 46, 59, 63] use zero or few-shot prompting and ask the model to predict which tables and columns are required to generate the SQL that corresponds to a given NLQ. The advantage of these approaches is that LLMs can be used without the need of fine-tuning, making them easier to transfer to a new and unseen DB, and do not require any knob tuning as they do not need to set any thresholds. However, this also means that they are harder to analyze and understand their behavior and mistakes.

3.2.2 Value Linking

The goal of value linking is, given an NLQ, to retrieve relevant values stored in the database that are necessary to create the corresponding SQL. This is a process similar to schema linking, but it carries additional challenges stemming mainly from the large volume of data that might be stored in the DB. Because this is only a pre-processing step in the entire Text-to-SQL pipeline, a low latency is required so that the user does not have to wait for large time periods to receive their answer. As such, effective value linking usually requires the use of additional data structures that can accelerate the retrieval process.

This problem is even more challenging when the NLQ expresses a condition (i.e., a reference to a DB value) in a different way than how the value is stored in the DB. For example, the word *"female"* might imply a condition such as *"gender=F"*. In this case, besides a link between *"female"* and the column *"gender"*, the system must also be given the value as it is stored in the DB (*"F"*), in order to use it when constructing the SQL prediction. Otherwise, it will most likely produce a condition like *"gender=female"*, which would return no results.

3.2.2.1 Match-based Value Linking

This approach to value linking is very similar to the corresponding techniques for schema linking (see Section 3.2.1.1). In this case, the value linking mechanism compares each word or n-gram of the NLQ to each value stored in the database. These comparisons can be performed with any of the metrics and techniques described in Section 3.2.1.1. While this is a straight-forward way to perform value linking, it has a major drawback concerning latency and efficiency. In contrast to columns and tables, the values stored in a database are much larger in number. As such, this exhaustive approach leads to very large number of comparisons that take a very long time to complete.

Early systems [57] focusing on the Spider dataset [71] would use this approach because the low number of values that are stored in its databases made the search time relatively small. However, newer datasets such as BIRD [35] and real-world databases in general contain much greater amounts of data. For this reason, this type of value linking is usually avoided.

3.2.2.2 Using Indexes for Value Linking

As mentioned before, the large volume of data usually stored in databases renders the exhaustive search over all the DB values a very expensive procedure. To tackle this challenge, systems create additional data structures (i.e., indexes) that allow for fast and efficient search over the data. Indexes have also been used in earlier Text-to-SQL systems, which do not rely on deep learning [23, 31], to accelerate the search.

An index for value linking must contain the values of the database and the table and column in which they are stored. The index might contain all the values of the DB, or only the text values as these are the ones that must be used in the generated SQL exactly as they appear in the DB.

Furthermore, there have been different index types used in Text-to-SQL systems which can be separated into sparse and dense vector indexes, based on the type of the used vectors. The difference between the two types is that sparse vectors are built such that each dimension of the vector corresponds to a specific word or sub-word and often contain multiple zero values, whereas dense vectors are generated with a learned model and contain a non-zero value in most or all dimensions. More specifically, indexes using sparse vectors have been used by systems such as CodeS [33] which uses BM25 [48] and CHESS [53], CHASE-SQL [45], and XiYan-SQL [20] which use MinHashLSH [9]. On the other hand, systems such as Chat2Data [64], CatSQL [17], and DART-SQL [41] use dense vector indexes which rely on learned embeddings of the DB values. The main difference between the two types of indexes is that dense vectors offer better generalization to synonyms and paraphrases, while sparse vectors rely on the term frequency of words and are less robust if the DB value is not written in a lexically similar way in the NLQ.

3.2.2.3 Value Reference Detection

In order to avoid checking all the words or n-grams of the NLQ for potential value links, some systems propose to first detect possible value references and only search these references. This extra step can help reduce the number of look-ups or comparisons while also increasing the quality of discovered value links.

Named Entities. ValueNet [3] performs Named Entity Recognition (NER) on the user's NLQ to discover possible value references. This technique is very effective in discovering candidates that refer to entities such as a location or a person but might not generalize to values references that are not named entities. Specifically, it searches for five types of entities, namely: *Person, Place, Country, Organization and Sport.*

LLM Detection. Systems such as CHESS [53], CHASE-SQL [45], and XiYan-SQL [20] also propose the use of an LLM to detect possible references to values. In this case, the LLM is prompted with the question and asked to identify parts of the NLQ that might refer to DB values. While this approach might yield more generalizable results than NER because of the NL understanding capabilities of LLMs, it also increases latency because an LLM must be prompted. Furthermore, the LLM can be prompted to generate alternative versions of the identified references (e.g., "L.A.“ from "Los Angeles“), which can increase the chances of finding value links when they are stored differently in the DB.

3.3 Input Construction

In order to use a neural network for Text-to-SQL, it is essential to consider how the problem's inputs are going to be passed to the model. There are different inputs that are useful for translating a NLQ to SQL. The NLQ and the names of the DB columns and tables could be considered the minimum required input. Other features that could improve the network performance include: (*a*) the relationships present in the DB schema, including primary/foreign key relationships and connections between columns and the tables they belong to, (*b*) samples values for each column of the DB, (*c*) descriptions and comments about the tables and columns of the DB, and (*d*) links and values that have been discovered during pre-processing.

The use of neural networks mandates the transformation of all inputs into a form that can be accepted by the network. This can be restrictive, given how heterogeneous these types of inputs are and how difficult it is to represent them all in a single type of input. In this section, we examine the most representative choices for input structuring, while also taking into account the additional features that each choice can incorporate. We distinguish four main choices: (*a*) structure NLQ and columns separately, (*b*) serialize all inputs, (*c*) structuring NLQ with each column separately, and (*d*) graph structuring. A schematic overview of the possible choices can be seen in Figure 3.3.

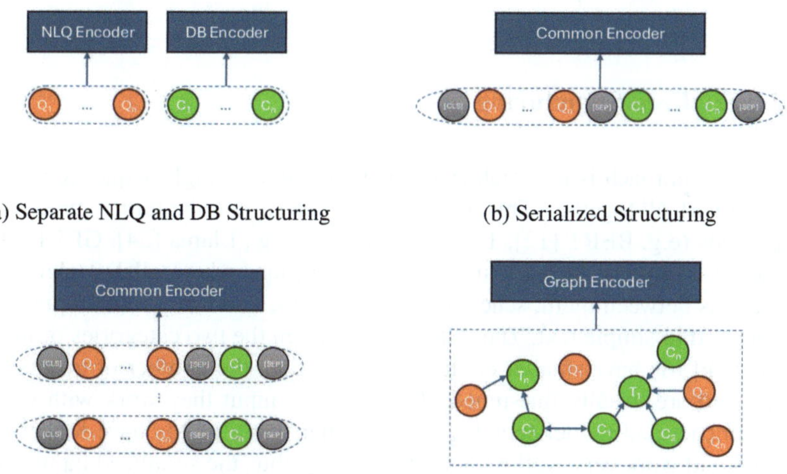

(a) Separate NLQ and DB Structuring

(b) Serialized Structuring

(c) Per-column Structuring

(d) Graph Structuring

Fig. 3.3: An overview of the possible input structuring choices. Orange tokens represent words of the NLQ, green tokens represent database elements and gray tokens are auxiliary tokens.

3.3.1 Separate NLQ and Column Structuring

A first approach, used mostly by early neural Text-to-SQL systems (e.g., Seq2SQL [76], SQLNet [65]), is to structure and process the NLQ separately from the table columns. The main reason for processing the two inputs separately is the shape mismatch between them; while the NLQ is a simple sentence (i.e., a sequence of words), the table header is a list of column names, where each name can contain multiple words, i.e., it is a sequence of sequences of words.

In Seq2SQL [76], SQLNet [65] and IncSQL [52], each word (embedding) of the NLQ is fed into a bi-directional LSTM (bi-LSTM) that produces a hidden state representation for each word. For column headers, since each column name can have multiple words, a bi-LSTM is used for each column name, and the final hidden state of each column is used as the initial representation for the column. Notice that by keeping only the last state of each column name, the representation of the header becomes a simple sequence and not a nested sequence. Since the two inputs are encoded separately, they must be combined at some point so that the output is influenced by both of them. This can be done by using cross-serial dot-product attention [38], concatenating the two representations, summing them or using a combination of the above.

None of the systems that follow this approach use any extra features besides the NLQ and DB columns. This may be attributed to the fact that these are some of the earliest neural Text-to-SQL proposals, which did not perform any pre-processing and focused on the simpler WikiSQL dataset.

3.3.2 Serialized Structuring

A different approach is to serialize all the inputs into a single sequence and pass it to the network all together. This is a very common (if not ubiquitous) practice when using PLMs (e.g. BERT [12], T5 [47]) or LLMs (e.g., Llama [54], GPT [43], etc.). In essence all inputs are structured in a text prompt, where all DB elements, the connections between them, schema and value links, and every other input type can be expressed in simple text. The difference between the two categories of models is that since PLMs have smaller context windows (i.e., the number of tokens the can handle) and are usually fine-tuned, the serialized input they work with is usually more compact and model-specific. On the other hand, LLMs have longer context windows and work very well without fine-tuning, thus the serialized inputs they are often used with are much more expressive, human-readable, and contain additional information (e.g., sample DB values).

Serializing the inputs simplifies the encoding process and benefits from the robustness of PLMs and LLMs. Since these models create a contextualized representation of their input, because if each input were to be encoded separately, the system would not benefit from their contextualization ability. However, it also carries disadvantages, such as losing schema structure information and being unable to easily represent relationships between the inputs (e.g., primary-foreign key relationships, schema links, etc.). As we go through some different serialization approaches, we will also examine how much information can be retained in each case.

3.3.2.1 Input Serialization for PLMs

PLMs usually work better when processing input sequences that follow a similar format to the format that was used to train them. For this reason, works using PLMs either use the same format the PLM creators propose, or fine-tune the model to the format they have chosen to use. It should also be noted that PLMs usually employ a few special tokens that are added to the serialized sequence to convey information about the structure of the sequence. For example, BERT [12] uses the classification [CLS] and the separating [SEP] special tokens. The [CLS] token is added at the start of the sequence. Its contextualized output, which gathers information from all the tokens in the sequence, can be used to make classification predictions that concern the entire sequence. The [SEP] special token can be used to separate different sentences in the same sequence. These tokens are also useful for the Text-to-SQL problem, while some systems also use additional tokens to provide information about the structure of the input.

The simplest serialization technique, used by several systems [22, 26, 40] that work on the WikiSQL dataset, creates a single input sequence that only contains the NLQ and all the column headers. The serialized sequence starts with the [CLS] token, as is common for BERT, then the NLQ tokens are appended, followed by a [SEP] token marking the end of the NLQ and then each column name is added followed by a [SEP] token. This input is processed by BERT, which creates a contextualized representation that has the same length as the input, and that can be processed by the rest of the network to make predictions. Since these systems only work with single tables, there is not a lot of information that needs to be preserved, but it could be argued that this approach separates the column names much less strictly compared to the separate encoding approach.

IRNet [21] (when using BERT) creates an input that starts with a [CLS] token, then continues with the NLQ's tokens followed by a [SEP] token, the name of each column of the database followed by a [SEP] token, and finally the table names of the schema, each separated with a [SEP] token as well. In order to encode discovered schema links along with the rest of the input, IRNet uses three extra tokens, namely [Column], [Table], [Value], that can be appended before a NLQ token or phrase, to mark that it was linked to a database candidate. Still, using this serialization format, there is a lot of schema information not captured. For example, it is not possible to extract any primary-foreign key relationships, or to which table each column belongs.

Finally, BRIDGE [36] constructs an input for a PLM that starts with a [CLS] token, followed by the NLQ and a [SEP] token, as well as the tables and columns of the DB, where a [T] and [C] token is added before each table and column name, respectively, so as to better preserve each attribute's role. The difference between IRNet's and BRIDGE's use of the special [C]/[Column] and [T]/[Table] tokens is that the former uses them in the NLQ part to indicate a schema link to a column or table, while the latter uses them to indicate that the tokens after a [C] or [T] token are a column or table name, respectively. BRIDGE also uses an extra third token [V] along with a value, after a column name, to mark that this value appears under the column at hand and was discovered as a possible value link to some NLQ candidate. In this case, BRIDGE uses the [V] token in the DB schema part of the input while also appending a value after it, while IRNet uses the [Value] token in the NLQ part, without providing the actual value. Additionally, all the columns belonging to a certain table are added right after the table's name in the sequence so as to better preserve the schema structure in this serialized representation. Nevertheless, all relationships between attributes (e.g., primary/foreign keys) are still lost when following this representation.

3.3.2.2 Input Serialization for LLMs

Serializing inputs for LLMs follows a similar intuition to the process described for PLMs, with the main difference being that LLMs can work with much larger inputs and usually do not need fine-tuning to achieve good performance in Text-to-SQL. As such, LLM prompts are usually much more expressive, similarly to how a human would be instructed to perform a task and contain much more information, leading to larger inputs. An example prompt can be seen in Figure 3.4. In essence, this Figure is not that different from the layout displayed in Figure 3.3b, because this text will also be tokenized and certain tokens will correspond to the NLQ and other tokens will correspond to the DB. The difference is that it can be much longer and contain more information.

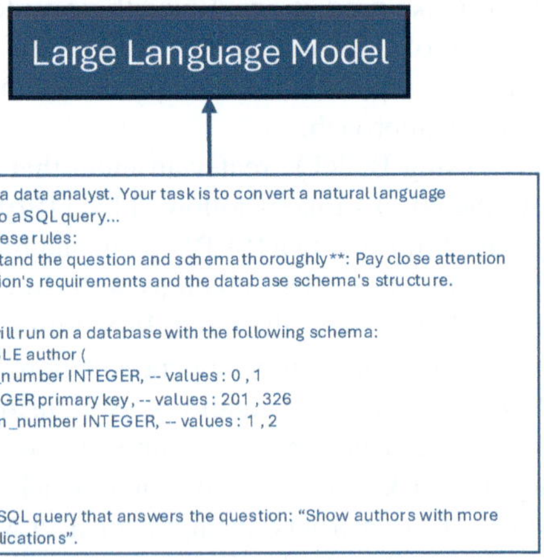

Fig. 3.4: An example of a Text-to-SQL prompt for an LLM.

A lot of works [6, 14, 19] have explored the best ways to prompt LLMs considering: (i) what instructions to provide to the LLM, (ii) how to represent the database schema and which parts of it to include, and (iii) what additional information to include. It must be noted, however, that even though this direction of research has managed to provide some general guidelines on how to prompt LLMs for this task, there is no golden rule for all the possible LLMs have and will continue to be created. As such, it is always wise to perform an experimental analysis when using a new LLM in order to understand the best ways to use it.

Firstly, when prompting LLMs (especially in a zero-shot setting) it is very beneficial to provide a set of general instructions and a role to the model. Instructions usually contain directions on how to construct the SQL, which might be generic (e.g., ”use aliases for all tables in the FROM clause”) or use-case-specific (e.g., ”avoid using LEFT JOIN, use JOIN instead”, ”use SQLite dialect”, etc.). For example, if a researcher knows that the test dataset does not need LEFT JOINs to answer its questions, they can instruct the LLM to avoid them. Such instructions are very likely lead to higher performance for this dataset but lower generalizability. It is also possible to provide more general instructions and roles [27] that have been shown to improve performance (”you are an expert database assistant”, ”you only answer with syntactically correct SQL”, etc.).

Furthermore, representing the DB schema in a text format can be done in multiple ways [6, 18]. A straightforward way is to present the actual SQL code that is used to create the schema (i.e., CREATE statements). This representation can also present the types of each column and the primary and foreign keys of the database in the same way the would be declared during its creation. Additionally, sample values that are present in the DB can be added to the representation in the form of comments or even as an INSERT statement. Another approach is to present the DB schema as a list. This can either be done in a more “natural” way, as a bullet list where each line starts with the name of a table followed by the columns appearing in the table, or in a more “pythonic” way where the name of the table is followed by a square-bracket list with the column names. In this approach, sample values and primary/foreign keys can also be represented in multiple ways, such as in parentheses next to the respective column names or separately, after all tables and columns have been listed.

Finally, there is additional information that can be given to the LLM in order to increase its performance such as schema and value links, hints, formulas, etc. Using this type of input structure allows the introduction of any type of information as long as it can be expressed in text. For example, a hint related to the NLQ might be expressed as “Take into account that online classes are stored in the table `virtual_class` instead of the table `class`”. Similarly, a value link discovered for a NLQ might be expressed as “The value `employee.gender = 'F'` might be relevant to the question”.

3.3.3 Per-Column Structuring

HydraNet [39] employs a unique approach: it processes the NLQ with each column separately and makes predictions for each column independently. For each table column, a different input is constructed by concatenating the NLQ with the column name and type and the table name. Using this input, the system predicts the probability of the column at hand appearing in the SELECT clause, the probability of the column appearing in the WHERE clause, the operation that will be used if this column appears in the WHERE clause, and so on. It could be argued that this approach does not allow the system to have a complete view of the problem instance, because the neural network makes predictions for each column separately, without being aware of the rest of the table columns.

This approach does not utilize any additional features (e.g., schema links). However, given that it also serializes its inputs (albeit, only keeping a single column each time), it could draw inspiration from the serialization techniques described in Section 3.3.2 to encode information about schema links. For example, it could append values similarly to BRIDGE [36], or use [Table] and [Column] tokens to explicitly mark column and table names in the input NLQ.

It should be noted, however, that generalizing this approach to a complete relational DB would not be an easy task. First of all, a DB usually has multiple tables, each containing multiple columns, which means that the network would have to make predictions for a much larger number of columns, greatly increasing time complexity for predicting a single SQL query. Furthermore, queries posed on complete DBs often contain JOIN clauses and other operations that depend on more than one entity; as such, processing each column separately becomes very counter-intuitive. Finally, this approach is based on a sketch-based decoder (more in Section 3.4), which is hard to extend for full DBs.

3.3.4 Graph Structuring

A graph is a very expressive approach for representing the DB elements and their relationships. Representing and encoding the input using a graph is used only by a handful of systems [1, 2, 34, 58]. Each node in the graph represents a database table or a column, while their relationships can be represented by edges that connect the respective nodes. It is also possible to add the NLQ words as nodes in the graph, and add edges that connect the query candidates with their equivalent database candidates for representing all the discovered schema links. Additionally, the used graph representation may allow for different classes of nodes and edges leading to even higher expressivity. There can be different classes of nodes to distinguish between tables, columns and NLQ words and different classes of edges to distinguish between edges that represent foreign-primary key relations, edges that indicate a column belonging to a table and edges that represent schema links.

Even though representing the system input as a graph allows for minimal loss of information and can include many types of additional inputs, processing a graph with a neural network is far more difficult than processing a sequence. This is the main reason why graphs have yet to see widespread use in the Text-to-SQL problem. However, recent advances in graph neural networks and the clever use of Transformers [56] proposed by RAT-SQL [58] and [50], are showing very promising and might be a good choice for future research.

3.4 SQL Generation

Generating SQL queries with neural networks can be achieved through multiple approaches. This is possible because SQL can viewed in different ways such as a simple sequence of text like any other NL sentence or as a program that follows a specific structure and grammar rules. Text-to-SQL systems can be divided into three categories based on how they generate SQL queries [7]: (a) sequence-based, (b) grammar-based, and (c) sketch-based slot-filling approaches.

3.4.1 Sequence-based approaches

This category includes systems that generate the predicted SQL, or a large part of it, as a sequence of words (comprising SQL tokens and schema elements) [4, 36, 76]. This decoding technique is the simplest, and was first adopted by Seq2SQL [76], which is one of the first deep-learning Text-to-SQL systems.

Subsequent systems steered away from sequence generation because it was prone to errors. The main drawback is that during prediction time the system generates SQL one token at a time and there are no measures to safeguard from producing syntactically or grammatically incorrect queries. When generating a query, it is not forced to follow the strict SQL grammatical rules, nor does it actively prevent generating incorrect column and table names that do not exist in the DB.

However, in 2021 sequence-based approaches started to be used again and proved to be very efficient thanks to the introduction of large pre-trained Transformer-based [56] models (e.g., T5 [47], BART [30]) and even more so a few years later with the popularization of LLMs (e.g., Llama [54], GPT [43], etc.). Since then, the indisputable success of LLMs sparked a return to this approach of SQL generation and a large decline to the use of any other approach. In fact, as most systems after 2021 rely on LLMs, it would be safe to say that sequence-based generation is the only used SQL generation approach in the age of LLMs.

3.4.1.1 Chain of Thought

Performing sequence-based generation with an LLM allows for calibrations on the way the LLM responds, usually through prompt engineering or by providing similar few-shot examples. Research has shown that LLMs perform better when asked to break down and explain their generation process step by step, also known as Chain of Thought (CoT) [61] prompting. In this paradigm, the LLM essentially attempts to build the SQL in an iterative way, explaining its "thought" process in each step. While this might seem intuitive for a SQL developer, guiding an LLM to work in such a way is not trivial. For this reason many researchers have worked towards automatically generating examples where the SQL is created in a CoT manner.

ACT-SQL [73] performs CoT generation by guiding the model to first state the needed tables and columns for the NLQ. Then, possible value that should be used in the SQL are explicitly stated by the LLM and finally, the LLM generates the SQL query. This process happens in a single LLM call, i.e., there are no uses of external schema or value linking components. The intuition in this case is that if the LLM is forced to generate a logical reasoning plan, it is more likely to take the intermediate "thoughts" into account and generate a correct SQL.

SELECT-SQL [51] proposes two CoT approaches for SQL: Structure-Synthesis CoT and Modular-Synthesis CoT. Structure-Synthesis CoT is a similar approach to the one followed by ACT-SQL where the LLM's reasoning starts by identifying relevant columns, tables, and values before attempting to generate the final SQL. Modular-Synthesis CoT attempts to decompose the original NLQ into simpler sub-questions, and build the SQL from the simplest sub-question iteratively expanding it until all sub-questions are covered and thus the original NLQ is answered.

FinSQL [72] also uses CoT prompting but in a simpler way, where the model is simply instructed to generate its reasoning process before generating the SQL. In order to achieve this, the authors perform synthetic CoT data generation, enriching the NLQ/SQL pairs of an existing dataset with CoT reasoning. These enriched examples are then used as few-shot examples to guide the LLM to also perform CoT.

3.4.2 Sketch-based approaches

Systems in this category [22, 26, 39, 40, 65, 70] aim at simplifying the difficult task of generating a SQL query to the easier task of predicting certain parts of the query, such as predicting the table columns that appear in the SELECT clause. In this way, the SQL generation task is transformed into a classification task. In particular, we consider a query sketch with a number of empty slots that must be filled in, and develop neural networks that predict the most probable elements for each slot. A basic prerequisite for such approaches is to have a query sketch that, when completed, will be able to capture the NLQ's intention.

While dividing the Text-to-SQL problem into small sub-tasks makes it easier to generate syntactically correct queries, sketch-based approaches may have two

```
SELECT <AGG> <COL>
WHERE <COL> <OP> <VAL>
(AND <COL> <OP> <VAL>)*
```

Fig. 3.5: The query sketch used by SQLNet, a system following a slot-filling approach to SQL generation

drawbacks. Firstly, the resulting neural network architecture may end up being quite complex since dedicated networks may be used for each slot or part of the query. Furthermore, it is hard to extend to complex SQL queries, because generating sketches for any type of SQL query is not trivial.

An example of such a sketch can be seen in Figure 3.5, which displays the query sketch used by SQLNet [65]. In this system, separate networks are used to predict: (i) the aggregation function in the SELECT clause, (ii) the column in the SELECT clause, (iii) the columns in the WHERE clause, (iv) the operators in the conditions of the WHERE clause, (v) the values in each condition, and (vi) the number of conditions in the WHERE clause. As mentioned earlier, each of these networks has a much simpler task than generating the entire query, but the expressivity of the sketch is quite limited. While this sketch worked well for the WikiSQL [76] benchmark, it does not support JOINS over multiple tables, nesting, ordering, and many other important capabilities of SQL.

3.4.3 Grammar-based approaches

Systems using a grammar-based decoder [7, 13, 21, 52, 58] are an evolution of sequence-to-sequence approaches, and produce a sequence of grammar rules instead of simple tokens in their output. These grammar rules are instructions that, when applied, can create a structured query.

The most often used grammar-based decoders by Text-to-SQL systems have been previously proposed for code generation as an Abstract Syntax Tree (AST) [68, 69]. These models take into account the grammar of the target code language (in our case, the SQL grammar) and consider the target program to be an AST, whose nodes are expanded at every tree level using the grammar rules, until all branches reach a terminal rule. When it reaches a terminal rule, the model might generate a token, for example, a table name, an operator or a condition value, in the case of Text-to-SQL. The decoder uses a LSTM-based architecture that predicts a sequence of actions, where each action is the next rule to apply to the program AST. Because the available predictions are based both on the given grammar and the current state of the AST, the possibility of generating a grammatically incorrect query is greatly reduced.

Grammar-based approaches were considered the most advantageous option for generating complex SQL queries before the widespread use of LLMs. At that time sequence-based approaches were too prone to errors and sketch-based approaches were difficult to be extended to complex queries, making grammar-based approaches the most reliable. However, as LLMs became larger and more powerful, they were more and more capable of generating valid SQL queries without errors, taking the place of grammar-based approaches, which slowly declined.

3.5 Neural Learning

Another dimension that must be examined when considering a neural Text-to-SQL system is how the model learns to perform the task of generating SQL queries. Earlier systems adopted the simple paradigm of training the network exclusively on a Text-to-SQL dataset, however, as systems evolved, they have used more sophisticated training approaches or have relied mainly or entirely on pre-training. In fact, the large success of LLMs has shown that a strong enough model can perform Text-to-SQL without any task-specific training.

3.5.1 Fresh Start

The most common approach is to train the network from scratch, i.e., initialize all the weights with a random initialization algorithm and train them on a downstream task. This was in fact the most common approach when using a neural network for most tasks. However, the popularity of Transformer-based [56] language models in the 2020s showed that pre-trained networks and self-supervised learning were able to achieve much better performance. This marked the end of such training approaches as they are usually not comparable with the performance of pre-trained models.

3.5.2 Transfer Learning

Transfer learning refers to when a model that is pre-trained on a different, usually more generic task or dataset, is then incorporated into a new model and further trained on a downstream task (e.g., Text-to-SQL). This means that a Pre-trained Language Model (e.g., BERT [11], T5 [47], etc.) or a Large Language Model (e.g., Llama [54], DeepSeek-Coder [10], etc.) that has already been trained as a general-purpose model, is adapted into a Text-to-SQL system and further Supervised Fine-tuning (SFT) is performed on a Text-to-SQL dataset. SFT can be used to update all the parameters of a language model, or in cases where the model is too large and SFT becomes too expensive, it is also possible to use parameter-efficient fine-tuning (PEFT) techniques. One such technique is Low-Rank Adaptation (LoRa) [24], which proposes to only update a sub-set of the model's parameters when fine-tuning, greatly reducing the computational costs and time required.

3.5.3 In-Context Learning

In-Context Learning (ICL) is a technique for prompting LLMs with task examples alongside the actual instance of the task that the model must perform. The large size and strong performance of LLMs allows them to perform very well on many specialist tasks such as Text-to-SQL even without ICL, i.e., in a zero-shot setting. However, to achieve even better results, researchers use ICL (or few-shot prompting) to steer the model into following the logic that is used in the demonstration examples.

ICL allows the use of a general-purpose LLM, which can be very beneficial in a setting where LLMs are used for multiple tasks. This is because it allows the reuse of the same LLM, cutting the cost of training and hosting different model instances for each task. However, ICL can only be effective if the underlying LLM has a very large number of parameters and such models are usually more expensive to host and use.

Furthermore, due to the effectiveness and popularity of ICL, researchers have also spent significant efforts into designing the most effective techniques for retrieving relevant few-shot demonstration examples. In an ICL paradigm, a (Text-to-SQL) dataset is used as a pool from which demonstration examples are retrieved. When a NLQ must be translated into SQL, a set of demonstration examples must be retrieved from the pool to be given to the model. Researchers have shown [18, 42, 73] that when the demonstration examples are more closely related to the NLQ at hand, the model's performance increases. Researchers use semantic, structural, and other similarity measures to compare the user NLQ to the NLQs from the pool and obtain the best possible examples. For example, if the retrieved examples contain a SQL query that shares a similar structure or logic to the SQL that the user NLQ requires, it is more likely for the model to generate it correctly.

3.5.4 Additional Objectives

Another interesting approach that follows the success of language models and self-supervised learning is that of using additional learning tasks while training for the Text-to-SQL problem. Some works [5, 25, 66] suggest that training neural models for more generic tasks besides the downstream task of Text-to-SQL that the model is designed to solve, can improve performance on the downstream task. When using additional objectives, one must decide whether the model should be trained on all the auxiliary objectives along the downstream task or whether it should be first trained on the auxiliary tasks and then fine-tuned on the downstream task. Some examples of additional objectives include:

- **Erosion**: The erosion task [66] consists of randomly permuting, removing and adding columns to the input schema and training the model to produce the correct SQL query using the eroded schema. Additionally, the system must learn to produce an unknown token when it has to use a column that has been removed from the given schema.

- **Shuffling**: The shuffle task [66] randomly changes the order of schema entities and condition values in the input SQL query and NLQ, training the model to correctly re-order them.
- **Graph Pruning**: The graph pruning task [5] trains the model to prune all the nodes of the input graph representation that are irrelevant to the given NLQ.
- **Schema Dependency Learning**: SDSQL [25] proposes an additional task to the Text-to-SQL task, that closely resonates to the schema linking problem. SDSQL is designed for the WikiSQL dataset. Schema Dependency Learning consists of predicting which words or phrases of the NLQ have a dependency to which columns of the table and the type of the dependency that connects them. The goal is to learn which parts of the NLQ signify that a specific column will appear in the SQL query and the role that the column will have in it (e.g., if it appears in the SELECT clause, if it implies the use of the MAX aggregation function, etc.).

3.5.5 Pre-training Specific Components

Another approach is to train specific parts of the network so that it can better adjust to the peculiarities of the task. For example, GP [75] proposes a framework that pre-trains the system decoder, before training the entire system, in order to better train it on the context-free parts of the SQL grammar it uses. For example, this would help the network learn that SQL queries always start with SELECT, the FROM clause is second, and so forth. For this purpose, the encoder's semantic information is replaced by zero vectors so that the decoder is pre-trained without any information about the particular NLQ.

3.6 Output Post-Processing

There is one last dimension to consider; that of output post-processing, i.e., additional techniques that can be applied on a model to produce even better results, or to avoid producing incorrect SQL queries.

3.6.1 None

An obvious approach is to use the model as is, without output refinement. The most important reason for this approach concerns time and resource availability; in some applications, it might be crucial to achieve low latency responses or to run on everyday machines. For example, if a refinement technique adds even a second of delay, this might be enough to make the user unhappy and unwilling to use the system. It must be noted however that almost all leader-board entries that achieve high results, use some refinement technique. This is mainly because when testing for a leader-board there is no user waiting for a response and thus no need to keep inference times low.

3.6.2 Execution-guided Decoding

Execution-guided Decoding [60] helps prevent sketch-based systems from predicting SQL queries that return execution errors. Even though sketch-based approaches are designed to avoid syntactical errors, the possibility for semantical errors is ever-present. Some examples of such errors include aggregation function mismatches (e.g., using AVERAGE on a string type column), condition type mismatches (e.g., comparing a float type column with a string type value), and so forth. To avoid these type of errors, execution-guided decoding can execute partially complete SQL queries at prediction time and decide to avoid a certain prediction if the execution fails or if it returns an empty output. Execution-guided decoding is system-agnostic and can be applied to most sketch-based systems (e.g., HydraNet [39], IE-SQL [40]), increasing their accuracy in almost all cases. Let us note that even though some systems presented in this book might not be proposed using execution-guided decoding in their original paper, they are subsequently shown to perform better when using it.

3.6.3 Constrained Decoding

While generative models with sequence-based outputs are becoming more powerful for NL generation, they are clearly prone to errors when it comes to generating structured language like SQL. *PICARD* [49] proposes a method for incrementally parsing and constraining auto-regressive decoders, to prevent them from producing grammatical or syntactical errors. For each token prediction, PICARD examines the generated sequence so far along with the k most probable next tokens and discards all tokens that would produce a grammatically incorrect SQL query, use an attribute that is not present in the DB at hand, or use a table column without having its table in the query scope (i.e., not having the appropriate table in the FROM clause). Using PICARD, a seq-to-seq pre-trained transformer model (T5-3B [47]) managed to reach the top of the Spider [71] leader-board, challenging the notion of the time that sequence-based decoders are unfit for Text-to-SQL.

Other systems with sequence-based decoders have also proposed similar decoding techniques to avoid errors. *SYNCROMESH* [44] uses completion engines to find the possible next tokens for a program given the program language grammar. Using the completion engine SYNCROMESH can decide which tokens to disqualify from prediction candidates in order to avoide erroneous SQL queries. Additional systems that use related techniques include SeaD [66] and BRIDGE [36].

3.6.4 Prediction Re-ranking

Given that neural networks are able to generate multiple predictions for a given input, some systems propose to search for the best SQL among these predictions.

The *Global-GNN* parser [2] proposes an additional network that re-ranks the top-k predictions of the main Text-to-SQL network and is trained separately from it. The discriminative re-ranker is a Graph Convolution Network that takes into account the NLQ and the database elements used by each of the k highest-confidence SQL predictions and re-ranks them based on how relevant it believes they are. Its authors argue that while the Text-to-SQL network usually predicts the correct structure for the target SQL query, it might not always predict the correct columns, tables and aggregation functions, because each of them is predicted only knowing already predicted elements and not future predictions. On the other hand, the re-ranker can look at the completed predictions and judge the use of each database element in hindsight, thus improving the prediction quality.

SQLFuse [74] performs prediction re-ranking using an LLM in a few-shot setting. The LLM is given the candidate predictions along with the DB schema, possible hints about the NLQ, and general instructions on how to choose the best prediction. Using an LLM for re-ranking allows for more additional inputs that can help the model make a better decision, but also increases the total system latency by adding an additional LLM call. Nevertheless, the authors of SQLFuse show that adding this re-ranking step significantly improves the model performance.

3.6.5 Execution-guided Selection

Some systems take advantage of a neural model's capability to generate multiple SQL predictions in combination with the execution of the predictions in order to improve their performance. *RESDSQL* [32] generates multiple SQL queries and only keeps the queries that are actually executable. This allows the system to avoid returning a query that would return an execution error. From the leftover queries the systems returns the query with the highest confidence score. *OpenSearch-SQL* [62] performs a similar procedure but uses voting based on the execution results of the queries. This means that the system groups the candidate queries in sets that produce the same results and keeps the set with the largest number of queries. The intuition behind this approach is that the result that is most often predicted is more likely to be the correct one. Finally, in order to keep a single query from the largest set, the system chooses the query with the shortest runtime. While such approaches have been proven to increase model performance, it should also be kept in mind that the execution of multiple candidate queries also increases the system latency.

3.6.6 Error Correction

Given that neural models might generate erroneous SQL queries, researchers have also proposed a set of techniques that attempt to correct an error after a query has failed to execute successfully, or in case of semantic errors. This can either be performed using a rule-based approach or an LLM-based approach.

DIN-SQL [46] prompts an LLM with a predicted SQL query and instructions that ask the model to look for and correct any possible errors that might appear in the query. In this case the LLM is also responsible for identifying that there is no error in the SQL query and abstaining from changing it.

OpenSearch-SQL [62] also uses LLM-based error correction but in a more fine-grained manner. It first tries to execute the generated SQL query and calls the LLM corrector only if the execution returns an error or an empty result set. Additionally, the authors define different prompts and different few-shot examples for each error category in order to better guide the LLM.

CHESS [53] performs a similar LLM-based error correction process. It prompts an LLM with the NLQ, DB schema, faulty SQL query, and the error message and asks the LLM to generate a corrected version.

CatSQL [17] employs a rule-based "semantics correction" technique that attempts to correct errors in three ways. First, it checks for simple mistakes such as the use of aggregation functions over columns that do not support them (e.g., an AVG over a string column). Second, it checks FROM clauses to verify that all used columns in the query have their table in the FROM clause. If a table is missing then it is automatically added. Third, it checks the join paths in the FROM clause to verify that the columns used to join tables are actually connected with a foreign key relationship. If an error is detected, then the join path is reconstructed based on the relationships in the DB.

FinSQL [72] also performs a rule-based check to ensure that all tables that are used in the generated SQL are also present in the FROM clause. If a table is missing, the model first attempts to match the used table to another table that appears in the FROM clause, assuming that the used table has been misspelled. If no similar table is found in the FROM clause, the system will search for a table in the DB schema and add it to the FROM clause in order to fix the query.

3.6.7 Execution-guided Refinement

DART-SQL [41] prompts an LLM with the generated SQL query, along with the initial NLQ and the data resulting from the SQL execution, instructing the model to change the SQL query if it is incorrect. The LLM can also choose to abstain from refining the SQL if it believes it is already correct and matches the user NLQ. Otherwise, a new refined SQL is generated and the process repeats, by providing the execution results of the refined SQL. If the SQL creates an execution error, the error message is also given to the LLM in order to correct the erroneous query. This iterative process repeats until the model decides not to refine the SQL or if multiple rounds of refinement pass (the authors suggest a max of 3 rounds) without convergence, in order to avoid being stuck in an infinite loop. The intuition behind this process follows the approach taken by SQL developer who might change a SQL program that they considered correct after receiving execution results that do not meet their expectations.

This is also similar to the error correction performed by OpenSearch-SQL [62], with the main difference being that DART-SQL attempts to refine the query even if it executes successfully.

References

1. Ben Bogin, Jonathan Berant, and Matt Gardner. Representing schema structure with graph neural networks for text-to-SQL parsing. In *Proceedings of the 57th Annual Meeting of the Association for Computational Linguistics*, pages 4560–4565, Florence, Italy, July 2019. Association for Computational Linguistics.
2. Ben Bogin, Matt Gardner, and Jonathan Berant. Global reasoning over database structures for text-to-SQL parsing. In *Proceedings of the 2019 Conference on Empirical Methods in Natural Language Processing and the 9th International Joint Conference on Natural Language Processing (EMNLP-IJCNLP)*, pages 3659–3664, Hong Kong, China, November 2019. Association for Computational Linguistics.
3. Ursin Brunner and Kurt Stockinger. Valuenet: A neural text-to-SQL architecture incorporating values. *ArXiv*, abs/2006.00888, 2020.
4. Ruichu Cai, Boyan Xu, Zhenjie Zhang, Xiaoyan Yang, Zijian Li, and Zhihao Liang. An encoder-decoder framework translating natural language to database queries. In Jérôme Lang, editor, *Proceedings of the Twenty-Seventh International Joint Conference on Artificial Intelligence, IJCAI 2018, July 13-19, 2018, Stockholm, Sweden*, pages 3977–3983. ijcai.org, 2018.
5. Ruisheng Cao, Lu Chen, Zhi Chen, Yanbin Zhao, Su Zhu, and Kai Yu. LGESQL: Line graph enhanced text-to-SQL model with mixed local and non-local relations. In *Proceedings of the 59th Annual Meeting of the Association for Computational Linguistics and the 11th International Joint Conference on Natural Language Processing (Volume 1: Long Papers)*, pages 2541–2555, Online, August 2021. Association for Computational Linguistics.
6. Shuaichen Chang and Eric Fosler-Lussier. How to prompt llms for text-to-sql: A study in zero-shot, single-domain, and cross-domain settings. *arXiv preprint arXiv:2305.11853*, 2023.
7. DongHyun Choi, Myeong Cheol Shin, EungGyun Kim, and Dong Ryeol Shin. RYANSQL: Recursively applying sketch-based slot fillings for complex text-to-sql in cross-domain databases, 2020.
8. Fred J. Damerau. A technique for computer detection and correction of spelling errors. *Commun. ACM*, 7(3):171–176, March 1964.
9. Mayur Datar, Nicole Immorlica, Piotr Indyk, and Vahab S. Mirrokni. Locality-sensitive hashing scheme based on p-stable distributions. In *Proceedings of the Twentieth Annual Symposium on Computational Geometry*, SCG '04, page 253–262, New York, NY, USA, 2004. Association for Computing Machinery.

10. Dejian Yang Zhenda Xie Kai Dong Wentao Zhang Guanting Chen Xiao Bi Y. Wu Y.K. Li Fuli Luo Yingfei Xiong Wenfeng Liang Daya Guo, Qihao Zhu. Deepseek-coder: When the large language model meets programming – the rise of code intelligence, 2024.
11. Jacob Devlin, Ming-Wei Chang, Kenton Lee, and Kristina Toutanova. BERT: pre-training of deep bidirectional transformers for language understanding. *CoRR*, abs/1810.04805, 2018.
12. Jacob Devlin, Ming-Wei Chang, Kenton Lee, and Kristina Toutanova. BERT: Pre-training of deep bidirectional transformers for language understanding, 2019.
13. Li Dong and Mirella Lapata. Coarse-to-fine decoding for neural semantic parsing, 2018.
14. Xuemei Dong, Chao Zhang, Yuhang Ge, Yuren Mao, Yunjun Gao, lu Chen, Jinshu Lin, and Dongfang Lou. C3: Zero-shot text-to-sql with chatgpt, 2023.
15. Timothy Dozat and Christopher D. Manning. Deep biaffine attention for neural dependency parsing, 2017.
16. Timothy Dozat and Christopher D. Manning. Simpler but more accurate semantic dependency parsing, 2018.
17. Han Fu, Chang Liu, Bin Wu, Feifei Li, Jian Tan, and Jianling Sun. Catsql: Towards real world natural language to sql applications. *Proc. VLDB Endow.*, 16(6):1534–1547, feb 2023.
18. Dawei Gao, Haibin Wang, Yaliang Li, Xiuyu Sun, Yichen Qian, Bolin Ding, and Jingren Zhou. Text-to-sql empowered by large language models: A benchmark evaluation, 2023.
19. Dawei Gao, Haibin Wang, Yaliang Li, Xiuyu Sun, Yichen Qian, Bolin Ding, and Jingren Zhou. Text-to-sql empowered by large language models: A benchmark evaluation. *Proc. VLDB Endow.*, 17(5):1132–1145, may 2024.
20. Yingqi Gao, Yifu Liu, Xiaoxia Li, Xiaorong Shi, Yin Zhu, Yiming Wang, Shiqi Li, Wei Li, Yuntao Hong, Zhiling Luo, Jinyang Gao, Liyu Mou, and Yu Li. Xiyan-sql: A multi-generator ensemble framework for text-to-sql. *arXiv preprint arXiv:2411.08599*, 2024.
21. Jiaqi Guo, Zecheng Zhan, Yan Gao, Yan Xiao, Jian-Guang Lou, Ting Liu, and Dongmei Zhang. Towards complex text-to-sql in cross-domain database with intermediate representation, 2019.
22. Pengcheng He, Yi Mao, Kaushik Chakrabarti, and Weizhu Chen. X-sql: reinforce schema representation with context, 2019.
23. Vagelis Hristidis, Luis Gravano, and Yannis Papakonstantinou. Efficient IR-style keyword search over relational databases. In *VLDB*, pages 850–861, 2003.
24. Edward J. Hu, Yelong Shen, Phillip Wallis, Zeyuan Allen-Zhu, Yuanzhi Li, Shean Wang, Lu Wang, and Weizhu Chen. Lora: Low-rank adaptation of large language models, 2021.
25. Binyuan Hui, Xiang Shi, Ruiying Geng, Binhua Li, Yongbin Li, Jian Sun, and Xiaodan Zhu. Improving text-to-SQL with schema dependency learning, 2021.
26. Wonseok Hwang, Jinyeong Yim, Seunghyun Park, and Minjoon Seo. A comprehensive exploration on wikisql with table-aware word contextualization, 2019.
27. Aobo Kong, Shiwan Zhao, Hao Chen, Qicheng Li, Yong Qin, Ruiqi Sun, Xin Zhou, Enzhi Wang, and Xiaohang Dong. Better zero-shot reasoning with role-play prompting. In Kevin Duh, Helena Gomez, and Steven Bethard, editors, *Proceedings of the 2024 Conference of the North American Chapter of the Association for Computational Linguistics: Human Language Technologies (Volume 1: Long Papers)*, pages 4099–4113, Mexico City, Mexico, June 2024. Association for Computational Linguistics.
28. Jayant Krishnamurthy, Pradeep Dasigi, and Matt Gardner. Neural semantic parsing with type constraints for semi-structured tables. In *Proceedings of the 2017 Conference on Empirical Methods in Natural Language Processing*, pages 1516–1526, Copenhagen, Denmark, September 2017. Association for Computational Linguistics.
29. John D. Lafferty, Andrew McCallum, and Fernando C. N. Pereira. Conditional random fields: Probabilistic models for segmenting and labeling sequence data. In *Proceedings of the Eighteenth International Conference on Machine Learning*, ICML '01, page 282–289, San Francisco, CA, USA, 2001. Morgan Kaufmann Publishers Inc.
30. Mike Lewis, Yinhan Liu, Naman Goyal, Marjan Ghazvininejad, Abdelrahman Mohamed, Omer Levy, Ves Stoyanov, and Luke Zettlemoyer. BART: Denoising sequence-to-sequence pre-training for natural language generation, translation, and comprehension, 2019.
31. Fei Li and H. V. Jagadish. Constructing an interactive natural language interface for relational databases. *PVLDB*, 8(1):73–84, September 2014.

32. Haoyang Li, Jing Zhang, Cuiping Li, and Hong Chen. Resdsql: decoupling schema linking and skeleton parsing for text-to-sql. In *Proceedings of the Thirty-Seventh AAAI Conference on Artificial Intelligence and Thirty-Fifth Conference on Innovative Applications of Artificial Intelligence and Thirteenth Symposium on Educational Advances in Artificial Intelligence*, AAAI'23/IAAI'23/EAAI'23. AAAI Press, 2023.
33. Haoyang Li, Jing Zhang, Hanbing Liu, Ju Fan, Xiaokang Zhang, Jun Zhu, Renjie Wei, Hongyan Pan, Cuiping Li, and Hong Chen. Codes: Towards building open-source language models for text-to-sql. *Proc. ACM Manag. Data*, 2(3), may 2024.
34. Jinyang Li, Binyuan Hui, Reynold Cheng, Bowen Qin, Chenhao Ma, Nan Huo, Fei Huang, Wenyu Du, Luo Si, and Yongbin Li. Graphix-t5: Mixing pre-trained transformers with graph-aware layers for text-to-sql parsing. In *Proceedings of the AAAI conference on artificial intelligence*, volume 37, pages 13076–13084, 2023.
35. Jinyang Li, Binyuan Hui, Ge Qu, Jiaxi Yang, Binhua Li, Bowen Li, Bailin Wang, Bowen Qin, Ruiying Geng, Nan Huo, Xuanhe Zhou, Ma Chenhao, Guoliang Li, Kevin Chang, Fei Huang, Reynold Cheng, and Yongbin Li. Can llm already serve as a database interface? a big bench for large-scale database grounded text-to-sqls. In A. Oh, T. Naumann, A. Globerson, K. Saenko, M. Hardt, and S. Levine, editors, *Advances in Neural Information Processing Systems*, volume 36, pages 42330–42357. Curran Associates, Inc., 2023.
36. Xi Victoria Lin, Richard Socher, and Caiming Xiong. Bridging textual and tabular data for cross-domain text-to-SQL semantic parsing. In *Findings of the Association for Computational Linguistics: EMNLP 2020*, pages 4870–4888, Online, November 2020. Association for Computational Linguistics.
37. Yinhan Liu, Myle Ott, Naman Goyal, Jingfei Du, Mandar Joshi, Danqi Chen, Omer Levy, Mike Lewis, Luke Zettlemoyer, and Veselin Stoyanov. Roberta: A robustly optimized bert pretraining approach, 2019.
38. Minh-Thang Luong, Hieu Pham, and Christopher D. Manning. Effective approaches to attention-based neural machine translation, 2015.
39. Qin Lyu, Kaushik Chakrabarti, Shobhit Hathi, Souvik Kundu, Jianwen Zhang, and Zheng Chen. Hybrid ranking network for text-to-sql. Technical Report MSR-TR-2020-7, Microsoft Dynamics 365 AI, March 2020.
40. Jianqiang Ma, Zeyu Yan, Shuai Pang, Yang Zhang, and Jianping Shen. Mention extraction and linking for SQL query generation. In *Proceedings of the 2020 Conference on Empirical Methods in Natural Language Processing (EMNLP)*, pages 6936–6942, Online, November 2020. Association for Computational Linguistics.
41. Wenxin Mao, Ruiqi Wang, Jiyu Guo, Jichuan Zeng, Cuiyun Gao, Peiyi Han, and Chuanyi Liu. Enhancing text-to-SQL parsing through question rewriting and execution-guided refinement. In Lun-Wei Ku, Andre Martins, and Vivek Srikumar, editors, *Findings of the Association for Computational Linguistics: ACL 2024*, pages 2009–2024, Bangkok, Thailand, August 2024. Association for Computational Linguistics.
42. Linyong Nan, Yilun Zhao, Weijin Zou, Narutatsu Ri, Jaesung Tae, Ellen Zhang, Arman Cohan, and Dragomir Radev. Enhancing text-to-SQL capabilities of large language models: A study on prompt design strategies. In Houda Bouamor, Juan Pino, and Kalika Bali, editors, *Findings of the Association for Computational Linguistics: EMNLP 2023*, pages 14935–14956, Singapore, December 2023. Association for Computational Linguistics.
43. OpenAI, Josh Achiam, Steven Adler, Sandhini Agarwal, Lama Ahmad, Ilge Akkaya, Florencia Leoni Aleman, Diogo Almeida, Janko Altenschmidt, Sam Altman, Shyamal Anadkat, Red Avila, Igor Babuschkin, Suchir Balaji, Valerie Balcom, Paul Baltescu, Haiming Bao, Mohammad Bavarian, Jeff Belgum, Irwan Bello, Jake Berdine, Gabriel Bernadett-Shapiro, Christopher Berner, Lenny Bogdonoff, Oleg Boiko, Madelaine Boyd, Anna-Luisa Brakman, Greg Brockman, Tim Brooks, Miles Brundage, Kevin Button, Trevor Cai, Rosie Campbell, Andrew Cann, Brittany Carey, Chelsea Carlson, Rory Carmichael, Brooke Chan, Che Chang, Fotis Chantzis, Derek Chen, Sully Chen, Ruby Chen, Jason Chen, Mark Chen, Ben Chess, Chester Cho, Casey Chu, Hyung Won Chung, Dave Cummings, Jeremiah Currier, Yunxing Dai, Cory Decareaux, Thomas Degry, Noah Deutsch, Damien Deville, Arka Dhar, David Dohan, Steve Dowling, Sheila Dunning, Adrien Ecoffet, Atty Eleti, Tyna Eloundou, David Farhi,

Liam Fedus, Niko Felix, Simón Posada Fishman, Juston Forte, Isabella Fulford, Leo Gao, Elie Georges, Christian Gibson, Vik Goel, Tarun Gogineni, Gabriel Goh, Rapha Gontijo-Lopes, Jonathan Gordon, Morgan Grafstein, Scott Gray, Ryan Greene, Joshua Gross, Shixiang Shane Gu, Yufei Guo, Chris Hallacy, Jesse Han, Jeff Harris, Yuchen He, Mike Heaton, Johannes Heidecke, Chris Hesse, Alan Hickey, Wade Hickey, Peter Hoeschele, Brandon Houghton, Kenny Hsu, Shengli Hu, Xin Hu, Joost Huizinga, Shantanu Jain, Shawn Jain, Joanne Jang, Angela Jiang, Roger Jiang, Haozhun Jin, Denny Jin, Shino Jomoto, Billie Jonn, Heewoo Jun, Tomer Kaftan, Lukasz Kaiser, Ali Kamali, Ingmar Kanitscheider, Nitish Shirish Keskar, Tabarak Khan, Logan Kilpatrick, Jong Wook Kim, Christina Kim, Yongjik Kim, Jan Hendrik Kirchner, Jamie Kiros, Matt Knight, Daniel Kokotajlo, Lukasz Kondraciuk, Andrew Kondrich, Aris Konstantinidis, Kyle Kosic, Gretchen Krueger, Vishal Kuo, Michael Lampe, Ikai Lan, Teddy Lee, Jan Leike, Jade Leung, Daniel Levy, Chak Ming Li, Rachel Lim, Molly Lin, Stephanie Lin, Mateusz Litwin, Theresa Lopez, Ryan Lowe, Patricia Lue, Anna Makanju, Kim Malfacini, Sam Manning, Todor Markov, Yaniv Markovski, Bianca Martin, Katie Mayer, Andrew Mayne, Bob McGrew, Scott Mayer McKinney, Christine McLeavey, Paul McMillan, Jake McNeil, David Medina, Aalok Mehta, Jacob Menick, Luke Metz, Andrey Mishchenko, Pamela Mishkin, Vinnie Monaco, Evan Morikawa, Daniel Mossing, Tong Mu, Mira Murati, Oleg Murk, David Mély, Ashvin Nair, Reiichiro Nakano, Rajeev Nayak, Arvind Neelakantan, Richard Ngo, Hyeonwoo Noh, Long Ouyang, Cullen O'Keefe, Jakub Pachocki, Alex Paino, Joe Palermo, Ashley Pantuliano, Giambattista Parascandolo, Joel Parish, Emy Parparita, Alex Passos, Mikhail Pavlov, Andrew Peng, Adam Perelman, Filipe de Avila Belbute Peres, Michael Petrov, Henrique Ponde de Oliveira Pinto, Michael, Pokorny, Michelle Pokrass, Vitchyr H. Pong, Tolly Powell, Alethea Power, Boris Power, Elizabeth Proehl, Raul Puri, Alec Radford, Jack Rae, Aditya Ramesh, Cameron Raymond, Francis Real, Kendra Rimbach, Carl Ross, Bob Rotsted, Henri Roussez, Nick Ryder, Mario Saltarelli, Ted Sanders, Shibani Santurkar, Girish Sastry, Heather Schmidt, David Schnurr, John Schulman, Daniel Selsam, Kyla Sheppard, Toki Sherbakov, Jessica Shieh, Sarah Shoker, Pranav Shyam, Szymon Sidor, Eric Sigler, Maddie Simens, Jordan Sitkin, Katarina Slama, Ian Sohl, Benjamin Sokolowsky, Yang Song, Natalie Staudacher, Felipe Petroski Such, Natalie Summers, Ilya Sutskever, Jie Tang, Nikolas Tezak, Madeleine B. Thompson, Phil Tillet, Amin Tootoonchian, Elizabeth Tseng, Preston Tuggle, Nick Turley, Jerry Tworek, Juan Felipe Cerón Uribe, Andrea Vallone, Arun Vijayvergiya, Chelsea Voss, Carroll Wainwright, Justin Jay Wang, Alvin Wang, Ben Wang, Jonathan Ward, Jason Wei, CJ Weinmann, Akila Welihinda, Peter Welinder, Jiayi Weng, Lilian Weng, Matt Wiethoff, Dave Willner, Clemens Winter, Samuel Wolrich, Hannah Wong, Lauren Workman, Sherwin Wu, Jeff Wu, Michael Wu, Kai Xiao, Tao Xu, Sarah Yoo, Kevin Yu, Qiming Yuan, Wojciech Zaremba, Rowan Zellers, Chong Zhang, Marvin Zhang, Shengjia Zhao, Tianhao Zheng, Juntang Zhuang, William Zhuk, and Barret Zoph. Gpt-4 technical report, 2024.

44. Gabriel Poesia, Oleksandr Polozov, Vu Le, Ashish Tiwari, Gustavo Soares, Christopher Meek, and Sumit Gulwani. Synchromesh: Reliable code generation from pre-trained language models. *arXiv preprint arXiv:2201.11227*, 2022.
45. Mohammadreza Pourreza, Hailong Li, Ruoxi Sun, Yeounoh Chung, Shayan Talaei, Gaurav Tarlok Kakkar, Yu Gan, Amin Saberi, Fatma Ozcan, and Sercan O. Arik. Chase-sql: Multi-path reasoning and preference optimized candidate selection in text-to-sql, 2024.
46. Mohammadreza Pourreza and Davood Rafiei. Din-sql: Decomposed in-context learning of text-to-sql with self-correction. *Advances in Neural Information Processing Systems*, 36, 2024.
47. Colin Raffel, Noam Shazeer, Adam Roberts, Katherine Lee, Sharan Narang, Michael Matena, Yanqi Zhou, Wei Li, and Peter J. Liu. Exploring the limits of transfer learning with a unified text-to-text transformer, 2020.
48. Stephen Robertson and Hugo Zaragoza. The probabilistic relevance framework: Bm25 and beyond. *Found. Trends Inf. Retr.*, 3(4):333–389, April 2009.
49. Torsten Scholak, Nathan Schucher, and Dzmitry Bahdanau. PICARD: Parsing incrementally for constrained auto-regressive decoding from language models, 2021.
50. Peter Shaw, Philip Massey, Angelica Chen, Francesco Piccinno, and Yasemin Altun. Generating logical forms from graph representations of text and entities. In *Proceedings of the 57th Annual*

Meeting of the Association for Computational Linguistics, pages 95–106, Florence, Italy, July 2019. Association for Computational Linguistics.
51. Ke Shen and Mayank Kejriwal. Select-sql: Self-correcting ensemble chain-of-thought for text-to-sql, 2024.
52. Tianze Shi, Kedar Tatwawadi, Kaushik Chakrabarti, Yi Mao, Oleksandr Polozov, and Weizhu Chen. Incsql: Training incremental text-to-sql parsers with non-deterministic oracles, 2018.
53. Shayan Talaei, Mohammadreza Pourreza, Yu-Chen Chang, Azalia Mirhoseini, and Amin Saberi. Chess: Contextual harnessing for efficient sql synthesis. *arXiv preprint arXiv:2405.16755*, 2024.
54. Hugo Touvron, Louis Martin, Kevin Stone, Peter Albert, Amjad Almahairi, Yasmine Babaei, Nikolay Bashlykov, Soumya Batra, Prajjwal Bhargava, Shruti Bhosale, et al. Llama 2: Open foundation and fine-tuned chat models. *arXiv preprint arXiv:2307.09288*, 2023.
55. Arif Usta, Akifhan Karakayali, and Özgür Ulusoy. Dbtagger: Multi-task learning for keyword mapping in NLIDBs using bi-directional recurrent neural networks. *Proc. VLDB Endow.*, 14(5):813–821, jan 2021.
56. Ashish Vaswani, Noam Shazeer, Niki Parmar, Jakob Uszkoreit, Llion Jones, Aidan N Gomez, L ukasz Kaiser, and Illia Polosukhin. Attention is all you need. In I. Guyon, U. Von Luxburg, S. Bengio, H. Wallach, R. Fergus, S. Vishwanathan, and R. Garnett, editors, *Advances in Neural Information Processing Systems*, volume 30. Curran Associates, Inc., 2017.
57. Bailin Wang, Richard Shin, Xiaodong Liu, Oleksandr Polozov, and Matthew Richardson. Rat-sql: Relation-aware schema encoding and linking for text-to-sql parsers. *arXiv preprint arXiv:1911.04942*, 2019.
58. Bailin Wang, Richard Shin, Xiaodong Liu, Oleksandr Polozov, and Matthew Richardson. RAT-SQL: Relation-aware schema encoding and linking for text-to-sql parsers, 2020.
59. Bing Wang, Changyu Ren, Jian Yang, Xinnian Liang, Jiaqi Bai, Linzheng Chai, Zhao Yan, Qian-Wen Zhang, Di Yin, Xing Sun, and Zhoujun Li. Mac-sql: A multi-agent collaborative framework for text-to-sql, 2024.
60. Chenglong Wang, Kedar Tatwawadi, Marc Brockschmidt, Po-Sen Huang, Yi Mao, Oleksandr Polozov, and Rishabh Singh. Robust text-to-sql generation with execution-guided decoding, 2018.
61. Jason Wei, Xuezhi Wang, Dale Schuurmans, Maarten Bosma, Brian Ichter, Fei Xia, Ed H. Chi, Quoc V. Le, and Denny Zhou. Chain-of-thought prompting elicits reasoning in large language models. In *Proceedings of the 36th International Conference on Neural Information Processing Systems*, NIPS '22, Red Hook, NY, USA, 2022. Curran Associates Inc.
62. Xiangjin Xie, Guangwei Xu, Lingyan Zhao, and Ruijie Guo. Opensearch-sql: Enhancing text-to-sql with dynamic few-shot and consistency alignment. *Proc. ACM Manag. Data*, 3(3), June 2025.
63. Yuanzhen Xie, Xinzhou Jin, Tao Xie, Matrixmxlin Matrixmxlin, Liang Chen, Chenyun Yu, Cheng Lei, Chengxiang Zhuo, Bo Hu, and Zang Li. Decomposition for enhancing attention: Improving LLM-based text-to-SQL through workflow paradigm. In Lun-Wei Ku, Andre Martins, and Vivek Srikumar, editors, *Findings of the Association for Computational Linguistics: ACL 2024*, pages 10796–10816, Bangkok, Thailand, August 2024. Association for Computational Linguistics.
64. Guoliang Li Xinyang Zhao, Xuanhe Zhou. Chat2data: An interactive data analysis system with rag, vector databases and llms, 2024.
65. Xiaojun Xu, Chang Liu, and Dawn Song. Sqlnet: Generating structured queries from natural language without reinforcement learning, 2017.
66. Kuan Xuan, Yongbo Wang, Yongliang Wang, Zujie Wen, and Yang Dong. Sead: End-to-end text-to-sql generation with schema-aware denoising, 2021.
67. Sun Yang, Qiong Su, Zhishuai Li, Ziyue Li, Hangyu Mao, Chenxi Liu, and Rui Zhao. Sql-to-schema enhances schema linking in text-to-sql, 2024.
68. Pengcheng Yin and Graham Neubig. A syntactic neural model for general-purpose code generation, 2017.

69. Pengcheng Yin and Graham Neubig. TRANX: A transition-based neural abstract syntax parser for semantic parsing and code generation. In *Proceedings of the 2018 Conference on Empirical Methods in Natural Language Processing: System Demonstrations*, pages 7–12, Brussels, Belgium, November 2018. Association for Computational Linguistics.
70. Tao Yu, Zifan Li, Zilin Zhang, Rui Zhang, and Dragomir Radev. Typesql: Knowledge-based type-aware neural text-to-sql generation, 2018.
71. Tao Yu, Rui Zhang, Kai Yang, Michihiro Yasunaga, Dongxu Wang, Zifan Li, James Ma, Irene Li, Qingning Yao, Shanelle Roman, Zilin Zhang, and Dragomir Radev. Spider: A large-scale human-labeled dataset for complex and cross-domain semantic parsing and text-to-SQL task. In Ellen Riloff, David Chiang, Julia Hockenmaier, and Jun'ichi Tsujii, editors, *Proceedings of the 2018 Conference on Empirical Methods in Natural Language Processing*, pages 3911–3921, Brussels, Belgium, October-November 2018. Association for Computational Linguistics.
72. Chao Zhang, Yuren Mao, Yijiang Fan, Yu Mi, Yunjun Gao, Lu Chen, Dongfang Lou, and Jinshu Lin. Finsql: Model-agnostic llms-based text-to-sql framework for financial analysis. In *Companion of the 2024 International Conference on Management of Data*, SIGMOD/PODS '24, page 93–105, New York, NY, USA, 2024. Association for Computing Machinery.
73. Hanchong Zhang, Ruisheng Cao, Lu Chen, Hongshen Xu, and Kai Yu. Act-sql: In-context learning for text-to-sql with automatically-generated chain-of-thought. *arXiv preprint arXiv:2310.17342*, 2023.
74. Tingkai Zhang, Chaoyu Chen, Cong Liao, Jun Wang, Xudong Zhao, Hang Yu, Jianchao Wang, Jianguo Li, and Wenhui Shi. Sqlfuse: Enhancing text-to-sql performance through comprehensive llm synergy. *arXiv preprint arXiv:2407.14568*, 2024.
75. Liang Zhao, Hexin Cao, and Yunsong Zhao. GP: Context-free grammar pre-training for text-to-sql parsers, 2021.
76. Victor Zhong, Caiming Xiong, and Richard Socher. Seq2sql: Generating structured queries from natural language using reinforcement learning, 2017.

70. Pengcheng Yin and Graham Neubig. TRANX: A transition-based neural abstract syntax parser for semantic parsing and code generation. In Proceedings of the 2018 Conference on [illegible] Brussels, Belgium, [illegible]

[illegible] Zhang [illegible] generation. [illegible]

[illegible]

Chapter 4
Text-to-SQL Systems

Abstract Neural Text-to-SQL systems have been appearing with increasing frequency since the introduction of the first large-scale benchmarks for the task. With multiple new systems being introduced each year, it is often hard to follow the research trends and new directions that arise. This chapter presents a walkthrough of different Text-to-SQL systems, grouping them in comprehensive groups based on common core ideas and research approaches. Using the taxonomy presented in the previous chapter, we aim to present and compare different systems and ultimately shed light into what has been done since the rise of neural Text-to-SQL.

4.1 Introduction

Using the taxonomy for deep learning Text-to-SQL systems established in Chapter 4, this chapter will zoom in on key systems that have introduced novel and interesting ideas and have shaped the area. This chapter provides insights and explanations on these systems while also grouping them based on important milestones. Figure 4.1 presents a chronological view on deep learning Text-to-SQL systems, along with important datasets and language representation advancements that have had a great impact on the domain. While certain systems could obviously fit in multiple sections, this specific categorization is based on the novelty introduced by each system at the time of its publishing, its influence on later systems, as well as the possible importance of each novelty given its capability to address future and open research problems.

4.2 The Dawn of an Era

As mentioned before, the era of deep learning Text-to-SQL systems essentially starts with the release of the first large annotated Text-to-SQL dataset. WikiSQL was

G. Katsogiannis-Meimarakis et al., *Natural Language Interfaces for Databases with Deep Learning*, Data-Centric Systems and Applications,
https://doi.org/10.1007/978-3-032-06905-4_4

System	Pre-processing	Input Construction	Output Generation	Neural Learning	Post-processing
Seq2SQL [59]	-	Separate	Sequence	FS	-
SQLNet [50]	-	Separate	Sketch	FS	-
IncSQL [42]	-	Separate	Grammar	FS	-
TypeSQL [54]	SL	Separate	Sketch	FS	-
Coarse2Fine [8]	-	Separate	Sketch	FS	-
SyntaxSQLNet [55]	-	Separate	Sketch	FS	-
SQLova [18]	-	Serialize	Sketch	TL	EG-Dec
IRNet [14]	SL	Serialize	Grammar	TL	-
X-SQL [15]	-	Serialize	Sketch	TL	EG-Dec
RAT-SQL [46]	SL + VL	Graph	Grammar	TL	-
GNN [1]	SL	Graph	Grammar	FS	-
Global-GNN [2]	SL	Graph	Grammar	FS	Re-rank
ValueNet [3]	SL	Serialize	Grammar	TL	-
BRIDGE [25]	SL	Serialize	Sequence	TL	C-Dec
HydraNet [28]	-	Per column	Sketch	TL	EG-Dec
IE-SQL [29]	SL	Serialize	Sketch	TL	EG-Dec
RYANSQL [5]	-	Serialize	Sketch	TL	-
SmBoP [39]	SL	Graph	Grammar	TL	-
SDSQL [17]	SL	Serialize	Sketch	TL + AO	EG-Dec
SeaD [51]	-	Serialize	Sequence	TL + AO	C-Dec
T5-3B+PICARD [40]	-	Serialize	Sequence	TL	C-Dec
RESDSQL [20]	SL	Serialize	Sequence	TL	-
ACT-SQL [57]	SL + VL	Serialize	Sequence	ICL	-
C3-SQL [9]	SL	Serialize	Sequence	ICL	EG-Sel
DAIL-SQL [12]	-	Serialize	Sequence	ICL	-
CodeS [21]	SL + VL	Serialize	Sequence	ICL + TL	-
DIN-SQL [35]	SL	Serialize	Sequence	ICL	EC
SENSE [52]	-	Serialize	Sequence	TL	-
FinSQL [56]	SL	Serialize	Sequence	ICL + PEFT	EC
DART-SQL [30]	SL + VL	Serialize	Sequence	ICL	EG-Ref
SQLFuse [58]	SL	Serialize	Sequence	ICL	Re-rank
CHESS [44]	SL + VL	Serialize	Sequence	ICL	EG-Ref + EG-Sel
SelECT-SQL [41]	-	Serialize	Sequence	ICL	EG-Ref + Re-rank
OpenSearch-SQL [49]	SL + VL	Serialize	Sequence	ICL	EC + EG-Sel

Table 4.1: Classification of Text-to-SQL systems based on the architecture presented in Chapter 3. For Input Pre-processing: SL stands for Schema Linking, VL stands for Value Linking. For Neural Learning: FS stands for Fresh Start, TL stands for Transfer Learning, AO stands for Additional Objectives, ICL stands for In-Context Learning, PEFT stands for Parameter-Efficent Fine-Tuning. For Output Post-processing: EG-Dec stands for Execution-Guided Decoding, C-Dec stands for Constrained Decoding, EG-Sel stands for Execution-Guided Selection, EG-Ref stands for Execution-Guided Refinement, EC stands for Error Correction.

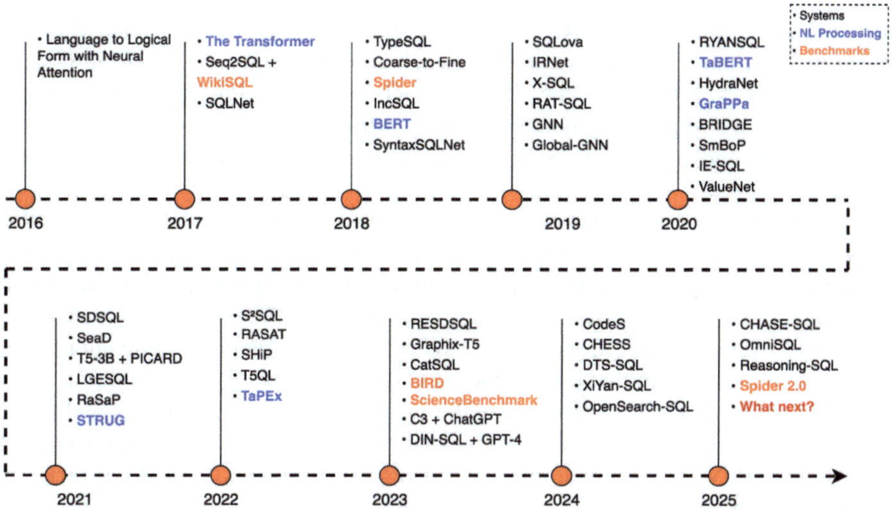

Fig. 4.1: A timeline of deep learning text-to-sql systems, datasets and language representation techniques

released along with *Seq2SQL* [59], which was one of the first neural networks for the Text-to-SQL task and was based on previous work focusing on generating logical forms using neural networks [7]. The system predicts the aggregation function and the column for the SELECT clause as classification tasks and generates the WHERE clause using a seq-to-seq pointer network. The latter part of the system is burdened with generating parts of the query that can lead to syntactic errors, which is its major drawback.

A big difference from almost all other systems is that Seq2SQL is partially trained using reinforcement learning. While the aggregation function and SELECT column predictors are trained using cross entropy loss, the WHERE clause predictor is trained using a reward function that returns a positive reward if the produced query returns the same results as the ground truth query and a negative reward if the query returns different results or if it cannot be executed due to errors. The reasoning behind using reinforcement learning, even though it generally performs worse than supervised learning, is that the WHERE clause can be expressed in multiple ways and still be correct.

To address these problems, i.e., that sequence decoders can produce errors and that reinforcement learning is not ideal, *SQLNet* [50] proposed using a query sketch with fixed slots that, when filled, form a SQL query. This sketch albeit being very simple, covers all the queries present in the WikiSQL dataset. Using a sketch allowed the problem to be formulated almost entirely as a classification problem, since the network has to predict: (*a*) the aggregation function between a fixed number of choices, (*b*) the SELECT column among a number of columns present in the table, (*c*) the number of conditions (between 0 and 4 in the WikiSQL dataset), (*d*) the columns present in the WHERE clause (as multi-label classification, since they can be more than one), (*e*) the operation of each condition among a fixed number of operations ($\leq, =, \geq$) and (*f*) the value of each condition. Predicting the value is achieved using a sequence generator network, which in this case is only responsible for the value and not for the SQL syntax or grammar, so syntactic mistakes are avoided.

Another improvement introduced in SQLNet is the use of a *column attention neural architecture* to the network. Given that SQLNet encodes the NLQ and table columns separately, the encoded representation of the NLQ does not have any information on the available columns and thus cannot inform the system on which words in the NLQ are important for generating the correct SQL query. Column attention is an attention mechanism that infuses the NLQ representation with information about the table columns, so as to emphasize the words that might be more related to the table. Other than that, the two systems share some common points with both of them using GloVe [33] embeddings for text representation and LSTM networks for encoding them.

4.3 Sketch Generation

While the use of a sketch greatly simplified the Text-to-SQL problem and made predictions simpler for neural networks, the complexity of SQL queries these systems could generate using a single sketch was restricted. Systems such as Coarse2Fine [8] and RYANSQL [5] have tried to generalize sketch-based decoding, by attempting to not only fill in the slots of a sketch but also generate the appropriate sketch for a given NLQ.

Coarse2Fine [8] is a semantic parser that can generate various types of programs, one of which is SQL. Its main highlight is that it decomposes the decoding process into two steps: first, it generates a rough (coarse) sketch of the target program without low-level details, and then it fills this sketch with the missing (fine) details. Its authors argue that a great advantage of this approach is that the network can disentangle high-level from low-level knowledge and learn each one of them more effectively. Unfortunately, this system is only used on the WikiSQL dataset and is not extended to more complex SQL queries, which is not trivial work. In fact, because Coarse2Fine is designed for the WikiSQL dataset, the sketches it generates only differ between them in the number of conditions that appear in the WHERE clause and the operations in each condition. As such, while the idea it proposes might be very interesting, in practice, it essentially achieves generating SQL queries of no greater complexity than what simple sketch-based systems do.

RYANSQL [5] is another system that generates the appropriate sketch before filling it, but in contrast to the previous, it manages to produce much more complex SQL queries such as the ones present in the Spider dataset. This is achieved by breaking down each SQL query into a non-nested form that consists of multiple, simpler, sub-queries. The authors propose 7 types of sub-queries, each with its own sketch, that can be combined to produce more complex queries. The network then learns to recursively predict the type of each sub-query and to subsequently fill in its sketch. RYANSQL achieved the first position in the Spider benchmark at the time of its publication, but has since been surpassed by other systems, while no other similar approach has been able to achieve comparable performance.

SyntaxSQLNet [55] follows a similar approach, but instead of generating the query sketch, it follows a pre-defined SQL grammar that determines which of its 9 slot-filling modules needs to be called to make a prediction. This allow the system to produce grammatically correct complex queries while enjoying the benefits of a sketch-based decoder. At each prediction step, the grammar and the prediction history from the previous steps are used to determine the module (e.g., COLUMN module, AGGREGATOR module, OPERATOR module, HAVING module, etc.) that needs to make a prediction in order to build the SQL query. Although this is a hybrid approach, the architecture of the decoder modules classifies SyntaxSQLNet as a sketch-based system. The main difference is that most sketch-based decoders call all their slot-filling modules simultaneously to fill the sketch, whereas SyntaxSQLNet calls specific modules recursively because the grammar defines what needs to be filled in at each prediction step. SyntaxSQLNet was one of the first systems proposed for Spider. Since then, many systems have achieved better performance scores while steering away from this methodology, hinting at its weaknesses. For example, one of the main challenges was to effectively pass all the information of the prediction history and the current state of the generated SQL to each module, at every prediction step.

4.4 Graph Representations

The use of graphs for input processing saw increased use between 2019 and 2023. Despite this approach's powerful capability to represent the DB schema and other useful task information, graph neural networks are complex to use and lost favor due to the effectiveness and ease of use of LLMs. This section explores key systems that showed new perspectives on how graphs could be represented and used in the Text-to-SQL task.

A natural option for processing graphs are Graph Neural Networks (GNNs). However, while being a good option for tasks such as node classification, node clustering and edge prediction, they are not as suitable for generative tasks like the Text-to-SQL problem. Two systems managed to leverage GNNs to encode the database schema and its elements: the GNN parser [1] and its successor Global-GNN parser [2]. To achieve this, the database schema is represented as a graph, where tables and columns are represented as nodes, and different types of edges represent the relationships between them (e.g., which columns appear in which table and which columns and tables are connected with a primary-foreign key relationship). For NLQ encoding, both systems use word embeddings and LSTM networks, while node encodings calculated by the GNNs are concatenated to each word embedding, based on the discovered schema links. For SQL generation, both systems use a grammar-based decoder [53] that generates a SQL query as an Abstract Syntax Tree (AST), which is often used by grammar-based systems [3, 14, 47]. Global-GNN [2] introduces the use of a re-ranker that, given *k* SQL predictions from the network, chooses the best interpretation based on the database elements used and the calculated graph representation.

In order to avoid the disadvantages of GNNs, other efforts modify architectures that have already shown their power in the Text-to-SQL task, such as the Transformer [45], so that they can accept edge information and process a graph. *RAT-SQL* [47] uses a graph representation of the input, but instead of using GNNs, it proposes a modified Transformer architecture named Relation Aware Transformer (RAT). Firstly, it creates a *question-contextualized schema graph*; i.e., a graph representing the database tables and columns as well as the words of the NLQ as nodes and the relationships between them as edges. An edge can appear either between two database nodes, similarly to the previous systems, or between a database node and a word node. In this graph, schema linking is performed to discover connections between a database node and a word node that might refer to it. The names of all the nodes in the graph are first encoded using BERT [6] and then processed by the RAT network, along with the edge information of each node. The RAT neural block performs *relation aware self-attention* on its inputs, which essentially biases the network towards the given relations (edges). This allows the system to use Transformers and even pre-trained language models to process the graph as a series while also utilizing the information present in the graph edges. Finally, it generates a SQL query as an AST using the method mentioned above [53].

In a similar manner, *Graphix-T5* [22] proposes to modify the architecture of the encoder of the T5 [37] PLM, to enable the encoding of graph inputs. By using "Graphix" encoding layers and retaining the pre-trained weights of the original encoder layers, this approach manages to preserve both the benefits of pre-training and the advanced representation of graphs. The input graph is constructed similarly to RAT-SQL, with DB nodes being connected based on schema relationships, NLQ and DB nodes are inter-connected based on discovered schema links. Additionally, NLQ nodes can be connected between each other with "modifier" and "argument" relationships (e.g., in the phrase "female student", female is a modifier to student).

4.5 Using Intermediate Languages

Following the success of the grammar-based methods in generating complex SQL queries over multi-table DBs, researchers also examined the use of intermediate languages during the SQL generation phase. The intuition behind this idea is that if a model can generate SQL grammar, it might achieve even better results if it is trained to generate a simpler intermediate language. Such languages can better align with NL than SQL making it easier for the system to make predictions, but at the same time they can be deterministically translated into SQL. This section examines key systems that use an Intermediate Language, either a pre-existing language or one created specifically for this task, as the target language for the neural decoder.

IRNet [14] is a grammar-based system capable of generating complex SQL queries, such as the ones in the Spider dataset. It uses the same AST decoding method [53] for code generation used in other grammar-based Text-to-SQL systems (e.g., RATSQL [47] and the GNN parser [1]). The main difference is that it predicts an AST of a SemQL program, which is an Intermediate Language created specifically for this system. Its authors argue that it is easier to generate queries in this language and then transform them to SQL. Furthermore, IRNet performs schema linking by considering all n-grams of length 1 to 6 as query candidates and all column and table names as DB candidates and uses exact and partial matches to discover links between them. It also searches for all query candidates that appear inside quotes in the ConceptNet knowledge graph [43] in order to link them to a database column or table.

SmBoP [39] is a grammar-based system that introduces various novelties in the SQL generation phase. The use of relational algebra as an Intermediate Language is one of them. Its authors argue that, along with being better aligned with NL, relational algebra is a language that is already used by DB engines, unlike SemQL. Additionally, in order to decode ASTs of queries in relational algebra, SmBoP uses a bottom-up parser, in contrast to the usual approach of generating ASTs by performing top-down depth-first traversal, followed by almost all Text-to-SQL systems. The bottom-up decoder generates at time step t, the top-k sub-trees of height $\leq t$, where k is a given parameter that represents the number of beams used during the decoding search. The main advantage of the bottom-up parsing is that at any given time-step, the generated sub-trees are meaningful and executable sub-programs, while in the top-down parsing, intermediate states are partial programs without a clear meaning.

NatSQL [11] is an intermediate language that was proposed to better align the output of Text-to-SQL systems with the input NLQs. In essence, NatSQL is a simplified version of SQL that overlooks complex clauses and structures that distance SQL from NL. For example, NatSQL does not contain any FROM and JOIN clauses, nesting and set operators (e.g., UNION, INTERSECT), as well as GROUP BY and HAVING clauses. On one hand, this means that any system using NatSQL can focus on satisfying the semantics of the NLQ by temporarily disregarding challenging parts of SQL. On the other hand, this high level of simplification does not allow NatSQL to have a deterministic translation to SQL, as other intermediate languages. In fact, transforming NatSQL to SQL requires a level of reasoning and SQL understanding, but it is arguably easier to do as a different step, thus simplifying the task of the system.

4.6 The Age of BERT

The introduction of the Transformer [45] in 2017 led to the quick rise in popularity of Pre-trained Language Models (PLMs). Much like in other NLP problems, replacing a conventional encoder with a PLM such as BERT [6] was shown to improve performance of a Text-to-SQL system. This led to a quick adoption of such models by many subsequent systems.

SQLova [18] is a sketch-based approach focused on the WikiSQL dataset. It employs a large and complex network almost identical to the one used by SQLNet, with its main difference being that instead of GloVe embeddings, it uses BERT to create a contextualized representation of the NLQ and table headers. The representations are then passed to 6 networks, each responsible for a different part of the query sketch, that are very similar to the sub-networks used by SQLNet. The result was a staggering, increase in execution accuracy on the test set of WikiSQL compared to systems using static word embeddings, indicating BERT's power in the Text-to-SQL task.

HydraNet [28] is another sketch-based approach on the WikiSQL benchmark taking advantage of the BERT language model. Its main difference from SQLova is that HydraNet aligns itself better to the way that BERT has been pre-trained and only uses a simple linear network after receiving the contextualized representations from BERT, instead of large networks with LSTMs and attention modules like SQLova. Furthermore, HydraNet processes each table header separately instead of jointly encoding them, an approach that is unique to this system. As a result, it can only make predictions for each column on its own, i.e., it decides if the column at hand will appear in the SELECT clause, if it will appear in the WHERE clause, what its operation will be if it appears in the WHERE clause and so on. HydraNet, with its simpler architecture leveraging BERT, achieves better accuracy on WikiSQL than SQLova, which employs a larger and more complex network.

X-SQL [15] is a sketch-based system using the MT-DNN pre-trained language model [27], that was built for the WikiSQL benchmark. Similarly to HydraNet, it uses much simpler networks than SQLova for filling the slots of the query sketch. However, it encodes all table headers simultaneously, along with the user question. Additionally, instead of using segment embeddings that originally indicate the span of different sentences in the language model's input, X-SQL uses *type embeddings*. These embeddings differentiate between the different types of elements in the input, such as the user's question, categorical columns and numerical columns. Furthermore, it uses an attention layer to create a single token representation for columns that have more than one token (i.e., more than one word in their name). X-SQL also outperforms the much more complex SQLova, achieving slightly lower scores than HydraNet.

4.7 Schema and Value Linking Focus

As discussed in Chapter 3, schema and value linking can play a major role creating a SQL query from a NLQ. This section looks into systems that have put extra effort on schema or value linking, or even based their entire workflow on this process.

TypeSQL [54] is one of the first systems to introduce a process similar to schema linking in its workflow, and one of the few systems working on WikiSQL that uses schema linking. Its methodology is described as *Type Recognition*, but closely resonates to the concept of schema linking. The goal of this methodology is to assign a "type" to every token of the NLQ. It considers all n-grams in the NLQ of length from 2 to 6 and tries to assign them one of the following "types": (*a*) *Column*, if it matches the name of a column or a value that appears under a column, (*b*) *Integer, Float, Date or Year*, if it a numerical n-gram, (*c*) *Person, Place, Country, Organization or Sport* by performing NER using the Freebase knowledge graph. Even though this process is unilateral, as its main goal is to classify the query candidates into a type category and not to explicitly link them to a DB candidate, it is one of the first attempts towards schema linking.

ValueNet [3] builds on the grammar-based system IRNet [14] focusing on schema and value linking. The main motivation of the system is that despite the constant improvement of Text-to-SQL systems, even the state-of-the-art was falling behind at predicting the correct values in the SQL conditions. Similarly to IRNet, ValueNet decodes a SQL query in a SemQL 2.0 AST. SemQL 2.0 extends the SemQL grammar with values. Additionally, since condition values might not be written by the user in the exact same way they appear in the DB, ValueNet employs an extended value linking workflow of five steps:

- *value extraction*: to recognize possible value mentions in the NLQ, it uses NER and heuristics;
- *value candidate generation*: to create additional candidate values, it uses string similarity, hand-crafted heuristics and n-grams;
- *value candidate validation*: to reduce the number of candidate values, it keeps only the candidates that appear in the DB;
- *value candidate encoding*: it appends each candidate to the input along with the table and the column it was found under, and
- *neural processing*: the encoded representations are processed by the neural network, which eventually decides if and where they will be used.

The authors also provide a classification of the Spider queries based on the difficulty of discovering the values. This is another important aspect of the Text-to-SQL problem usually overlooked by other works.

SDSQL [17] is a sketch-based system designed for the WikiSQL task. What is special about this system is that it can be viewed as two neural networks tackling two tasks at the same time. The first network predicts SQL queries using the same architecture used by SQLova [18], while the second network performs *schema dependency* predictions. The schema dependency network uses bi-affine networks [10] to predict dependencies between the words of the NLQ and the table headers. Such dependencies include: (*a*) the *select-column* dependency that connects a query candidate that maps to a column that will appear in the SELECT clause with the corresponding column of the table, and (*b*) the *where-value* dependency that connects the query candidate that refers to a value that will appear in the WHERE clause to the table column it belongs to. It must be noted that even though the second network performs schema linking, its predictions are not directly used by the first network to construct the SQL query. Instead, a combined loss from the predictions of both tasks is used to train the weights of the networks, which allows the *schema dependency learning* to improve the first network's performance indirectly.

IE-SQL [29] proposes a unique approach to the Text-to-SQL problem almost completely based on schema and value linking. It uses two instances of BERT [6] to perform two different tasks: a *mention extractor* and a *linker*. The mention extractor recognizes which query candidates are mentions of columns that will be used in the SELECT and WHERE clauses of the SQL query, mentions of aggregation functions, condition operators and condition values. Additionally, the mention extractor recognizes mentions that should be grouped together. For example, the mentions of the column, the operator and the value that belong to the same condition are grouped together. Having extracted the mentions, the linker maps the mentions of column names to the actual columns of the table they are referring to. The linker also maps value mentions without a grouped column to the appropriate table column. By using the predictions of the mention extractor and the linker, IE-SQL can predict an SQL query, without any additional neural component. Even though this approach may not be a clear match with any of the three decoding categories, we classify it as a sketch-based system because its methodology is heavily based on the existence of a query sketch similar to the one used by SQLNet [50]. IE-SQL can better learn the dependencies between the slots and uses a more robust approach. Still, the mention types it recognizes are a direct match to the slots of the query sketch. Therefore, extending it to queries beyond the sketch is not trivial.

The subsequent release of the BIRD benchmark [23] brought a new wave of interest to schema linking and even more to value linking. The reason is that BIRD contained DBs with more complex schemas and, more importantly, a much larger number of stored values. This made the exhaustive value linking approaches of the time too slow for BIRD. Following this, many systems like *CodeS* [21], *CHESS* [44], *CHASE-SQL* [34], and *XiYan-SQL* [13] started using indexing (see Chapter 3.2.2) to retrieve relevant values. Additionally, at this time a lot of systems adopted external models to perform schema linking. Some examples include *RESDSQL* which used an additional cross-encoder model to predict the most relevant columns to a question and *DIN-SQL* [35] which proposed the use of an LLM to perform schema linking.

4.8 The Return of the Sequence

Generating SQL queries using a sequence-based decoder was initially avoided as it could produce syntax and grammar errors, as discussed in Section 3.4. Grammar-based decoders were instead regarded as the best choice for a system to effectively generate complex SQL queries. However, starting at 2021, new works [25, 40, 51] shifted the landscape by introducing a series of techniques that minimize the possibility of errors by sequence-based decoders. These techniques made the use of very powerful pre-trained encoder-decoder models [19, 37] a viable and high-performing option, allowing the systems that use them to achieve top performance in both the Spider and WikiSQL benchmarks.

SeaD [51] is a system based on the BART [19] encoder-decoder PLM designed for WikiSQL. To overcome the drawbacks of its sequence-based decoder, SeaD employs two techniques: *(a)* it introduces two additional tasks on which the model is trained at the same time with the Text-to-SQL task, and *(b)* it uses execution-guided decoding [48], slightly modified to work with its sequence-based decoder. Its main contribution is the use of the two additional training tasks named *erosion* and *shuffle* (see Section 3.5), which are designed specifically to help the model better understand the nature of the Text-to-SQL problem and the tables used by the WikiSQL dataset. The use of additional training tasks is also closely aligned with how language models are pre-trained to understand the more general notion of natural language before being fine-tuned to a specific task. Nevertheless, while SeaD managed to overcome the limitations of sequence-based decoders and achieve the best performance on the WikiSQL benchmark, both the decoding technique and the additional objectives it employs are designed with the WikiSQL dataset in mind. Extending them to full relational databases would not be a trivial matter.

BRIDGE [25] is another system with a sequence-based decoder that works on Spider, although it does not use an encoder-decoder language model. Instead, it uses BERT [6] and LSTM networks for input encoding and enriches the input representation using linear networks that use metadata such as foreign and primary key relationships, as well as column type information. Additionally, the system performs schema linking using fuzzy string matching between query candidates and the values of columns that only take values from a pre-defined list (i.e., picklist attributes). The discovered values are added in the input sequence to help the network create better SQL queries. Finally, the sequence-based decoder used by BRIDGE is a pointer generator network using *Schema-consistency Guided Decoding*, a constraining strategy to avoid the aforementioned drawbacks of sequence-based decoders. In order to use schema-consistency guided decoding, BRIDGE is trained (and makes predictions) on SQL queries written in *execution order*, i.e. all queries start with the FROM clause, followed by the WHERE, GROUP BY, HAVING, SELECT, ORDER BY and LIMIT clauses, strictly in that order. This means that all columns that appear in the query, must appear after the table that they belong to has been generated. Based on this, BRIDGE can limit the search space of columns and avoid using columns that will produce invalid SQL queries.

PICARD [40] is a constraining technique for auto-regressive decoders of language models, that is specifically created to improve their performance on the Text-to-SQL task. Essentially, at each prediction step, it constrains the model's set of possible predictions by removing tokens that could produce syntactically and grammatically incorrect SQL queries. It is used at inference time, by looking at the confidence scores of the model's prediction and the schema of the underlying DB, and it operates at three levels:

- it rejects misspelled attributes and keywords, as well as tables and columns that are invalid for the given schema,

- it parses the output as an AST to reject grammatical errors, such as an incorrect order of keywords and clauses or an incorrect query structure,
- it checks that all used tables have been brought into scope by being included in the FROM clause and that all used columns belong to exactly one table that has been brought into scope.

When PICARD was used with the T5 [37] pre-trained language model (the 3B parameters version), it ranked first on the Spider leaderboard for execution with values. This of course does not come without any drawbacks, such as the increased prediction time due to the constrained decoding, as well as the tremendous computational and memory requirements for training and running such a large model as T5-3B.

4.9 Hail to the LLM

As PLMs kept growing to the point where they started being called Large Language Models (LLMs), a new era of models had been established relying mostly or entirely on such models. By 2023, almost all Text-to-SQL systems were using LLMs, reaching new levels of performance and rendering the once challenging Spider benchmark into a walk in the park. At that time, the more challenging and complex BIRD [23] benchmark was introduced, offering new challenges for researchers and models alike. Early efforts [26, 38] of using LLMs for the Text-to-SQL task showed that, although a thorough experimentation of the prompt design is required to achieve maximum performance, these models have the potential to outperform existing methods and take on more challenging datasets like BIRD.

A significant line of research explored how to optimally structure the input prompt for in-context learning. Various studies investigated different prompt structures, for example, with alternative ways to express the DB schema, or various methods for few-shot example selection. One such approach [32] proposed representing the schema as CREATE statements rather than plain text descriptions, while instructions were formatted as comments. This approach is said to be closer to an actual code file and to increase uniformity in the prompt. This method also introduced a few-shot example selection strategy based on the SQL similarity. More specifically, the pool of the available annotated examples is divided based on the Spider categorization. When a user asks a question, with the use of a preliminary predictor, an initial SQL prediction is retrieved and used to select similar examples that belong to the same category. To ensure the diversity of the provided examples, they implement k-means clustering and select the k diverse examples that are closest to each centroid. Another example is *ACT-SQL* [57], which adopts a hybrid approach to select few-shot examples. It combines a static set of randomly chosen examples with dynamically retrieved examples based on question similarity. Additionally, it proposes the use of manually labeled CoT examples to enhance the model's performance.

There are several other formats that have been proposed in the literature for prompt design and example selection. While extensive experimentation [4, 12] has also been conducted, results often vary across different LLMs making it difficult to adopt a universally optimal prompt configuration So even though these studies provide valuable insights and good practices into how to prompt an LLM for Text-to-SQL, some experimentation is always required when applying such systems.

As open-source LLMs increased, researchers also began exploring various training strategies to further improve Text-to-SQL performance. *CodeS* [21] introduced additional pre-training stages to enhance SQL generation and natural language understanding. The LLM was trained on three distinct data sources: (1) SQL-related data extracted from StarCoder's [24] pre-training corpus, (2) high-quality natural language dialogue data, and (3) NL-to-code datasets containing natural language paired with both SQL and other programming languages (e.g., Python). The training process involved two epochs on SQL-related data and one epoch each on NL-related and NL-to-code data, employing a modified language modeling objective to maximize the likelihood of generating correct SQL sequences.

SENSE [52] proposed a two-step process: supervised fine-tuning on synthetic GPT-4-generated data, followed by direct preference optimization (DPO) [36]. This second phase presented the model with positive and negative SQL examples, improving its alignment with user preferences and enhancing its robustness against common errors.

To reduce the computational cost of fine-tuning and enable fine-tuning in scenarios where less data are available, parameter-efficient fine-tuning (PEFT) methods can also be used. These techniques update only a part of the model's weights or introduce new weight matrices that are combined with the model and have been used in several tasks. Towards this direction, *FinSQL* [56] proposes the use of Low-Rank Adaptation (LoRA) [16] to create an LLM-based Text-to-SQL model. More specifically, they use LoRA to uniformly train the model on three specialized SQL-related tasks: (1) chain-of-thought SQL generation, where the LLM first explains its reasoning before generating a query, (2) synonymous question-driven SQL generation, which replaces original questions with semantically equivalent variants to improve generalization, and (3) skeleton-aware SQL generation, in which the model first generates an SQL query "skeleton" (omitting schema elements and values) before completing the full query.

Finally, there is a lot of research that focuses on auxiliary tasks that can be performed before or after the SQL generation and can increase the quality of the generated queries. This often includes sub-tasks such as schema and value linking, paraphrasing and analyzing the NLQ, or correcting and refining the generated SQL. This research trend can be attributed to two reasons. First, LLMs are hard and expensive to train or modify and most researchers and practitioners would prefer to use them out of the box. Second, the most powerful LLMs are often closed source and only allow for prompting with an API, providing no training options.

The goal of such systems is to provide a prompt to the LLM that will contain helpful information discovered by the auxiliary tasks to the LLM, or use additional models or LLMs to improve the generated SQL. *RESDSQL* [20] and *CodeS* [21] focus on discovering schema and value links with independent models and data structures. The retrieved links are then added to the prompt, facilitating the LLMs task of generating SQL without having to discover these links. *DIN-SQL* [35], decomposes the task of Text-to-SQL into four sub-tasks: schema linking, question classification, SQL generation, and self-correction. They are all performed by prompting an LLM, resulting to four LLM calls per NLQ, but nevertheless achieving state of the art performance at its time of publication. Similarly, *DART-SQL* [31] breaks the task into three components: question rewriting, context-aware prompt generation, and execution-guided refinement. The first is LLM-based and is responsible for paraphrasing a given natural language question to increase the relatedness with the database. The second component performs the main translation task. The third component is again based on LLMs and is responsible for detecting erroneous translations based on the execution results of the predicted query and repeating the translation process by providing hints of the error.

References

1. Ben Bogin, Jonathan Berant, and Matt Gardner. Representing schema structure with graph neural networks for text-to-SQL parsing. In *Proceedings of the 57th Annual Meeting of the Association for Computational Linguistics*, pages 4560–4565, Florence, Italy, July 2019. Association for Computational Linguistics.
2. Ben Bogin, Matt Gardner, and Jonathan Berant. Global reasoning over database structures for text-to-SQL parsing. In *Proceedings of the 2019 Conference on Empirical Methods in Natural Language Processing and the 9th International Joint Conference on Natural Language Processing (EMNLP-IJCNLP)*, pages 3659–3664, Hong Kong, China, November 2019. Association for Computational Linguistics.
3. Ursin Brunner and Kurt Stockinger. Valuenet: A neural text-to-SQL architecture incorporating values. *ArXiv*, abs/2006.00888, 2020.
4. Shuaichen Chang and Eric Fosler-Lussier. How to prompt llms for text-to-sql: A study in zero-shot, single-domain, and cross-domain settings. *arXiv preprint arXiv:2305.11853*, 2023.
5. DongHyun Choi, Myeong Cheol Shin, EungGyun Kim, and Dong Ryeol Shin. RYANSQL: Recursively applying sketch-based slot fillings for complex text-to-sql in cross-domain databases, 2020.
6. Jacob Devlin, Ming-Wei Chang, Kenton Lee, and Kristina Toutanova. BERT: Pre-training of deep bidirectional transformers for language understanding, 2019.
7. Li Dong and Mirella Lapata. Language to logical form with neural attention, 2016.
8. Li Dong and Mirella Lapata. Coarse-to-fine decoding for neural semantic parsing, 2018.
9. Xuemei Dong, Chao Zhang, Yuhang Ge, Yuren Mao, Yunjun Gao, lu Chen, Jinshu Lin, and Dongfang Lou. C3: Zero-shot text-to-sql with chatgpt, 2023.
10. Timothy Dozat and Christopher D. Manning. Deep biaffine attention for neural dependency parsing. In *5th International Conference on Learning Representations, ICLR 2017, Toulon, France, April 24-26, 2017, Conference Track Proceedings*. OpenReview.net, 2017.
11. Yujian Gan, Xinyun Chen, Jinxia Xie, Matthew Purver, John R. Woodward, John Drake, and Qiaofu Zhang. Natural SQL: Making SQL easier to infer from natural language specifications. In *Findings of the Association for Computational Linguistics: EMNLP 2021*, pages 2030–2042, Punta Cana, Dominican Republic, November 2021. Association for Computational Linguistics.
12. Dawei Gao, Haibin Wang, Yaliang Li, Xiuyu Sun, Yichen Qian, Bolin Ding, and Jingren Zhou. Text-to-sql empowered by large language models: A benchmark evaluation. *Proc. VLDB Endow.*, 17(5):1132–1145, may 2024.
13. Yingqi Gao, Yifu Liu, Xiaoxia Li, Xiaorong Shi, Yin Zhu, Yiming Wang, Shiqi Li, Wei Li, Yuntao Hong, Zhiling Luo, Jinyang Gao, Liyu Mou, and Yu Li. Xiyan-sql: A multi-generator ensemble framework for text-to-sql. *arXiv preprint arXiv:2411.08599*, 2024.

14. Jiaqi Guo, Zecheng Zhan, Yan Gao, Yan Xiao, Jian-Guang Lou, Ting Liu, and Dongmei Zhang. Towards complex text-to-sql in cross-domain database with intermediate representation, 2019.
15. Pengcheng He, Yi Mao, Kaushik Chakrabarti, and Weizhu Chen. X-sql: reinforce schema representation with context, 2019.
16. Edward J. Hu, Yelong Shen, Phillip Wallis, Zeyuan Allen-Zhu, Yuanzhi Li, Shean Wang, Lu Wang, and Weizhu Chen. Lora: Low-rank adaptation of large language models, 2021.
17. Binyuan Hui, Xiang Shi, Ruiying Geng, Binhua Li, Yongbin Li, Jian Sun, and Xiaodan Zhu. Improving text-to-SQL with schema dependency learning, 2021.
18. Wonseok Hwang, Jinyeong Yim, Seunghyun Park, and Minjoon Seo. A comprehensive exploration on wikisql with table-aware word contextualization, 2019.
19. Mike Lewis, Yinhan Liu, Naman Goyal, Marjan Ghazvininejad, Abdelrahman Mohamed, Omer Levy, Ves Stoyanov, and Luke Zettlemoyer. BART: Denoising sequence-to-sequence pre-training for natural language generation, translation, and comprehension, 2019.
20. Haoyang Li, Jing Zhang, Cuiping Li, and Hong Chen. Resdsql: decoupling schema linking and skeleton parsing for text-to-sql. In *Proceedings of the Thirty-Seventh AAAI Conference on Artificial Intelligence and Thirty-Fifth Conference on Innovative Applications of Artificial Intelligence and Thirteenth Symposium on Educational Advances in Artificial Intelligence*, AAAI'23/IAAI'23/EAAI'23. AAAI Press, 2023.
21. Haoyang Li, Jing Zhang, Hanbing Liu, Ju Fan, Xiaokang Zhang, Jun Zhu, Renjie Wei, Hongyan Pan, Cuiping Li, and Hong Chen. Codes: Towards building open-source language models for text-to-sql. *Proc. ACM Manag. Data*, 2(3), may 2024.
22. Jinyang Li, Binyuan Hui, Reynold Cheng, Bowen Qin, Chenhao Ma, Nan Huo, Fei Huang, Wenyu Du, Luo Si, and Yongbin Li. Graphix-t5: Mixing pre-trained transformers with graph-aware layers for text-to-sql parsing. In *Proceedings of the AAAI conference on artificial intelligence*, volume 37, pages 13076–13084, 2023.
23. Jinyang Li, Binyuan Hui, Ge Qu, Jiaxi Yang, Binhua Li, Bowen Li, Bailin Wang, Bowen Qin, Ruiying Geng, Nan Huo, Xuanhe Zhou, Ma Chenhao, Guoliang Li, Kevin Chang, Fei Huang, Reynold Cheng, and Yongbin Li. Can llm already serve as a database interface? a big bench for large-scale database grounded text-to-sqls. In A. Oh, T. Naumann, A. Globerson, K. Saenko, M. Hardt, and S. Levine, editors, *Advances in Neural Information Processing Systems*, volume 36, pages 42330–42357. Curran Associates, Inc., 2023.
24. Raymond Li, Loubna Ben Allal, Yangtian Zi, Niklas Muennighoff, Denis Kocetkov, Chenghao Mou, Marc Marone, Christopher Akiki, Jia Li, Jenny Chim, et al. Starcoder: may the source be with you! *arXiv preprint arXiv:2305.06161*, 2023.
25. Xi Victoria Lin, Richard Socher, and Caiming Xiong. Bridging textual and tabular data for cross-domain text-to-SQL semantic parsing. In *Findings of the Association for Computational Linguistics: EMNLP 2020*, pages 4870–4888, Online, November 2020. Association for Computational Linguistics.
26. Aiwei Liu, Xuming Hu, Lijie Wen, and Philip S Yu. A comprehensive evaluation of chatgpt's zero-shot text-to-sql capability. *arXiv preprint arXiv:2303.13547*, 2023.
27. Xiaodong Liu, Pengcheng He, Weizhu Chen, and Jianfeng Gao. Multi-task deep neural networks for natural language understanding, 2019.
28. Qin Lyu, Kaushik Chakrabarti, Shobhit Hathi, Souvik Kundu, Jianwen Zhang, and Zheng Chen. Hybrid ranking network for text-to-sql. Technical Report MSR-TR-2020-7, Microsoft Dynamics 365 AI, March 2020.
29. Jianqiang Ma, Zeyu Yan, Shuai Pang, Yang Zhang, and Jianping Shen. Mention extraction and linking for SQL query generation. In *Proceedings of the 2020 Conference on Empirical Methods in Natural Language Processing (EMNLP)*, pages 6936–6942, Online, November 2020. Association for Computational Linguistics.
30. Wenxin Mao, Ruiqi Wang, Jiyu Guo, Jichuan Zeng, Cuiyun Gao, Peiyi Han, and Chuanyi Liu. Enhancing text-to-SQL parsing through question rewriting and execution-guided refinement. In Lun-Wei Ku, Andre Martins, and Vivek Srikumar, editors, *Findings of the Association for Computational Linguistics: ACL 2024*, pages 2009–2024, Bangkok, Thailand, August 2024. Association for Computational Linguistics.

31. Wenxin Mao, Ruiqi Wang, Jiyu Guo, Jichuan Zeng, Cuiyun Gao, Peiyi Han, and Chuanyi Liu. Enhancing text-to-sql parsing through question rewriting and execution-guided refinement. In *Findings of the Association for Computational Linguistics ACL 2024*, pages 2009–2024, 2024.
32. Linyong Nan, Yilun Zhao, Weijin Zou, Narutatsu Ri, Jaesung Tae, Ellen Zhang, Arman Cohan, and Dragomir Radev. Enhancing text-to-SQL capabilities of large language models: A study on prompt design strategies. In Houda Bouamor, Juan Pino, and Kalika Bali, editors, *Findings of the Association for Computational Linguistics: EMNLP 2023*, pages 14935–14956, Singapore, December 2023. Association for Computational Linguistics.
33. Jeffrey Pennington, Richard Socher, and Christopher D. Manning. Glove: Global vectors for word representation. In *Empirical Methods in Natural Language Processing (EMNLP)*, pages 1532–1543, 2014.
34. Mohammadreza Pourreza, Hailong Li, Ruoxi Sun, Yeounoh Chung, Shayan Talaei, Gaurav Tarlok Kakkar, Yu Gan, Amin Saberi, Fatma Ozcan, and Sercan O. Arik. Chase-sql: Multi-path reasoning and preference optimized candidate selection in text-to-sql, 2024.
35. Mohammadreza Pourreza and Davood Rafiei. Din-sql: Decomposed in-context learning of text-to-sql with self-correction. *Advances in Neural Information Processing Systems*, 36, 2024.
36. Rafael Rafailov, Archit Sharma, Eric Mitchell, Stefano Ermon, Christopher D. Manning, and Chelsea Finn. Direct preference optimization: Your language model is secretly a reward model, 2024.
37. Colin Raffel, Noam Shazeer, Adam Roberts, Katherine Lee, Sharan Narang, Michael Matena, Yanqi Zhou, Wei Li, and Peter J. Liu. Exploring the limits of transfer learning with a unified text-to-text transformer, 2020.
38. Nitarshan Rajkumar, Raymond Li, and Dzmitry Bahdanau. Evaluating the text-to-sql capabilities of large language models. *arXiv preprint arXiv:2204.00498*, 2022.
39. Ohad Rubin and Jonathan Berant. Smbop: Semi-autoregressive bottom-up semantic parsing, 2020.
40. Torsten Scholak, Nathan Schucher, and Dzmitry Bahdanau. PICARD: Parsing incrementally for constrained auto-regressive decoding from language models, 2021.
41. Ke Shen and Mayank Kejriwal. Select-sql: Self-correcting ensemble chain-of-thought for text-to-sql, 2024.
42. Tianze Shi, Kedar Tatwawadi, Kaushik Chakrabarti, Yi Mao, Oleksandr Polozov, and Weizhu Chen. Incsql: Training incremental text-to-sql parsers with non-deterministic oracles, 2018.
43. R. Speer and Catherine Havasi. Representing general relational knowledge in conceptnet 5. In *LREC*, 2012.
44. Shayan Talaei, Mohammadreza Pourreza, Yu-Chen Chang, Azalia Mirhoseini, and Amin Saberi. Chess: Contextual harnessing for efficient sql synthesis. *arXiv preprint arXiv:2405.16755*, 2024.
45. Ashish Vaswani, Noam Shazeer, Niki Parmar, Jakob Uszkoreit, Llion Jones, Aidan N Gomez, L ukasz Kaiser, and Illia Polosukhin. Attention is all you need. In I. Guyon, U. Von Luxburg, S. Bengio, H. Wallach, R. Fergus, S. Vishwanathan, and R. Garnett, editors, *Advances in Neural Information Processing Systems*, volume 30. Curran Associates, Inc., 2017.
46. Bailin Wang, Richard Shin, Xiaodong Liu, Oleksandr Polozov, and Matthew Richardson. Rat-sql: Relation-aware schema encoding and linking for text-to-sql parsers. *arXiv preprint arXiv:1911.04942*, 2019.
47. Bailin Wang, Richard Shin, Xiaodong Liu, Oleksandr Polozov, and Matthew Richardson. RAT-SQL: Relation-aware schema encoding and linking for text-to-sql parsers, 2020.
48. Chenglong Wang, Kedar Tatwawadi, Marc Brockschmidt, Po-Sen Huang, Yi Mao, Oleksandr Polozov, and Rishabh Singh. Robust text-to-sql generation with execution-guided decoding, 2018.
49. Xiangjin Xie, Guangwei Xu, Lingyan Zhao, and Ruijie Guo. Opensearch-sql: Enhancing text-to-sql with dynamic few-shot and consistency alignment. *Proc. ACM Manag. Data*, 3(3), June 2025.
50. Xiaojun Xu, Chang Liu, and Dawn Song. Sqlnet: Generating structured queries from natural language without reinforcement learning, 2017.

51. Kuan Xuan, Yongbo Wang, Yongliang Wang, Zujie Wen, and Yang Dong. Sead: End-to-end text-to-sql generation with schema-aware denoising, 2021.
52. Jiaxi Yang, Binyuan Hui, Min Yang, Jian Yang, Junyang Lin, and Chang Zhou. Synthesizing text-to-SQL data from weak and strong LLMs. In Lun-Wei Ku, Andre Martins, and Vivek Srikumar, editors, *Proceedings of the 62nd Annual Meeting of the Association for Computational Linguistics (Volume 1: Long Papers)*, pages 7864–7875, Bangkok, Thailand, August 2024. Association for Computational Linguistics.
53. Pengcheng Yin and Graham Neubig. A syntactic neural model for general-purpose code generation, 2017.
54. Tao Yu, Zifan Li, Zilin Zhang, Rui Zhang, and Dragomir Radev. Typesql: Knowledge-based type-aware neural text-to-sql generation, 2018.
55. Tao Yu, Michihiro Yasunaga, Kai Yang, Rui Zhang, Dongxu Wang, Zifan Li, and Dragomir Radev. Syntaxsqlnet: Syntax tree networks for complex and cross-domaintext-to-sql task, 2018.
56. Chao Zhang, Yuren Mao, Yijiang Fan, Yu Mi, Yunjun Gao, Lu Chen, Dongfang Lou, and Jinshu Lin. Finsql: Model-agnostic llms-based text-to-sql framework for financial analysis. In *Companion of the 2024 International Conference on Management of Data*, SIGMOD/PODS '24, page 93–105, New York, NY, USA, 2024. Association for Computing Machinery.
57. Hanchong Zhang, Ruisheng Cao, Lu Chen, Hongshen Xu, and Kai Yu. Act-sql: In-context learning for text-to-sql with automatically-generated chain-of-thought. *arXiv preprint arXiv:2310.17342*, 2023.
58. Tingkai Zhang, Chaoyu Chen, Cong Liao, Jun Wang, Xudong Zhao, Hang Yu, Jianchao Wang, Jianguo Li, and Wenhui Shi. Sqlfuse: Enhancing text-to-sql performance through comprehensive llm synergy. *arXiv preprint arXiv:2407.14568*, 2024.
59. Victor Zhong, Caiming Xiong, and Richard Socher. Seq2sql: Generating structured queries from natural language using reinforcement learning, 2017.

Chapter 5
Describing SQL queries in Natural Language

Abstract Structured Query Language (SQL) is a powerful tool for data retrieval, but its complexity often renders databases inaccessible to non-technical users. While natural language interfaces can help bridge this gap by translating user questions into SQL queries, these users may still struggle to understand or verify the generated queries. This chapter addresses the SQL-to-Text problem: the task of converting SQL queries back into natural language descriptions. An introduction of the problem and its key challenges is given and the earlier template-based approaches are presented, before diving into the neural era of SQL-to-Text. Finally, we present the benchmarks and metrics that are used to train and evaluate neural SQL-to-Text models and present key systems that have been proposed.

5.1 Introduction

As we discussed in previous chapters, a lot of effort has been put towards creating Text-to-SQL systems that can translate a NLQ from the user to SQL and retrieve the desired data. Translating SQL to NL is equally significant for a number of reasons. First, given that the user of a NLIDB might not be familiar with SQL, a NL description of the SQL generated can help the user validate that the SQL actually matches their intent. Providing NL explanations for these queries increases the confidence of casual users that the results they are getting are what they were looking for, while also creating a more complete NL experience.

Generating NL explanations of SQL queries can also be beneficial for other use cases, both inside and outside the scope of a NLIDB. A more advanced NLIDB might also offer recommendations of SQL queries, in order to help the user discover interesting data stored in the database. Once again, it is easier for the user to understand the recommended queries if they are described in NL rather than given in SQL. SQL-to-Text systems can also help experienced users speed up their work. Software developers and DB administrators often come across complicated queries

G. Katsogiannis-Meimarakis et al., *Natural Language Interfaces for Databases with Deep Learning*, Data-Centric Systems and Applications,
https://doi.org/10.1007/978-3-032-06905-4_5

that are directed to DBs with schemata they are not familiar with. Getting a quick NL explanation of such queries would save a lot of time.

Finally, SQL-to-Text systems are also essential for data augmentation pipelines for training Text-to-SQL systems [7, 29]. In such a pipeline, SQL queries will be generated automatically, either using a predefined grammar or by modifying a set of given SQL queries, and a SQL-to-Text system will be used to generate their NL counterparts. This process will produce augmented NL/SQL pairs that can be used to train and evaluate Text-to-SQL systems.

Unfortunately, the SQL-to-Text problem has not seen the same level of research as the Text-to-SQL problem. Previous efforts at generating SQL query explanations can be divided into two categories: rule-based systems [4, 8, 11, 13, 25, 28] that create explanations using pre-defined templates, and neural systems [7, 16, 29, 31]. The former approaches tend to create explanations that appear "robotic" and need human effort to be applied to an unseen DB (e.g., to construct new rules or templates), while the latter approaches cannot guarantee to produce correct explanations every time.

5.2 The SQL-to-Text Problem

Given a SQL query on a relational database with a specific schema, the objective of the SQL-to-Text problem is to build an explanation in natural language that has the same semantic meaning with the formal query language. Apart from *semantic accuracy*, a NL explanation should have the following desired properties. It should (a) be fluent and human-like, mimicking a human speaker so as not to seem robotic (*fluency*), and (b) be brief and avoid unnecessary repetitions (*brevity*).

The SQL-to-Text problem falls under the wider Query-to-Text task which aims at providing a NL explanation of a structured query in a given query language (e.g., SPARQL, Cypher, etc.) and executed against different types of data stores. For example, some works have studied the SPARQL-to-Text problem [5, 17] using template-based approaches for SQL-to-Text, which create a representation of the query (e.g., a query graph), and apply a pre-defined set of rules to simplify the representation, and eventually verbalize each of its components. Such approaches have also been applied to the SQL-to-Text problem, as we will discuss in Section 5.3.

Additionally, the SQL-to-Text problem can be seen as an instance of the code summarization problem, which aims at verbalizing fragments of code from any programming language to NL. This is a highly complicated task, given the intricacies, expressiveness and levels of abstractions of modern programming languages. We will provide additional information on this task in Chapter 7, along with other code generation and understanding tasks.

5.2.1 Challenges

The SQL-to-Text problem hides several challenges, that stem from two parts: the complexity of SQL and DBs, and the difficulty of generating fluent and accurate NL utterances. The intertwining of these two very different worlds creates some very peculiar challenges for this problem.

Query Understanding. First and foremost, a SQL-to-Text system might encounter very complex queries that join multiple tables, use multiple attributes, have nested queries, and other complicated clauses. These complex elements require a good understanding of their purpose in order to be explained, because they do not serve the same purpose every time. For example, the SELECT clause always determines the attributes that will be returned but a nested query might be used to get the students with the best grades in one case or to get the students that passed a certain class in another case. Additionally, in order to explain complicated queries, the system must be able to understand what needs to be verbalized and in which cases. For example, most joins may not need an explicit verbalization, but some queries might perform a join over a certain key that has a large impact on the query meaning.

Domain Adaptation. Similarly, another challenge is correctly identifying the DB domain and using the appropriate vocabulary. In some cases different verbs should be used according to the domain and the entities that are explained (e.g., "Which artist made the soundtrack of each movie" should be "Which artist composed the soundtrack of each movie"). Additionally, some SQL operators such as the `MAX` aggregation function must be translated in a different way, depending on the context and the attribute on which it is applied. In a DB containing sport data, the `MAX(lap_time)` refers to the *"slowest lap time"*, while in a database containing products, the `MAX(price)` refers to the *"highest product price"*.

Fluent Explanations. Furthermore, generating natural language explanations that are fluent, coherent, and do not appear "robotic" is a difficult task when dealing with SQL. While SQL queries contain elements that appear multiple times, such as attribute names, there must be no unnecessary repetitions in the generated explanation. For example, "projects starting after 2014 and projects starting before 2020" should be "projects starting between 2014 and 2020". Similarly, some queries might present complex combinations of tables and entities, but there must not be unnecessary over-complications in the NL. For example, "show me actors that play in a movie and other actors who play in the same movie" should be "show me actors who have played in the same movie".

5.3 Template-based Approaches

Template-based approaches require the design of special templates and rules that are used to compose sentences (e.g., [4, 13]). Due to the non-ambiguous nature of the

SQL queries, templates can help limit the syntactic variability of their output and smooth explanations out [23]. Logos [12] is a representative system in this category.

Logos' approach to NL generation comprises graph representations of the database and the queries, template phrases associated with parts of the graph, and graph traversal in particular directions to compose the templates found on the way into the final text creation.

The *database graph* captures the relationships between the database relations and attributes (nodes of the graph). Its edges are divided into three types: (a) *membership edges* (attributes to relations), representing attribute projections in queries, (b) *selection edges* (relations to attributes), representing attributes in predicates, and (c) *join edges* (attribute to attribute), representing joins.

The *query graph* of a query is the part of the database graph that the query refers to, extended with additional nodes (e.g., for functions) and edges (e.g., for group-by's) in order to capture the entire query meaning. Each node or edge of the query graph can be annotated with a *label* that signifies its meaning in natural language. There are default labels that can be used for any database. Additionally, labels can be provided by a domain expert.

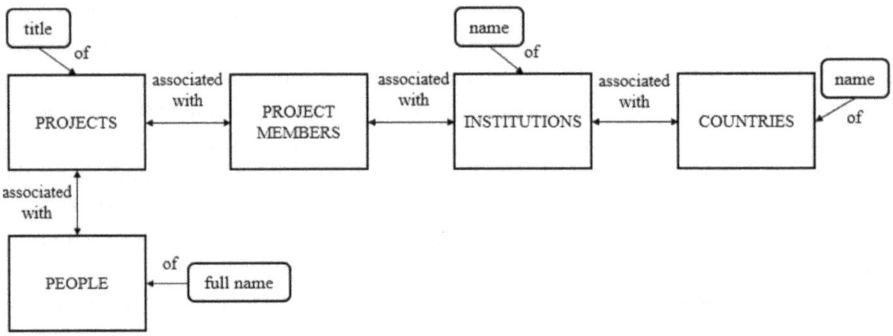

Fig. 5.1: A subgraph of the CORDIS database graph.

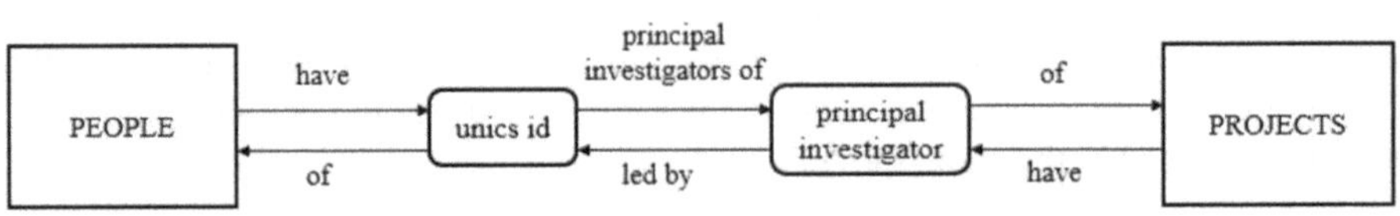

Fig. 5.2: A join on the CORDIS database graph.

For example [4], in Figure 5.1, we see a subgraph of the CORDIS[1] database, which stores information about research projects funded by the European Union. Note that

[1] https://data.europa.eu/euodp/en/data/dataset/cordisH2020projects

for simplicity, we do not show the attributes used to join the various relations. Nodes and edges are annotated with default labels. They can also get hand-crafted labels. For instance, for the relation *Project_Members*, instead of the system's default label *"project members"*, we can use the short label *"participants"*. Figure 5.2 zooms in on the join path connecting relation *People* with relation *Projects* and provides a more detailed view. A possible label which expresses this connection is *"principal investigators of"*, while the default one is *"associated with"*. Such designer labels are stored in special tables called *designer tables*.

NL explanations are created by traversing the query graph accompanied with a *template mechanism* [26]. The template mechanism uses the provided labels (designer or default) to form meaningful phrases. A *template label* $l(u)$ or $l((u, v))$ is assigned to a node u or a path (u, v), respectively. For instance, a join template label may have the form: $l((u, v)) = l(u) + expr + l(u, v) + l(v)$, where u and v are relation nodes of the query graph. Using Figure 5.2), a template for the path connecting the tables *People* and *Projects* is the following: $l((\text{People}, \text{Projects})) = l(\text{People})$ + *" as "* + *"principal investigators of"* +$l(\text{Projects})$ = *"people as principal investigators of projects"* .

Synthesis of the NL explanations is performed as graph traversal of the query graph. There are three traversal strategies: (a) Binary Search Tree (BST) algorithm, where the translation consists of a composition of clauses each one of them focusing on specific query semantics, (b) Multiple Reference Points (MRP) algorithm, where information from all parts of the query graph is blended in the translation, (c) Template composition (TMT) algorithm, where predefined, richer templates corresponding to different query parts are used in an effort to produce more concise translations.

5.4 The Evolution of Neural Approaches

After the introduction of the Transformer [27] and the rapid advancements in deep learning and NLP, researchers started considering how to incorporate these approaches in SQL-to-Text systems. This evolution came in similar fashion to the Text-to-SQL area (see Chapter 4), albeit in a much smaller scale of published research and systems. Nevertheless, adopting neural approaches meant that appropriate benchmarks and evaluation metrics were in need, in order to measure the models' performance and to improve it. This section describes the datasets that are most often used for this problem and how systems can be evaluated on them.

5.4.1 Benchmarks

The main source of data for SQL explanation systems have been Text-to-SQL benchmarks. In fact, because there are no benchmarks created specifically for the SQL-to-Text systems, researchers resort to using Text-to-SQL benchmarks for training and evaluation. Even though these datasets were not created specifically for the SQL-to-Text problem, they can be adapted by using their inputs (i.e. NLQs) as outputs and their outputs (i.e. SQL queries) as inputs. However, this approach should not be seen as a panacea, as it can be problematic (a further discussion of this can be found in Section 5.5).

Neural SQL-to-Text systems have used only two benchmarks for a large majority of their evaluations: WikiSQL [34] and Spider [32]. In this area we see a similar pattern to the Text-to-SQL problem, where despite having a large pool of available datasets, researchers only tend to use a few of them in their works. *WikiSQL* contains simple NLQs and SQL over single tables taken from Wikipedia. Arguably, this task is relatively simple as it does not contain full relational DB that reflect real-world scenarios and the quality of the NL questions is low as they were created by crowd-sourcing. *Spider* contains NLQs, SQL queries, and relational DBs that were manually created for the Text-to-SQL task and is more complex than WikiSQL but still does not reflect the complexity of real-world DBs. A more in-depth discussion of both datasets can be found in Section 2.5.1, along with multiple other datasets created for the Text-to-SQL task.

5.4.2 Evaluation Metrics

It is also important to consider how to measure the correctness of a predicted NL explanation of a query against the ground truth explanation provided by a benchmark. Most works so far have relied on automatic translation metrics such as the BLEU score [18]. However such metrics might not be ideal for this problem, as we will discuss in Section 5.5. On the other hand, some works [9, 31] have also resorted to manual evaluation of the generated explanations. In this case, human annotators are asked to rate the explanations on axes such as "grammatical correctness", "naturalness" (i.e., the fluency level of the NL), and "correctness" or "informativeness" (i.e., if the explanation correctly describes all parts of the SQL code). However this is a costly and time-consuming approach that is far from ideal when working with deep learning models where incremental changes must constantly be evaluated.

In this section, we present various automatic metrics that are available and could be suitable for the problem at hand, grouping them in two large categories based on how they work: (i) n-gram based metrics and (ii) learned metrics. It should also be noted that readability metrics could also be considered for evaluating SQL explanations, however no system so far has used them. These metrics consider features such as the length of a text, the number of unique words, the number of "hard" words (using a pre-defined set of words), etc. to derive a score. This score is designed to represent how difficult it is to read and understand the given text passage Some examples of readability metrics include the Flesch-Kincaid [10] readability formula and the Dale-Chall readability formula [3].

5.4.2.1 N-Gram-Based Metrics

Metrics based on n-grams, focus on comparing the overlap of n-grams appearing in the prediction to the n-grams of the ground truth. This means that this type of metrics are favorable to predictions that use the same vocabulary as the ground truth, but are not robust to synonyms and paraphrases.

BLEU (BiLingual Evaluation Understudy) score [18] is an automatic evaluation metric that was originally proposed for machine translation. Besides machine translation, this is a very frequently-used evaluation metric for text generation tasks such as text summarization and image captioning. It evaluates the quality of a candidate translation against one or more reference translations based on n-gram precision. More specifically, n-gram precision is the number of n-grams of the candidate translation that are also present in the reference translation. Since its introduction, many different implementations have been published, which has been shown [21] to impede the consistent comparison of different works. **ROUGE** (Recall-Oriented Understudy for Gisting Evaluation) [15] score is an automatic evaluation metric proposed for text summarization. Similarly to n-gram precision, n-gram recall refers to the number of n-grams in the reference that also appear in the candidate translation.

chrF [19] and **chrF++** [20] are automatic translation metrics that take into account character n-grams along with word n-grams. More specifically, the initial chrF metric is based completely on character n-gram matching while the later chrF++ combines both character and word n-grams.

METEOR (Metric for Evaluation of Translation with Explicit Ordering) score [1] is another automatic metric for machine translation based on n-gram matching. It combines both n-gram precision and recall and also takes into account the ordering of the candidate translation compared to the reference.

5.4.2.2 Learned Metrics

Learned metrics rely on trained neural models to predict a similarity score between the prediction and the ground truth. For this reason they are capable of capturing the connections between synonyms and different wordings but are usually regarded as black box component, making it difficult to understand why they produce a certain score for a given input.

Sentence Transformers [22] is a state of the art technique for creating sentence embeddings using siamese networks of BERT-like models. Essentially, a BERT-like model is used to create a sentence embedding for the candidate and reference query explanations and the cosine similarity of their embeddings is used as a metric of their semantic similarity.

BLEURT [24] use the BERT's [CLS] token and a linear layer to predict a score. The main difference to Sentence Transformers is that BLEURT, processes the two inputs (i.e., reference and candidate) at the same time, and not separately. The output [CLS] token contains a contextualized representation based on both inputs, which is then used to predict a score through a linear layer. Although the model is trained to produce outputs in the range of $[-1, 1]$, it is not possible to guarantee that its output will always be in this range, due to the nature of the model.

BERTScore [33] uses BERT to compute contextual embeddings of both the candidate and reference translations and uses cosine similarity to produce a score based on the embeddings.

5.5 Limitations & Research Opportunities

Given the comparatively underdeveloped status of the neural SQL-to-Text field, we can make a few observations of current limitations and research opportunities, drawing inspiration from the nature of the problem as well as the development of neural Text-to-SQL systems.

5.5.1 Limitations of Current Metrics

Even though all works rely on the BLEU score [18] to evaluate their systems, this metric is not ideal for the SQL-to-Text problem. Given that metrics like BLEU rely on n-gram matching, they are not robust to the use of different vocabulary, expressions, and syntax that could convey the same meaning. For example, the explanations "*How many singers do we have?*" and "*What is the number of singers?*" are semantically equivalent, despite only sharing one common word. Additionally, as the authors of BLEU state: *"[...] quantity leads to quality"*, that is, BLEU is most efficient when applying it on large texts and corpora. However, query explanations are usually short texts loaded with very specific information, and changing even a single word can completely alter their meaning, rendering them incorrect. For example, "*How many singers do we have?*" describes a different query than "*How many songs do we have?*". The scores given to the aforementioned examples can be seen in Table 5.1. It is clear that n-gram based metrics will favor the wrong explanation when it uses similar vocabulary and syntax.

On the other hand, learned metrics are more robust at capturing the semantics of their inputs due to their training. As such, they could be more promising for the SQL-to-Text task, but can not be seen as a panacea. For this category, we identify two drawbacks. Firstly, since these metrics usually rely on deep learning models, the scores they produce are not explainable and in some cases not reproducible. Additionally, even though these metrics can provide a semantic comparison between texts, they are not guaranteed to rate candidate explanations, on the exact criteria of the SQL-to-Text problem. For example, the ground truth "*Tell me the age of the oldest dog.*" and the prediction "*Tell me the age of the youngest dog.*", are arguably semantically similar, but do not describe the same query. In fact, the Sentence Transformer metric gives a higher score to the wrong prediction, as shown in Table 5.1. Finally, given that high performance usually requires large neural models, evaluating a large number of examples with learned metrics can be computationally expensive and time consuming.

Table 5.1: Examples of NL explanations of SQL queries and their respective scores. Notice how classic automatic translation metrics can favor the wrong explanation.

Reference	Candidates	BLEU	chrF++	METEOR	s-Trans
How many singers do we have?	How many songs do we have?	48.89	68.49	80.66	61.07
	What is the number of singers?	7.80	24.15	0.00	89.09
Tell me the age of the oldest dog.	Tell me the age of the youngest dog.	66.06	72.83	86.47	90.28
	How old is the eldest dog?	5.66	37.42	16.12	81.16

For these reasons, there is currently no clear solution for the problem of accurately and efficiently evaluating query explanations. As such, this remains an open problem that would greatly benefit any research on this topic going forward.

5.5.2 The need for dedicated benchmarks

As we mentioned earlier, there is a lack of a benchmark specifically for the SQL-to-Text and all papers on this problem have resorted to using Text-to-SQL datasets. However, using such datasets in reversed order can often be problematic and creating a dedicated benchmark would greatly help research efforts on this problem. Firstly, these datasets are created specifically for the Text-to-SQL task and can carry dataset construction biases. For example, the NL parts of some examples might be intentionally malformed or incomplete in order to make them more challenging for Text-to-SQL systems. However, when these examples are used as ground truths for SQL-to-Text systems, we are essentially training systems to generate low quality explanations. Additionally, a benchmark should provide fine-grained categories of explanations and queries that help developers evaluate the capabilities of their systems and to uncover their drawbacks. Spider [32] and BIRD [14], have a categorization of examples based on SQL query difficulty, but in the case of the SQL-to-Text task, there is also a need for NL-based categorization.

5.5.3 What is truly a Query Explanation?

There are three basic types of linguistic expressions that can be employed to express a query in NL: (i) a statement describing the expected data results (e.g., "Actors from Greece."), (ii) a question about the existence of the queried data (e.g., "Which actors are from Greece?"), and (iii) a command requesting the queried data (e.g., "Show all actors from Greece.") [5]. However, a query explanation can have additional levels of variation that need to be considered, in order to truly achieve progress. Let us consider the following query, taken from the Spider dataset's dev set, as a running example to demonstrate our point:

```
SELECT name, location, district
FROM shop
ORDER BY number_products DESC
```

If we were to closely follow each element of the query, similarly to how template-based approaches generate explanations, we could produce the following query explanation: *"Return the shop name, shop location and shop district of all shops. Order the results by shop number of products, in descending order"*. While this explanation includes every single element of the query, it is unlikely that a human would explain it in this way, as it includes many repetitions, it is unnecessarily long, and could be expressed much more fluently. A more "relaxed" take on explaining the query could produce the following utterance: *"Show me the shops, ordered by their number of products"*. One could argue, however, that this explanation does not describe the query in an exact manner, and could also cover other similar queries. For example, it does not specify exactly which attributes must be presented (i.e., name, location and district), nor how the results will be ordered (i.e., in descending order of product number), both of which are explicitly specified in the SQL query. On the other hand, it is also valid to argue that this additional information might be redundant for certain queries and omiting it increases the quality of the explanation. A more generally accepted approach would be the following explanation: *"Show me the name, location and district of all shops, in descending order of number of products"*.

Let us now consider a query that contains a GROUP BY clause with a COUNT aggregation function. The following example is also taken from the Spider dev set and is posed on a database containing information about concerts and stadiums where the concerts took place:

```
SELECT T2.name , COUNT(*)
FROM concert AS T1
JOIN stadium AS T2
    ON T1.stadium_id = T2.stadium_id
GROUP BY T1.stadium_id
```

A simple and fluent explanation could be *"How many concerts took place in each stadium?"*. However, in the same spirit as previously, one could say that this explanation does not complete encapsulate the intent of the SELECT clause. Instead, it would be valid to say that the correct interpretation should also include *"Show me the number of concerts per stadium along with the name of the stadium"*. This might seem excessive to some, given that a query that would return a list of numbers without the stadium that corresponds to each number of concerts. However, this depends on the precision and strictness required for describing the SQL query.

Finally, the proper explanation of the asterisk operator and the level of detail it requires are debatable. Let us consider the following SQL query as a motivating example:

```
SELECT *
FROM project
WHERE start_year > 2014
```

First of all, the explanation *"Show me projects that started after 2014"* is simple and straight-forward, but one could point out that a query with a clause such as `SELECT project.title` would have the same explanation and, as such, more detail is needed. Something along the lines of *"Show information about projects starting after 2014"* or *"Show everything about projects that start after 2014"*, might be more precise, but could still be vague to a non-technical user (e.g., what is "everything"?). A more strict explanation, that would also be clear for non-technical users, could be *"Show me all information stored in the database about projects starting after 2019."*. But it might be possible that there are other tables in the DB that contain information related to projects. Maybe *"Show me all information about projects starting after 2019, that is stored in the table named projects"* is the strictest explanation, but at this point we are clearly drifting away from our main goal of providing fluent and user-friendly explanations.

While all the above remain open questions in how to formulate query explanations, there are some valuable insights to gain. First of all, it is once again evident that evaluating query explanations is not a trivial task, and even human might disagree on the correctness of an explanation. More importantly, however, when designing a SQL-to-Text system, it is important to understand the style and level of detail that is expected to adhere to. To do so, it is often necessary to consider the type of domain and users that it is addressed to. For example, in a medical use case, it might be more important to be precise than brief. After all, it is not only necessary to review the accuracy of the system but also the expectations of the user.

5.6 Neural SQL-to-Text Systems

Deep learning SQL-to-Text models fall under two categories, based on how they process the input query: graph-to-sequence models and sequence-to-sequence models. Graph-to-Sequence approaches create a graph or abstract syntax tree representation of the SQL query, and process it as a structured input. This leads to more complex neural models but allows for better representation of the query structure and the dependencies between its parts. Sequence-to-sequence approaches process the input as a text sequence, leading to simpler models that are not explicitly given the query structure, but can be effective nevertheless. This category also includes the use of LLMs which are quite powerful without the need for graph representations. Another approach belonging to this category also considers the use of an intermediate language that is simpler than SQL and can help the model generate an explanation with more ease.

5.6.1 Graph-based Systems

Graph-to-Sequence (or Tree-to-Sequence) approaches [16, 31] create an abstract syntax tree of the SQL query, and process it as a structured input. One of the first neural systems [31] uses an existing graph-to-seq framework [30] that employs GNNs to process the input SQL graph and RNNs to generate the output explanation. However, this approach is only tested on queries taken from the WikiSQL [35] dataset, which are written for single tables and not entire databases, and thus are of relatively low complexity. A later approach [16] takes advantage of Transformer [27] networks to create a *Relation-Aware Graph Transformer* (RGT) encoder, that is more robust at encoding large query graphs, such as the ones resulting from complex SQL queries with multiple clauses. The RGT can encode both the syntax and the relations between the nodes of the tree, in order to provide a more informative representation of the query. However, using a graph encoder rejects the opportunity to use a sequence-to-sequence PLM, and leverage its power at understanding and generating NL, since it is not efficient to tweak the input types of a already pre-trained model.

5.6.2 Sequence-based Systems

Sequence-to-sequence models [2, 7, 29] process the input as a text sequence, either in its entirety [7] or in multiple runs [29], resulting in a hierarchical generation. The first approach [7] uses a simple sequence-to-sequence network with GRU networks. The network is then randomly initialized and trained on the WikiSQL [34] dataset in order to learn how to generate NL explanations.

The latter approach [29] follows a hierarchical methodology where each clause of the SQL query is processed independently. More specifically, an explanation is generated for each clause (i.e., SELECT, FROM, WHERE, etc.) and the generated texts are the merged in the same order as their clauses appear in the query. On one hand, this method reduces the length of the input for the neural model because it never has to process the entire query at once. Intuitively, this would allow the model to generate better explanations for each clause independently. On the other hand, there are some drawbacks to consider. Firstly, this would result in multiple invocations of the network, leading to additional computational costs. Additionally, processing each clause independently might lead to a loss of the general context of the query. For example, the explanation of the SELECT clause might depend on a different clause that the model can not read at the same time. Finally, there is no guarantee that the merging of all the sub-texts will lead to a coherent NL explanation.

The aforementioned sequence-to-sequence systems, also incorporate a copy-mechanism [6] in their decoder, which allows them to directly copy tokens from their inputs to the generated explanation (e.g., to use a table or column name in the explanation).

5.6.3 Using an Intermediate Language

In order to simplify the task of understanding the SQL query for the neural network, researchers have proposed the use of intermediate languages. One such example is EzSQL [2], an intermediate language for SQL that is closer to natural language and easier to read. For example, EzSQL simplifies complex structures such as UNIONs and INTERSECTs, it removes JOINs, and replaces most SQL keywords with phrases that are closer to natural language. This intermediate language is of course not executable, but it is much easier to read.

A system using this approach will deterministically translate the input SQL query into the intermediate language before passing it to the neural network. The network will then be tasked to translate the intermediate language to a natural language explanation, similarly to the aforementioned sequence-to-sequence approaches. Given the simplicity of the intermediate language, this task is expected to be easier for the network. However, it is likely that the network will need some additional training (or few-shot examples if a LLM is used) in order to understand this intermediate language that it might not be familiar with.

References

1. Satanjeev Banerjee and Alon Lavie. METEOR: An automatic metric for MT evaluation with improved correlation with human judgments. In *Proceedings of the ACL Workshop on Intrinsic and Extrinsic Evaluation Measures for Machine Translation and/or Summarization*, pages 65–72, Ann Arbor, Michigan, June 2005. Association for Computational Linguistics.
2. Meher Bhardwaj, Hrishikesh Ethari, and Dennis Singh Moirangthem. Ezsql: An sql intermediate representation for improving sql-to-text generation, 2025.
3. Edgar Dale and Jeanne S Chall. A formula for predicting readability: Instructions. *Educational research bulletin*, pages 37–54, 1948.
4. Stavroula Eleftherakis, Orest Gkini, and Georgia Koutrika. Let the database talk back: Natural language explanations for sql. *Proceedings of the 2nd Workshop on Search, Exploration, and Analysis in Heterogeneous Datastores, co-located with VLDB 2021*, 2021.
5. Basil Ell, Denny Vrandečić, and Elena Simperl. Spartiqulation: Verbalizing sparql queries. In Elena Simperl, Barry Norton, Dunja Mladenic, Emanuele Della Valle, Irini Fundulaki, Alexandre Passant, and Raphaël Troncy, editors, *The Semantic Web: ESWC 2012 Satellite Events*, pages 117–131, Berlin, Heidelberg, 2015. Springer Berlin Heidelberg.
6. Jiatao Gu, Zhengdong Lu, Hang Li, and Victor O.K. Li. Incorporating copying mechanism in sequence-to-sequence learning. In *Proceedings of the 54th Annual Meeting of the Association for Computational Linguistics (Volume 1: Long Papers)*, pages 1631–1640, Berlin, Germany, August 2016. Association for Computational Linguistics.

7. Daya Guo, Yibo Sun, Duyu Tang, Nan Duan, Jian Yin, Hong Chi, James Cao, Peng Chen, and Ming Zhou. Question generation from SQL queries improves neural semantic parsing. In *Proceedings of the 2018 Conference on Empirical Methods in Natural Language Processing*, pages 1597–1607, Brussels, Belgium, October-November 2018. Association for Computational Linguistics.
8. Yannis Ioannidis. From databases to natural language: The unusual direction. In Epaminondas Kapetanios, Vijayan Sugumaran, and Myra Spiliopoulou, editors, *Natural Language and Information Systems*, pages 12–16, Berlin, Heidelberg, 2008. Springer Berlin Heidelberg.
9. Srinivasan Iyer, Ioannis Konstas, Alvin Cheung, and Luke Zettlemoyer. Summarizing source code using a neural attention model. In *Proceedings of the 54th Annual Meeting of the Association for Computational Linguistics (Volume 1: Long Papers)*, pages 2073–2083, Berlin, Germany, August 2016. Association for Computational Linguistics.
10. J Peter Kincaid, Robert P Fishburne Jr, Richard L Rogers, and Brad S Chissom. Derivation of new readability formulas (automated readability index, fog count and flesch reading ease formula) for navy enlisted personnel. 1975.
11. Andreas Kokkalis, Panagiotis Vagenas, Alexandros Zervakis, Alkis Simitsis, Georgia Koutrika, and Yannis Ioannidis. Logos: A system for translating queries into narratives. In *Proceedings of the 2012 ACM SIGMOD International Conference on Management of Data*, SIGMOD '12, page 673–676, New York, NY, USA, 2012. Association for Computing Machinery.
12. Andreas Kokkalis, Panagiotis Vagenas, Alexandros Zervakis, Alkis Simitsis, Georgia Koutrika, and Yannis E. Ioannidis. Logos: a system for translating queries into narratives. In K. Selçuk Candan, Yi Chen, Richard T. Snodgrass, Luis Gravano, and Ariel Fuxman, editors, *Proceedings of the ACM SIGMOD International Conference on Management of Data, SIGMOD 2012, Scottsdale, AZ, USA, May 20-24, 2012*, pages 673–676. ACM, 2012.
13. Georgia Koutrika, Alkis Simitsis, and Yannis E. Ioannidis. Explaining structured queries in natural language. In *2010 IEEE 26th International Conference on Data Engineering (ICDE 2010)*, pages 333–344, 2010.
14. Jinyang Li, Binyuan Hui, Ge Qu, Jiaxi Yang, Binhua Li, Bowen Li, Bailin Wang, Bowen Qin, Ruiying Geng, Nan Huo, Xuanhe Zhou, Ma Chenhao, Guoliang Li, Kevin Chang, Fei Huang, Reynold Cheng, and Yongbin Li. Can llm already serve as a database interface? a big bench for large-scale database grounded text-to-sqls. In A. Oh, T. Naumann, A. Globerson, K. Saenko, M. Hardt, and S. Levine, editors, *Advances in Neural Information Processing Systems*, volume 36, pages 42330–42357. Curran Associates, Inc., 2023.
15. Chin-Yew Lin. ROUGE: A package for automatic evaluation of summaries. In *Text Summarization Branches Out*, pages 74–81, Barcelona, Spain, July 2004. Association for Computational Linguistics.
16. Da Ma, Xingyu Chen, Ruisheng Cao, Zhi Chen, Lu Chen, and Kai Yu. Relation-aware graph transformer for sql-to-text generation. *Applied Sciences*, 12(1), 2022.
17. Axel-Cyrille Ngonga Ngomo, Lorenz Bühmann, Christina Unger, Jens Lehmann, and Daniel Gerber. Sorry, i don't speak sparql: Translating sparql queries into natural language. In *Proceedings of the 22nd International Conference on World Wide Web*, WWW '13, page 977–988, New York, NY, USA, 2013. Association for Computing Machinery.
18. Kishore Papineni, Salim Roukos, Todd Ward, and Wei-Jing Zhu. Bleu: a method for automatic evaluation of machine translation. In *Proceedings of the 40th annual meeting of the Association for Computational Linguistics*, pages 311–318, 2002.
19. Maja Popović. chrF: character n-gram F-score for automatic MT evaluation. In *Proceedings of the Tenth Workshop on Statistical Machine Translation*, pages 392–395, Lisbon, Portugal, September 2015. Association for Computational Linguistics.
20. Maja Popović. chrF++: words helping character n-grams. In *Proceedings of the Second Conference on Machine Translation*, pages 612–618, Copenhagen, Denmark, September 2017. Association for Computational Linguistics.
21. Matt Post. A call for clarity in reporting BLEU scores. In *Proceedings of the Third Conference on Machine Translation: Research Papers*, pages 186–191, Brussels, Belgium, October 2018. Association for Computational Linguistics.

22. Nils Reimers and Iryna Gurevych. Sentence-bert: Sentence embeddings using siamese bert-networks. In *Proceedings of the 2019 Conference on Empirical Methods in Natural Language Processing*. Association for Computational Linguistics, 11 2019.
23. Ehud Reiter and Robert Dale. Building applied natural language generation systems. *Nat. Lang. Eng.*, 3(1):57–87, 1997.
24. Thibault Sellam, Dipanjan Das, and Ankur Parikh. BLEURT: Learning robust metrics for text generation. In *Proceedings of the 58th Annual Meeting of the Association for Computational Linguistics*, pages 7881–7892, Online, July 2020. Association for Computational Linguistics.
25. Alkis Simitsis and Yannis Ioannidis. DBMSs should talk back too, 2009.
26. Alkis Simitsis, Georgia Koutrika, Yannis Alexandrakis, and Yannis Ioannidis. Synthesizing structured text from logical database subsets. In *EDBT*, pages 428–439, 2008.
27. Ashish Vaswani, Noam Shazeer, Niki Parmar, Jakob Uszkoreit, Llion Jones, Aidan N Gomez, L ukasz Kaiser, and Illia Polosukhin. Attention is all you need. In I. Guyon, U. Von Luxburg, S. Bengio, H. Wallach, R. Fergus, S. Vishwanathan, and R. Garnett, editors, *Advances in Neural Information Processing Systems*, volume 30. Curran Associates, Inc., 2017.
28. Nathaniel Weir, Prasetya Utama, Alex Galakatos, Andrew Crotty, Amir Ilkhechi, Shekar Ramaswamy, Rohin Bhushan, Nadja Geisler, Benjamin Hättasch, Steffen Eger, Ugur Cetintemel, and Carsten Binnig. Dbpal: A fully pluggable NL2SQL training pipeline. In *Proceedings of the 2020 ACM SIGMOD International Conference on Management of Data*, SIGMOD '20, page 2347–2361, New York, NY, USA, 2020. Association for Computing Machinery.
29. Kun Wu, Lijie Wang, Zhenghua Li, Ao Zhang, Xinyan Xiao, Hua Wu, Min Zhang, and Haifeng Wang. Data augmentation with hierarchical SQL-to-question generation for cross-domain text-to-SQL parsing. In *Proceedings of the 2021 Conference on Empirical Methods in Natural Language Processing*, pages 8974–8983, Online and Punta Cana, Dominican Republic, November 2021. Association for Computational Linguistics.
30. Kun Xu, Lingfei Wu, Zhiguo Wang, Yansong Feng, and Vadim Sheinin. Graph2seq: Graph to sequence learning with attention-based neural networks. *ArXiv*, abs/1804.00823, 2018.
31. Kun Xu, Lingfei Wu, Zhiguo Wang, Yansong Feng, and Vadim Sheinin. SQL-to-text generation with graph-to-sequence model. In *Proceedings of the 2018 Conference on Empirical Methods in Natural Language Processing*, pages 931–936, Brussels, Belgium, October-November 2018. Association for Computational Linguistics.
32. Tao Yu, Rui Zhang, Kai Yang, Michihiro Yasunaga, Dongxu Wang, Zifan Li, James Ma, Irene Li, Qingning Yao, Shanelle Roman, Zilin Zhang, and Dragomir Radev. Spider: A large-scale human-labeled dataset for complex and cross-domain semantic parsing and text-to-SQL task. In Ellen Riloff, David Chiang, Julia Hockenmaier, and Jun'ichi Tsujii, editors, *Proceedings of the 2018 Conference on Empirical Methods in Natural Language Processing*, pages 3911–3921, Brussels, Belgium, October-November 2018. Association for Computational Linguistics.
33. Tianyi Zhang*, Varsha Kishore*, Felix Wu*, Kilian Q. Weinberger, and Yoav Artzi. Bertscore: Evaluating text generation with bert. In *International Conference on Learning Representations*, 2020.
34. Victor Zhong, Caiming Xiong, and Richard Socher. Seq2sql: Generating structured queries from natural language using reinforcement learning. *CoRR*, abs/1709.00103, 2017.
35. Victor Zhong, Caiming Xiong, and Richard Socher. Seq2sql: Generating structured queries from natural language using reinforcement learning, 2017.

Chapter 6
Multi-turn NLIDBs

Abstract Enabling interaction with users in a chatbot environment is an important step toward building natural and intuitive NLIDBs. This chapter explores the problem of multi-turn Text-to-SQL, focusing on its two main subcategories: interactive and conversational Text-to-SQL. For each subcategory, the chapter outlines the core challenges and offers a comprehensive overview of the systems' architecture. The chapter also presents existing datasets and evaluation metrics, providing a holistic understanding of how progress in the field is assessed. Finally, it presents a set of representative systems for the conversational Text-to-SQL task, illustrating how various design choices are implemented in practice.

6.1 Overview

The primary goal of natural language interfaces to databases (NLIDBs) is to enable users to access and interact with databases without requiring technical expertise. As Text-to-SQL, the core component of NLIDB systems, continues to advance, new research directions have emerged to further enhance the usability of these systems.

One such direction is multi-turn Text-to-SQL, which allows systems to engage in iterative interactions with users. Within this domain, two primary tasks have been identified and studied: **interactive Text-to-SQL** and **conversational Text-to-SQL**. Interactive Text-to-SQL engages with users in multiple steps to verify or correct the SQL translation, ensuring alignment with user intent. On the other hand, conversational Text-to-SQL systems aim to handle context-dependent follow-up queries, allowing users to build on previous questions.

The following sections provide an in-depth exploration of these tasks. We begin by examining the interactive Text-to-SQL problem, discussing the proposed solutions, the datasets and the metrics used in this research area. Subsequently, we analyze the conversational Text-to-SQL problem using the same structured approach.

G. Katsogiannis-Meimarakis et al., *Natural Language Interfaces for Databases with Deep Learning*, Data-Centric Systems and Applications,
https://doi.org/10.1007/978-3-032-06905-4_6

6.2 Interactive Text-to-SQL

6.2.1 The Interactive Text-to-SQL problem

For over a decade, the scientific community has been engaged in the development of systems that not only translate natural language questions (NLQs) into SQL queries in a single step but also support interactive dialogue with users. This dual capability—combining accurate query translation with dynamic user interaction—represents a significant step toward more intelligent, accessible, and user-friendly database interfaces [13]. With advancements in Text-to-SQL systems, which have brought the prospect of widespread adoption closer, interactive Text-to-SQL systems have emerged as a promising research domain. These systems aim to address erroneous translations by enabling users to verify and correct the Text-to-SQL output, thereby enhancing both accuracy and user confidence. The goal of an interactive Text-to-SQL system, given a NLQ, is twofold: (*a*) to convey the system's understanding of the question to the user, and (*b*) to integrate user feedback to refine the translation process.

Challenges. Achieving objective (a) presents challenges in ensuring that the system's feedback is both understandable to the user and useful for the refinement process, without imposing unnecessary complexity or requiring significant effort from the user. Objective (b) introduces further challenges, which are largely dependent on the nature of the user feedback. For instance, if the feedback is provided in natural language, the challenges discussed in Chapter 3 related to natural language become relevant to this problem as well.

6.2.2 Architecture

Interactive Text-to-SQL systems build upon standard Text-to-SQL models by integrating additional components that facilitate communication with users. The architecture of such systems is typically divided into three sequential phases: **Translation**, **Error Detection**, and **SQL Correction**.

The process begins with the Translation phase, where the user inputs a NLQ, which is translated into SQL using a Text-to-SQL model. Following translation, the system enters the Error Detection phase, where it identifies possible errors in the generated SQL. Finally, in the SQL Correction phase, the system modifies the SQL based on the detected errors of the previous phase. This cycle of detection and correction may be repeated iteratively until the output aligns with the user's intent.

Given that we have already elaborated on the Text-to-SQL systems' architecture, in Chapter 3, this chapter focuses on the Error Detection and SQL Correction phases, providing a comprehensive analysis of the components built in each phase.

We are going to categorize the systems into two main types that determine their architecture. The distinction is based on who initiates and drives the interaction.

For that reason, we define the *(a)* model-driven interaction systems, in which the system detects potential issues and solicits clarification from the user, and *(b)* the user-driven interaction systems, in which users have the responsibility to detect the errors by reviewing the system-generated translation.

6.2.2.1 Model-driven interaction

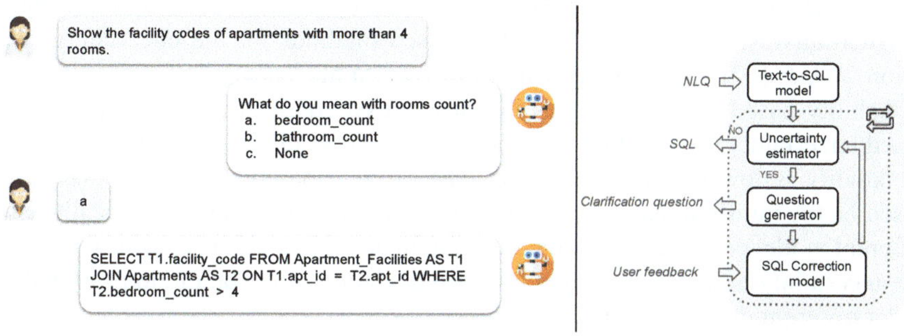

Fig. 6.1: Left: Example of user interaction. Right: model-driven interaction system architecture.

In the model-driven interaction systems, the Error Detection phase is composed of (1) an *uncertainty estimator* that spots parts of the translation which possibly have an error and (2) a *question generator* that creates clarification questions based on the found uncertainties. Once feedback is collected, a *SQL correction* model mechanism is defined to refine the query. Figure 6.1 provides an example of a model-driven interaction scenario along with the architecture of the system.

Uncertainty estimator. There are two main strategies that have been used for the uncertainty calculation in interactive Text-to-SQL systems: (1) the *misalignment-based uncertainty*, which detects inconsistencies between the NLQ and the generated SQL, and (2) the *information-based uncertainty*, which uses the translation model's internal information, such as the output probability distribution, to estimate confidence in specific translation parts.

PIIA [15] tries to align the predicted SQL query with the NLQ and considers the unaligned tokens as uncertain tokens. To do that, a SQL-to-Text Restatement and a Token-to-Token Alignment module are implemented. The SQL-to-Text Restatement transforms the predicted SQL query to the corresponding NLQ, under the assumption that it is easier to detect alignments between two NL questions. Then, a template-based approach is used to apply the transformation.

For the implementation of the Token-to-Token Alignment, the two sentences are concatenated and encoded with BERT. Then, the output of BERT is given to a Multi-Layer Perceptron (MLP) to further distil useful information. After that, a similarity matrix that contains the pairwise cosine similarities of the tokens in the two sentences is computed. Stop words and words that exist in the templates of the SQL-to-Text Representation module are not considered in the comparison. Finally, the Hungarian maximum matching algorithm is applied, over the generated bipartite graph, to find one-to-one alignments. The tokens with alignment scores less than a threshold are considered as uncertain tokens.

Similarly, *Nalir* [13] tries to match the nodes of the linguistic parse tree created from the user question to SQL components. For the schema elements and the values, it uses a similarity score that is defined as the maximum of the WUP similarity [24], to capture semantic similarity, and the jaccard similarity, to capture lexical similarity. Then, nodes with multiple candidates over a threshold are considered uncertain.

Alternatively, leveraging information-based methods for the uncertainty calculation, *MISP* [27] experiments with two uncertainty calculation measures, (1) a probability-based uncertainty and (2) a dropout-based uncertainty. The probability-based uncertainty decides that a prediction needs user clarification if the prediction probability is lower than a threshold. The dropout-based uncertainty measure is based on the intuition that if a probability on a prediction varies dramatically across different model perturbations under dropout, then the model is uncertain about it. So, the uncertainty is calculated as the standard deviation of the prediction's probability under different dropout perturbations.

Another information-based approach is *DialSQL* [10], in which two components are implemented to identify the error category and the position of the error. To determine the error category, i.e., whether it is a selection, projection or aggregation error, a probability distribution over all the error categories is calculated, based on the categories embeddings and the predicted SQL query. The start position of the error span is determined by the probability distribution over query tokens.

Question generator. The question generator is implemented using template-based approaches that create a multiple choice natural language clarification question based on the found uncertainties. *PIIA* [15] creates a multiple-choice question for each uncertain token. The question is always the "What do you mean by that?". For the creation of the candidate answers, all the schema elements names are added. If the uncertain token is about an aggregation, all the aggregation operators are added, too. Then, to create the final set of options, a ranking method is created. The candidates are ranked based on their similarity with the uncertain token. The similarity is calculated as the summation of the lexical and semantic similarity. The lexical similarity is calculated with the Jaccard similarity in the tokens, while the semantic similarity is calculated as the Euclidean distance between the tokens embeddings. After ranking the options, the top are selected for the multiple-choice question and two more are additionally added. These are the Value option, whose selection indicates that the uncertain token is a database value, and the None option, which ensures that uncertain tokens will not be modified unexpectedly.

MISP [27] creates binary questions regarding the uncertain tokens. More specifically, the questions are created with a rule-based natural language generator that consists of a seed lexicon, which defines NL descriptions for basic SQL elements (e.g., equals →=), and a grammar, which defines rules to derive questions (e.g., Does the system need to return information about $COL[col]? \rightarrow Q[col||SELECTagg?col]$).

DialSQL [10] leverages an uncertainty estimator to identify both the error category and the specific error span in a generated SQL query. Based on this information, it decodes a list of candidate replacements for the erroneous span. For each error category, a dedicated scoring method is defined, and a model is trained to rank the candidates such that the top-ranked choice aligns with the ground truth.

NaLiR [13] addresses uncertainty in NLQs by generating clarification questions for ambiguous or uncertain words. It presents users with multiple-choice options, where the candidates are derived from its uncertainty detection module, allowing users to select the most appropriate interpretation.

SQL Correction. In model-driven interaction settings, the SQL correction model takes as input the user's selected option from a predefined multiple-choice question. Because these options are predetermined, the correction mechanism is typically rule-based, executing specific actions based on the user's selection.

For instance, PIIA [15] defines a set of modifier rules that leverage part-of-speech (POS) tags and the types of answer options—namely, column name, table name, aggregation, and value—along with the context of the user's natural language (NL) question. These rules are applied to modify the original NL question, which is then retranslated into SQL based on the revised input. Similarly, MISP [27] integrates user feedback directly into the decoding process of the SQL generation model. It does so by constraining the output of the base model during decoding, preventing it from reproducing the same translation if the user has indicated that it is incorrect.

Furthermore, some systems adopt more straightforward approaches by posing clarification questions whose answers can be directly used to modify the SQL query. For example, NaLiR [13] utilizes user feedback to resolve ambiguities in mapping natural language (NL) phrases to elements of the database schema. When a user selects one of the candidate mappings for a specific NL span, the system discards the remaining alternatives and uses the selected mapping to refine the query accordingly.

6.2.2.2 User-driven interaction

The user-driven interaction systems expect feedback from the user regarding the translation. Since the user might not have the technical knowledge to understand the SQL translation, the systems implement an *SQL explanation* model that transforms the SQL query in natural language. Then, the *SQL correction* model kicks-in by considering the given user feedback to rectify the translation. Figure 6.2 provides an example of a user-driven interaction system alongside the architecture in these systems' category.

SQL Explanation. The task of explaining a produced SQL query closely aligns with the SQL-to-Text task. Due to the reliability of template-based approaches, which ensure accurate translations for the supported queries and avoid the uncertainty associated with neural models, systems that select to explain the translation rely on templates. Despite the fact that there are existing template-based systems that

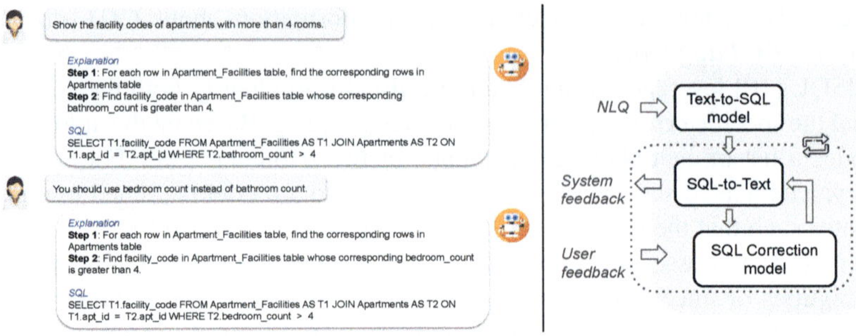

Fig. 6.2: Left: Example of user interaction. Right: user-driven interaction system architecture.

describe the SQL query [11], the systems in this research area prefer to create approaches that split the explanation into multiple steps, making the process of detecting and explaining the error easier.

SPLASH [6] defines 57 templates based on the queries existing in Spider, and manually creates a step-wise explanation for each template. Similarly, *STEPS* [21] provides the explanation of each SQL clause. It uses predefined templates for the generation of the natural language explanation in each clause.

SQL Correction. Similar to the model-driven interaction systems, for the correction phase, a single model responsible to refine the SQL query is defined. The difference in this case is that it takes as input a free-form natural language feedback from the user. Consequently, it is implemented with the use of language models, leveraging their ability to process and interpret unconstrained language input effectively.

NL-Edit [7] implements a model that takes user feedback in the form of natural language and translates it to a set of edit steps that will be applied deterministically to the incorrect SQL query. The system consists of an encoder that takes as input the concatenation of the user feedback, the explanation, the question and the database schema and a decoder that predicts the required edit steps. To train this model, a dataset is created, based on Spider with synthetic feedback on erroneous examples produced by applying edit rules. Another example of the neural-based approach is SPLASH [6]. Even though this work only presents the dataset for the interactive Text-to-SQL problem, it provides experiments with a set of baseline models for the correction task. Except for a re-ranking model that is proposed, the rest of the baseline models are existing Text-to-SQL parsers in which feedback is incorporated by concatenating it to the input.

Finally, in an effort to create a more efficient system for correcting errors, *STEPS* [21] adopts a *hybrid* approach that combines a rule-based system along with a neural one to reduce the computational cost. More specifically, three types of edits are defined that can be fixed by a rule-based system. These are replacing a column/table name or a literal value, adding a new column name in the select clause and removing a column name. The natural language correction feedback provided by the user is compared with the original clause explanation to determine if the edit falls into one of those categories. If it is not, the more costly neural-based alternative is triggered. For its implementation, the SmBoP [17] model is trained with an automatically created dataset based on Spider, that takes the explanations of each clause and returns the SQL translation. To combine those clauses, three rewriting rules are defined for correcting errors due to missing tables in the FROM clause, multiple clauses (e.g., two select clauses) in the same query.

6.2.3 Datasets

While Text-to-SQL datasets [14, 31] are not specifically designed for interactive Text-to-SQL tasks, they still provide valuable information, such as the ground truth SQL query that a system should aim to produce. This ground truth query serves as the target output for an interactive Text-to-SQL system, making these datasets a foundational resource for evaluating systems built for this task.

In addition to these general datasets, there are also datasets specifically crafted for the interactive Text-to-SQL task. These specialized datasets facilitate research by incorporating user feedback, either addressing specific errors or providing additional input for questions not adequately covered in standard Text-to-SQL datasets. For example, they may include feedback on ambiguous queries, capturing both system responses and user corrections. These datasets focus on user-driven interaction scenarios, as they contain the natural language description of the error as the feedback.

The *SPLASH* dataset [6] is the first dataset specifically designed for the interactive Text-to-SQL task. It includes NLQs, the corresponding SQL queries, erroneous SQL queries, and user feedback in natural language explaining the errors. SPLASH leverages the Spider dataset [31] as its primary source for questions. Erroneous SQL translations were generated using incorrect outputs from the Seq2Struct parser [19] trained on the Text-to-SQL task. User feedback was collected through crowdsourcing. More specifically, ten annotators were presented with the original question and an explanation of the generated SQL and were asked to identify errors, if any, and provide feedback to correct the SQL. To enhance feedback diversity, a second group of annotators paraphrased the feedback.

Despite its value, SPLASH has notable limitations. One key issue is the low variability of the queries and the restrictive range of error cases in the translated SQL queries. Since the queries originate from the Spider dataset, the challenges addressed are only a subset of those encountered in real-world scenarios, where queries often feature multiple nestings or a high number of operators—elements largely absent in Spider [16]. Moreover, Spider is among the Text-to-SQL datasets with the highest exact references of schema elements [16, 20], minimizing errors related to incorrect schema linking. Another limitation stems from the reliance on errors generated by a single parser, which narrows the dataset's focus to the specific weaknesses of this parser [26]. Given the rapid advancements in the Text-to-SQL field, many of these errors may no longer align with commonly observed issues in subsequent systems.

PRACTIQ [5] is an effort to create an interactive Text-to-SQL dataset that focuses on ambiguous and unanswerable questions. It contains the initial user questions, user clarification responses, SQL responses, SQL execution results and natural language explanations of the results. The databases of the questions are derived from Spider and the generation of the rest information is done in three stages. In the first stage, the column and cell values from existing SQL queries in the Spider dataset are extracted, and the database schema is modified to transform the question corresponding to that SQL to ambiguous or unanswerable. For example, to generate ambiguous queries, an LLM is requested to replace an existing requested column with two alternatives. Similarly, to create unanswerable questions, records or columns that are related to the question are removed from the database. In the second stage, the system's clarification question is generated using a template-based method or a prompting method. Then, the final SQL response is created by modifying the SQL, based on designed rules. Finally, the user response is simulated through prompting an LLM with the initial user question, the system's clarification questions and the final SQL query. In the third step, post-processing steps are applied to ensure the quality of the produced data. More specifically, the conversation is refined by creating a prompt with three default manually curated examples to improve the naturalness and coherence of the conversation and to add the natural language explanation to the execution results. Additionally, an LLM is used to evaluate the ambiguities that are created in the database, and only the data that pass the evaluation are kept. Furthermore, the SQL queries that are not executable in the modified databases are filtered out. Finally, the user question and the altered database are given to an LLM to perform binary classification of whether the given pair belongs to the specified category (ambiguous or unanswerable). Only the queries that pass the evaluation checks are kept in the dataset. The final dataset comprises 2812 conversations, with 1802 being ambiguous and unanswerable questions and 1034 queries derived from the Spider dev set and augmented with natural language explanations based on their execution results. To further verify the quality of the dataset, two tasks with human annotations are conducted. In the first one, 20 question-database pairs were selected from each category and four SQL experts were asked to classify them in the existing categories. In the second one, the annotators assess the factuality, helpfulness and naturalness of 10 randomly selected conversations per category. Both evaluations suggest that the created dataset is of good quality.

Despite the fact that PRACTIQ focuses on errors that unveil the value of interactive Text-to-SQL systems — the capability of answering ambiguous or unanswerable initial user questions — it still falls short of describing the wide range of errors that can arise from Text-to-SQL model predictions.

Thus, the need for a dedicated dataset for the interactive Text-to-SQL task is clear. Such a dataset can serve as a benchmark for comparing different models, providing a clear indication of their performance and fostering further development in interactive systems. By offering a standardized framework, it can help researchers assess how effectively models handle interactive scenarios and contribute to improving the robustness of these systems.

However, the development of a benchmark for this task carries several challenges. One major difficulty lies in the diversity of feedback scenarios. There is no universal standard for representing user feedback, making it challenging to represent user feedback in a way that will be usable with all different methods. Additionally, the rapid progress in the Text-to-SQL domain complicates the task of creating a dataset capable of encompassing the wide range of errors these systems may generate. Addressing these challenges is essential for ensuring the dataset's usability and relevance for the interactive Text-to-SQL task.

6.2.4 Metrics

The value of interactive approaches can be assessed by the performance improvements that they offer compared to single-turn translation scenarios. Therefore, the most commonly reported metrics are the **exact match** or the **execution accuracy** that are the main metrics for assessing a Text-to-SQL system, as shown in Chapter 3. In addition to these metrics, it has been argued that interactive systems should additionally capture translation improvements even when they do not result in a correct translation. To address this, a new metric is defined, named **Progress** [7], which measures the relative reduction in the number of edits required to transform an incorrect SQL query to the correct one, before and after an interactive step.

Another important factor for interactive Text-to-SQL evaluation is the **number of interaction turns**, since maintaining a low number of turns is vital for resource efficiency and user experience.

6.3 Conversational Text-to-SQL

6.3.1 The Conversational Text-to-SQL Problem

In real-world applications, users often seek information through multi-turn interactions with systems, posing a series of related questions rather than a single question [36]. This is common in practical settings such as customer support, data exploration, or business analytics, where each question builds upon previous ones to refine or extend the user's intent. Conversational Text-to-SQL systems are designed to address this scenario by translating NLQs within the context of a multi-turn dialogue. Unlike single-turn Text-to-SQL models, these systems should understand and process question sequences, where later queries may depend on earlier ones.

In the following section, we explore the architectural approaches employed by systems developed for this task, and we examine the datasets and evaluation metrics used to assess progress in conversational Text-to-SQL research.

6.3.1.1 Challenges

While many of the challenges present in traditional Text-to-SQL systems persist in this setting, conversational Text-to-SQL introduces additional complexities specific to dialogue-based interactions.

Question dependencies. A primary challenge in this task is handling dependencies between questions. Two primary types of dependencies referenced in the literature are *co-reference* and *ellipsis*. Co-reference occurs when two or more expressions refer to the same entity. For example, in the questions "Which movies did Quentin Tarantino write?" and "And which did he direct?", the term "he" in the second question refers to "Quentin Tarantino". Ellipsis is the omission of one or several words that are nevertheless understood in the context of the remaining elements. In the above example, the word "movies" is omitted from the second question but is understood based on the previous turn.

Error propagation. Another critical issue is error propagation. If a system produces an incorrect SQL translation in an early turn, subsequent queries—often dependent on the output or understanding of previous ones—may compound the initial mistake. This cascading effect makes error handling and recovery particularly important in conversational settings.

6.3.2 Architecture

Two main directions have emerged in addressing the conversational Text-to-SQL problem. The more widely adopted approach involves **adapting existing Text-to-SQL architectures** to incorporate dialogue context by considering previous questions. Systems in this category typically retain the core architecture described in Chapter 3 but extend it to handle the conversation history. The second approach takes a different route by **transforming the conversational problem into a single-turn Text-to-SQL task**. This is achieved by introducing a specialized model that rewrites each user question to remove dependencies on prior dialogue turns.

As the development of conversational and single-turn Text-to-SQL systems has progressed in parallel, we will not revisit the full range of architectural designs already covered in Chapter 3. Instead, this section focuses on two key areas:

- The **extensions in the single-turn Text-to-SQL taxonomy** introduced in Chapter 3, that adapt standard models to handle conversation context.
- The **dependency-resolution models** used in the reformulation-based approach, which aim to convert multi-turn interactions into single-turn queries.

6.3.2.1 Extending single turn Text-to-SQL taxonomy

The difference that a conversational Text-to-SQL task introduces, compared to single-turn, is the incorporation of the history. The history can include the previous NLQs, their corresponding SQL queries, or even the execution results of those queries. This contextual information requires new techniques that will be able to extend the single-turn scenario, where only a NLQ and the corresponding schema are required for the translation.

Conversational Text-to-SQL systems focus on two main axes from the single-turn Text-to-SQL taxonomy to create a model capable of using the conversation history: input construction and neural learning. While other components, such as schema linking, can also be affected by conversational context, most existing work does not introduce fundamentally new techniques in these areas, nor do they shift focus away from well-established single-turn methodologies.

Input construction. In conversational systems, the most substantial change is in the input, which must be extended to encode contextual information. Two main approaches have been followed for integrating the history into the input, which extend the corresponding categories of the input construction of Chapter 3: serialized structuring and separate structuring.

Serialized structuring. The most dominant approach is the extension of the serialized input discussed in Chapter 3. In this approach, all relevant information is concatenated into a single input sequence. In conversational settings, this includes the current NLQ, the database schema and additionally, the dialogue history. The content included in the history varies across systems. Some models include both previous NLQs and their corresponding SQL queries [8, 12, 35, 37], while others include only the previous NLQs with the most recent SQL query [2], or exclude SQL altogether and rely solely on natural language [30].

Separate structuring. Another strategy parallels the separate structuring paradigm used in single-turn models. However, in conversational systems, the separation between inputs is less clearly defined. A common approach is to use a dedicated encoder for the conversation history, while encoding the current question and schema together [1, 36], or encoding each input separately [23]. Alternatively, the input encoding can be divided based on the type of the input [38]. In this framework, one encoder processes all NLQs, another processes the SQL queries, and a third processes the database schema.

Neural learning. The neural learning techniques used in conversational Text-to-SQL generally mirror those employed in single-turn settings. This section reviews how the methods described in Chapter 3 are adapted or extended to accommodate the conversational context.

Fresh start. There are systems, mostly earlier ones, that train the model from scratch [23, 36, 38], due to the unique architectures that they propose. For example, models that use multiple input encoders cannot easily benefit from pre-trained language models, as these models are not trained in these settings.

Transfer learning. Transfer learning remains a central strategy, although its standalone use is less common in the conversational setting. Rather than relying solely on fine-tuning, many systems incorporate additional objectives to better adapt the model to the complexities of conversational interactions. An interesting variation on conventional fine-tuning is curriculum learning, where the model is trained on examples of increasing complexity. This gradual exposure mirrors the cognitive learning sequence found in human curricula and has been shown to be effective in enhancing the generalization capabilities and convergence speed of models [37].

In-context learning. In-context learning is widely adopted in systems that utilize large language models (LLMs). This approach leverages the generalization ability of LLMs without the need for additional training. Models that use in-context learning are not fine-tuned on the downstream task; instead, they are given a prompt that describes the task along with examples to demonstrate expected behavior [12, 33, 35].

Additional objectives. A common trend in both single-turn and conversational Text-to-SQL systems is the incorporation of auxiliary training objectives, used either during a pre-training stage or in parallel with fine-tuning on the downstream task. Several objectives focus on improving alignment with the database schema. For instance, schema grounding consistency [25] and related schema prediction [8] train the model to identify relevant tables and columns. Others, such as column contextual semantics [30] and schema state tracking [2], train the model to predict the appropriate position of schema elements within the SQL structure. These objectives are similar to the schema linking objectives used in single-turn systems but are enriched by the inclusion of conversational context.

Other objectives aim to model contextual relationships across dialogue turns. A common technique is masked language modeling [2, 30], where tokens in the input are masked, and the model is trained to reconstruct them. Another approach requires the model to generate a NLQ that summarizes the entire interaction [8]. In addition, some objectives attempt to capture more complex aspects of a conversation. For instance, models are trained to predict the differences between the current and previous SQL queries [8, 30], or to predict if there is a semantic dependency between NLQs [2].

6.3.2.2 Dependency-resolution models.

The task of dependency resolution in conversational Text-to-SQL systems is formulated as a paraphrasing problem, where the objective is to rewrite a follow-up NLQ into a fully independent one. The input to this task consists of the current question along with the dialogue history, and the output is a paraphrased version that no longer has contextual dependencies. To implement this functionality, systems use language models, leveraging their advanced natural language understanding and generation capabilities. This can mean employing large language models (LLMs) with few-shot prompting [34] or training smaller language models [3]. This strategy allows conversational Text-to-SQL systems to retain the architectural structure of state-of-the-art single-turn models by simply integrating an external paraphrasing module.

Despite its advantages, this approach presents a significant drawback: increased computational overhead in latency and resource consumption. This overhead results not only from the additional inference step required for paraphrasing, but also from the inherent limitation of the method itself. In real-world applications, follow-up questions frequently depend not only on prior natural language inputs but also on the results of previous queries. For example, consider the dialogue: "Which European city has the highest population density?" followed by "And how many citizens does it have?". While it is possible to reformulate the question as "What is the population of the European city with the highest population density?", doing so would require re-executing the first query, thereby introducing inefficiency and redundancy.

6.3.3 Metrics

The evaluation of the conversational Text-to-SQL systems is similar to the non-conversational task. The **execution accuracy** or the **exact match** have been used as the main metrics to count the accuracy. Building on that, it is also important to track accuracy in the context of a dialogue. For this reason, also use metrics such as the **question match** of each question in a dialogue, which is equal to 1 if a question is answered correctly, and the **interaction match** of a dialogue, which is equal to 1 if all the questions in a dialogue are answered correctly. To gain more insight into their system performance, similarly to the context-independent Text-to-SQL problem, some works report their accuracy in specific categories. These categories can be a hardness category similarly to the one defined in Spider [31] and/or categories based on the number of interaction turns that a dialogue has [1].

6.3.4 Datasets

Initial datasets for conversational Text-to-SQL. The first datasets developed to support training and evaluation in conversational Text-to-SQL tasks are SParC [32] and CoSQL [29]. SparC is derived from the Spider dataset. Fifteen annotators were asked to provide inter-connected questions aimed at achieving a specific goal, which originated from a Spider question. Annotators were required to generate at least two questions per goal to ensure multi-turn interactions. CoSQL was created using the Wizard-of-Oz methodology. More specifically, for the creation of the dialogues, there was a user asking the questions and an SQL expert that provided the answers. The users were crowdworkers and the experts comprised 25 graduate and undergraduate computer science students proficient in SQL. For each dialogue, users familiarized themselves with a database schema and received a goal question sourced from Spider's medium, hard, or extra-hard categories. Then, they were requested to create questions that were either interconnected with the given goal or questions to further explore the database. Experts labelled each question (e.g., AMBIGUOUS) and provided the appropriate SQL response. The resulting dataset contains the type of each question, the corresponding SQL, and the system's explanation of the SQL, when available.

While both datasets have been instrumental in advancing the field, they have notable limitations. As highlighted in the literature [2, 9], they include limited inter-question dependencies and SQL queries of relatively low complexity.

Increasing contextual complexity. To address the limited contextual dependencies in existing datasets CHASE [9] was introduced, a Chinese dataset containing question sequences and their corresponding SQL queries. The databases used are a processed subset of the DuSQL [22] databases. The question generation was implemented with two methods, manual annotation and translation of existing data. In the first method, 12 Chinese college students familiarized themselves with a database, and then generated sequences of queries related to the database. The first question in each sequence was freely created, while subsequent questions were guided by assigned intent categories (e.g., reuse entities with an additional column), promoting context-dependent interactions. In the second method, a processed subset of the questions in the SparC dataset was translated into Chinese. Another effort to create a dataset with enriched conversational complexity is STAR [2], a conversational Text-to-SQL dataset with 480K context-dependent Text-to-SQL conversations. The dataset has been constructed from single-turn questions taken from the Spider, CoSQL and SParC datasets, while the context dependent questions have been created with the use of 100 manually created templates for follow-up questions.

Extending SQL coverage. Recognizing the need to represent the full breadth of SQL operations beyond simple SELECT statements, MultiSQL [12] was introduced. This dataset incorporates additional SQL statements, such as CREATE and UPDATE, to reflect a wider range of database interactions. MultiSQL consists of 800 dialogue groups, with over 9000 turns from 166 databases. The databases are the databases of the CoSQL dataset, while the dialogues were generated with the use of GPT-4 under different prompt frameworks. After deduplication of the produced dataset, manual changes were applied to the dataset to ensure its quality. More specifically, the process includes (1) grammar correction of the produced SQL, (2) semantic correction between NL and SQL pairs, and (3) contextual relevance improvement, by inserting 334 NL-SQL query interactions to improve semantic coherence within dialogues. On average, MultiSQL dialogues contain approximately three times more query turns than those in SParC and CoSQL, offering richer conversational depth.

Limitations of current datasets. Despite the diversity of these datasets, most of them rely partially or entirely on the queries and databases of the Spider dataset. As discussed in previous chapters, Spider exhibits several limitations, including small database schemas and relatively simple query structures. These constraints inherently affect the complexity and variability of the datasets, underscoring the need for future datasets to diversify beyond Spider's questions and databases.

6.3.5 Systems

In this section, we describe a representative set of systems that exhibit distinct architectural and methodological characteristics. These systems illustrate the broad spectrum of strategies explored in the literature to address the challenges of conversational Text-to-SQL.

6.3.5.1 Custom Architectures

A significant line of research, particularly among earlier systems in the field, introduces custom architectures designed to explicitly model the complexities of conversation. These systems often focus on input encoding and propose novel encoding mechanisms.

HIE-SQL [38] (History Information Enhanced Text-to-SQL) introduces a three-part architecture: (1) a multimodal encoder, (2) the HIE-Layers, and (3) a Decoder. The multimodal encoder consists of two types of encoders. The first is a language model responsible for encoding the history and current NLQs, as well as, the database schema. The second, named SQLBERT, is the module that encodes the previous SQL query and is trained with data from the Spider, SparC and CoSQL benchmarks. The HIE-Layers consist of eight transformer layers with relative self-attention [18] based on the relations present in the schema-linking graph. This graph is a directed graph containing the schema relations, in addition to the relations between the current NLQ, the previous NLQs and the last predicted SQL query. The Decoder is a tree-based decoder proposed in [28].

EditSQL [36] is a system with three main components: (1) an utterance-table encoder, (2) an interaction-level encoder with turn attention and (3) a table-aware decoder. The utterance-table encoder encodes the NLQ and the database schema jointly using BERT and Bi-LSTMs with co-attention. The interaction-level encoder is used to capture the information across different NLQs. It is implemented with an LSTM that takes as input the output of the utterance encoder and a turn-attention mechanism responsible for capturing the correlation between the current and previous NLQs. Finally, the table-aware decoder uses an LSTM to generate the SQL query with attention mechanisms over the question representation, the schema representation and the previously generated queries. Additionally, the table-aware encoder is extended with a query editing mechanism, because the user might often ask closely related questions in an interaction, that can be answered by copy or insert operations over the previously translated SQL queries.

IGSQL [1] adopts an encoder-decoder framework composed of four main components: (1) a database schema interaction graph encoder, which captures context dependencies by incorporating historical representations of schema items across dialogue turns, (2) a text encoder, which encodes the current NLQ considering the previous ones, (3) a co-attention module between the database schema items representations and the NLQ representation and (4) a decoder, which generates the SQL query for the current turn based on the NLQ representation, the database schema items representations and the previously predicted SQL query representation. The main contribution of the paper is the database schema interaction graph encoder. The nodes of the graph represent the columns of the database, and edges include self-links, foreign-primary key relations, and intra-table column relations. At each interaction turn, the representations of the schema items are updated through two mechanisms: one that updates a node based on the neighboring schema item representations of the previous turn (cross-turn layer), and another that uses the adjacent item representations in the current turn (intra-turn layer).

IST-SQL [23] is a system that consists of four main components: (1) a BERT embedder, that generates the representations of the NLQ and the database schema, (2) an utterance encoder, that incorporates the previous NLQs into the representation of the current one, (3) an interaction state tracking module, that encodes and updates the representations of the database schema and the previous SQL queries, and (4) a decoder, that generates the SQL query. The main contribution is the use of the interaction states that include the *schema-state*, that represents the database schema, and the *SQL-state*, that represents the state of the previous SQL queries. For the representation of the schema-state, a RGNN is used, based on a graph where the nodes are the database columns along with the corresponding SQL keywords (e.g., SELECT, WHERE) in which they appeared in the previous SQL queries. The edges represent column relations, either direct foreign-primary key relations between two columns, or table-level foreign key paths connecting columns across related tables. For the representation of the SQL-state a dictionary is constructed, where the keys are all the SQL keywords and the values are the schema items that have been used with this SQL keyword in prior interactions. This dictionary is passed through a non-linear layer that produces the SQL-state representation. During each dialogue turn, the state updaters extract information from the previous SQL query to update both schema and SQL states.

6.3.5.2 Training PLMs

Another common strategy involves adapting pre-trained language models (PLMs) to the conversational Text-to-SQL task by applying extra training. These systems typically share a base architecture, but differ in how they are trained.

In *MIGA* [8] three pretraining tasks are used on the T5 model to create a conversational Text-to-SQL system. In all pretraining tasks the input is the same with the downstream task: a concatenation of the previous NLQs and the corresponding SQL queries, the database schema, and the current NLQ. The tasks are: (1) Related schema prediction, in which the model is trained to output all the tables and columns that are related with the NLQ, (2) Turn Switch Prediction, in which the model is expected to output the clauses in which the SQL must change compared to the previous one, and (3) Final Utterance Prediction, where the model is requested to summarize the whole dialogue in one NLQ. Additionally, to mitigate the phenomenon of error propagation — when the previous SQL in the dialogue is not correct and the model has learned to depend on it — the model is fine-tuned with examples in which the previous SQL queries have been shuffled.

In *STAR* [2] two pre-training objectives are proposed: (1) schema state tracking and (2) utterance dependency tracking, that are combined with the masked language modeling [4] to create a model capable of predicting context-dependent SQL queries. The schema state tracking objective aims to predict how the schema is used in the current query, given all the previous NLQs and the information about how the schema is used in the previous SQL query. Utterance dependency tracking aims to capture the dependency of sequential NLQs within each Text-to-SQL conversation.

To train with this objective, NLQs from different conversations are used as negative examples and the NLQs from the same conversation as positive examples with varying similarity scores. The similarity score is the weighted average of the SQL semantic similarity and the SQL structure similarity. The SQL semantic similarity is the Jaccard similarity between the schema-states of two SQL queries, while the SQL structure similarity is calculated with the use of the Weisfeiler-Lehman subtree kernel in the SQL trees of two queries. In addition to the introduced objectives, the masked language modeling objective is used to assist the model to learn the contextual representation of NLQs and schema.

SCoRe [30] (Structured and Sequential Context Representation) is a pre-training framework for the conversational Text-to-SQL task. For the proposed method, two pre-training objectives are introduced: (1) Column Contextual Semantics and (2) Turn Contextual Switch. The Column Contextual Semantics objective aims to capture the alignment between the NLQ and the database schema, by predicting the operations that should be performed to a column given a conversational turn. Turn Contextual Switch captures the conversational context flow by predicting the one of the 26 turn difference operations defined. The turn difference operations encode changes between turns of user queries (e.g., insert a new WHERE condition or remove an aggregate operator from the SELECT clause). Finally, the masked language modeling objective is used to facilitate contextual representation learning. The training loss is defined as the sum of the three objectives.

6.3.5.3 The LLM Era

After the broad usage of LLMs in several tasks and specifically in single-turn Text-to-SQL, approaches that are based in LLMs became popular in the conversational context as well. These methods vary on how they formulate the problem, but all of them rely on LLMs.

ACT-SQL [33] experiments with prompts for the single-turn Text-to-SQL task. More specifically, various representations for the database schema are used and an exemplar selection method is introduced. More specifically, half of the few-shot examples are randomly picked, while the rest are selected based on the similarity between their NLQs and the user's NLQ. Additionally, the similar examples included in the prompt are formulated with a chain-of-thought technique that analyses the production of the requested SQL query step by step. To adjust their approach to the conversational Text-to-SQL scenario, a model that removes the dependencies from the last NLQ is implemented, transforming the problem into a single-turn Text-to-SQL translation. More specifically, an LLM is prompted to remove the history dependencies from the question by providing it the conversation and ten random examples that perform this task.

MultiSQL [12] proposes a framework, consisting of (1) a system initialization, which contains the creation of the prompt, (2) an integration of dialogue history, and (3) a self-refinement, which is responsible to execute the translations and provide feedback to correct the SQL. Additionally, due to the new challenges introduced by the dataset they proposed — caused by the existence of statements other than SELECT —, they defined two new metrics to assess system performance. The first one, called context-aware match, tackles the issue of naming discrepancies due to changes in the database schema. To do that, fuzzy matching is applied to allow more flexible match of the predicted and expected schema element names. Additionally, a mapping dictionary is created to keep track of the changes made by CREATE and ALTER statements. Context-aware matching is equal to 1 if all the schema element names match (accounting for fuzzy matching and mapping dictionary) and the rest of SQL query matches exactly, otherwise it is 0. The second one is database state matching, and it is used to evaluate the non-SELECT statements as they do not return a list of values an thus can not be evaluated using execution accuracy. To assess the correctness of these statements, the database states after the execution of the predicted SQL and the gold SQL are compared. More specifically, in case of the CREATE, ALTER and DELETE statements, the structure of the databases (table names, column names, etc) is compared, while in case of INSERT or UPDATE, the content of the databases is compared.

Finally, following a different approach by formulating the task as an editing task over the previous SQL query, *CoE-SQL* [35] proposes a prompt design strategy created to tackle the conversational Text-to-SQL task. More specifically, an LLM is used to predict a chain of edit rules that can be applied to an SQL query to create the follow-up SQL query in a multi-turn scenario. This approach is based on the assumption that, when two consecutive questions are related, the later SQL query can be obtained by edit the previous one, rather than generating it from scratch. For the implementation, fourteen unit edit rules are defined by analyzing the training set. The similar examples used are constructed by randomly selecting four databases from the training dataset and four examples from each database. To extract the edit chains, the abstract syntax trees of the SQL queries are compared.

6.4 Conclusions

The field of multi-turn Text-to-SQL has seen substantial progress, with a wide range of research efforts exploring both conversational and interactive system capabilities. However, an important question remains: *Can current systems fully support a chatbot-like NLIDB?* Despite the significant advancements reviewed in this chapter, the answer remains unclear due to a lack of research that focuses on all types of user interaction (i.e., follow-up questions and feedback for refinement) with the system.

While existing approaches have made progress in handling multi-turn scenarios, there is still a lack of unified systems that seamlessly integrate both interactive and conversational functionalities. One of the question that arises is how the systems will differentiate between independent questions, follow-up queries, and requests for modifications to previous answers to provide efficient and correct translations. This area remains underexplored. Moreover, the evaluation of such systems presents a major bottleneck. Current benchmarks do not capture the full range of capabilities required for a robust, chatbot-like NLIDB.

In summary, while the research landscape is rich and evolving, there is still a gap between current capabilities and the goal of a fully functional, conversational NLIDB.

References

1. Yitao Cai and Xiaojun Wan. IGSQL: Database schema interaction graph based neural model for context-dependent text-to-SQL generation. In Bonnie Webber, Trevor Cohn, Yulan He, and Yang Liu, editors, *Proceedings of the 2020 Conference on Empirical Methods in Natural Language Processing (EMNLP)*, pages 6903–6912, Online, November 2020. Association for Computational Linguistics.
2. Zefeng Cai, Xiangyu Li, Binyuan Hui, Min Yang, Bowen Li, Binhua Li, Zheng Cao, Weijie Li, Fei Huang, Luo Si, and Yongbin Li. STAR: SQL guided pre-training for context-dependent text-to-SQL parsing. In Yoav Goldberg, Zornitsa Kozareva, and Yue Zhang, editors, *Findings of the Association for Computational Linguistics: EMNLP 2022*, pages 1235–1247, Abu Dhabi, United Arab Emirates, December 2022. Association for Computational Linguistics.
3. Zhi Chen, Lu Chen, Hanqi Li, Ruisheng Cao, Da Ma, Mengyue Wu, and Kai Yu. Decoupled dialogue modeling and semantic parsing for multi-turn text-to-SQL. In Chengqing Zong, Fei Xia, Wenjie Li, and Roberto Navigli, editors, *Findings of the Association for Computational Linguistics: ACL-IJCNLP 2021*, pages 3063–3074, Online, August 2021. Association for Computational Linguistics.
4. Jacob Devlin, Ming-Wei Chang, Kenton Lee, and Kristina Toutanova. BERT: pre-training of deep bidirectional transformers for language understanding. *CoRR*, abs/1810.04805, 2018.
5. Mingwen Dong, Nischal Ashok Kumar, Yiqun Hu, Anuj Chauhan, Chung-Wei Hang, Shuaichen Chang, Lin Pan, Wuwei Lan, Henghui Zhu, Jiarong Jiang, Patrick Ng, and Zhiguo Wang. PRACTIQ: A practical conversational text-to-sql dataset with ambiguous and unanswerable queries. *CoRR*, abs/2410.11076, 2024.
6. Ahmed Elgohary, Saghar Hosseini, and Ahmed Hassan Awadallah. Speak to your parser: Interactive text-to-SQL with natural language feedback. In Dan Jurafsky, Joyce Chai, Natalie Schluter, and Joel Tetreault, editors, *Proceedings of the 58th Annual Meeting of the Association for Computational Linguistics*, pages 2065–2077, Online, July 2020. Association for Computational Linguistics.
7. Ahmed Elgohary, Christopher Meek, Matthew Richardson, Adam Fourney, Gonzalo Ramos, and Ahmed Hassan Awadallah. NL-EDIT: Correcting semantic parse errors through natural language interaction. In Kristina Toutanova, Anna Rumshisky, Luke Zettlemoyer, Dilek Hakkani-Tur, Iz Beltagy, Steven Bethard, Ryan Cotterell, Tanmoy Chakraborty, and Yichao Zhou, editors, *Proceedings of the 2021 Conference of the North American Chapter of the Association for Computational Linguistics: Human Language Technologies*, pages 5599–5610, Online, June 2021. Association for Computational Linguistics.
8. Yingwen Fu, Wenjie Ou, Zhou Yu, and Yue Lin. Miga: a unified multi-task generation framework for conversational text-to-sql. In *Proceedings of the AAAI Conference on Artificial Intelligence*, volume 37, pages 12790–12798, 2023.
9. Jiaqi Guo, Ziliang Si, Yu Wang, Qian Liu, Ming Fan, Jian-Guang Lou, Zijiang Yang, and Ting Liu. Chase: A large-scale and pragmatic Chinese dataset for cross-database context-dependent text-to-SQL. In Chengqing Zong, Fei Xia, Wenjie Li, and Roberto Navigli, editors, *Proceedings of the 59th Annual Meeting of the Association for Computational Linguistics and the 11th International Joint Conference on Natural Language Processing (Volume 1: Long Papers)*, pages 2316–2331, Online, August 2021. Association for Computational Linguistics.

10. Izzeddin Gur, Semih Yavuz, Yu Su, and Xifeng Yan. DialSQL: Dialogue based structured query generation. In Iryna Gurevych and Yusuke Miyao, editors, *Proceedings of the 56th Annual Meeting of the Association for Computational Linguistics (Volume 1: Long Papers)*, pages 1339–1349, Melbourne, Australia, July 2018. Association for Computational Linguistics.
11. Andreas Kokkalis, Panagiotis Vagenas, Alexandros Zervakis, Alkis Simitsis, Georgia Koutrika, and Yannis Ioannidis. Logos: A system for translating queries into narratives. In *Proceedings of the 2012 ACM SIGMOD International Conference on Management of Data*, SIGMOD '12, page 673–676, New York, NY, USA, 2012. Association for Computing Machinery.
12. Chunhui Li, Yifan Wang, Zhen Wu, Zhen Yu, Fei Zhao, Shujian Huang, and Xinyu Dai. MultiSQL: A schema-integrated context-dependent Text2SQL dataset with diverse SQL operations. In Lun-Wei Ku, Andre Martins, and Vivek Srikumar, editors, *Findings of the Association for Computational Linguistics: ACL 2024*, pages 13857–13867, Bangkok, Thailand, August 2024. Association for Computational Linguistics.
13. Fei Li and Hosagrahar V Jagadish. Nalir: an interactive natural language interface for querying relational databases. In *Proceedings of the 2014 ACM SIGMOD international conference on Management of data*, pages 709–712, 2014.
14. Jinyang Li, Binyuan Hui, Ge Qu, Jiaxi Yang, Binhua Li, Bowen Li, Bailin Wang, Bowen Qin, Ruiying Geng, Nan Huo, Xuanhe Zhou, Ma Chenhao, Guoliang Li, Kevin Chang, Fei Huang, Reynold Cheng, and Yongbin Li. Can llm already serve as a database interface? a big bench for large-scale database grounded text-to-sqls. In A. Oh, T. Naumann, A. Globerson, K. Saenko, M. Hardt, and S. Levine, editors, *Advances in Neural Information Processing Systems*, volume 36, pages 42330–42357. Curran Associates, Inc., 2023.
15. Yuntao Li, Bei Chen, Qian Liu, Yan Gao, Jian-Guang Lou, Yan Zhang, and Dongmei Zhang. "what do you mean by that?" a parser-independent interactive approach for enhancing text-to-SQL. In Bonnie Webber, Trevor Cohn, Yulan He, and Yang Liu, editors, *Proceedings of the 2020 Conference on Empirical Methods in Natural Language Processing (EMNLP)*, pages 6913–6922, Online, November 2020. Association for Computational Linguistics.
16. Anna Mitsopoulou and Georgia Koutrika. Analysis of text-to-sql benchmarks: Limitations, challenges and opportunities. 2025.
17. Ohad Rubin and Jonathan Berant. Smbop: Semi-autoregressive bottom-up semantic parsing, 2020.
18. Peter Shaw, Jakob Uszkoreit, and Ashish Vaswani. Self-attention with relative position representations. In Marilyn Walker, Heng Ji, and Amanda Stent, editors, *Proceedings of the 2018 Conference of the North American Chapter of the Association for Computational Linguistics: Human Language Technologies, Volume 2 (Short Papers)*, pages 464–468, New Orleans, Louisiana, June 2018. Association for Computational Linguistics.
19. Richard Shin. Encoding database schemas with relation-aware self-attention for text-to-sql parsers. *arXiv preprint arXiv:1906.11790*, 2019.
20. Alane Suhr, Ming-Wei Chang, Peter Shaw, and Kenton Lee. Exploring unexplored generalization challenges for cross-database semantic parsing. In Dan Jurafsky, Joyce Chai, Natalie Schluter, and Joel Tetreault, editors, *Proceedings of the 58th Annual Meeting of the Association for Computational Linguistics*, pages 8372–8388, Online, July 2020. Association for Computational Linguistics.
21. Yuan Tian, Zheng Zhang, Zheng Ning, Toby Li, Jonathan K. Kummerfeld, and Tianyi Zhang. Interactive text-to-SQL generation via editable step-by-step explanations. In Houda Bouamor, Juan Pino, and Kalika Bali, editors, *Proceedings of the 2023 Conference on Empirical Methods in Natural Language Processing*, pages 16149–16166, Singapore, December 2023. Association for Computational Linguistics.
22. Lijie Wang, Ao Zhang, Kun Wu, Ke Sun, Zhenghua Li, Hua Wu, Min Zhang, and Haifeng Wang. DuSQL: A large-scale and pragmatic Chinese text-to-SQL dataset. In Bonnie Webber, Trevor Cohn, Yulan He, and Yang Liu, editors, *Proceedings of the 2020 Conference on Empirical Methods in Natural Language Processing (EMNLP)*, pages 6923–6935, Online, November 2020. Association for Computational Linguistics.

23. Run-Ze Wang, Zhen-Hua Ling, Jingbo Zhou, and Yu Hu. Tracking interaction states for multi-turn text-to-sql semantic parsing. In *Proceedings of the AAAI Conference on Artificial Intelligence*, volume 35, pages 13979–13987, 2021.
24. Zhibiao Wu and Martha Palmer. Verb semantics and lexical selection. In *32nd Annual Meeting of the Association for Computational Linguistics*, pages 133–138, Las Cruces, New Mexico, USA, June 1994. Association for Computational Linguistics.
25. Dongling Xiao, LinZheng Chai, Qian-Wen Zhang, Zhao Yan, Zhoujun Li, and Yunbo Cao. CQR-SQL: Conversational question reformulation enhanced context-dependent text-to-SQL parsers. In Yoav Goldberg, Zornitsa Kozareva, and Yue Zhang, editors, *Findings of the Association for Computational Linguistics: EMNLP 2022*, pages 2055–2068, Abu Dhabi, United Arab Emirates, December 2022. Association for Computational Linguistics.
26. Hao Yan, Saurabh Srivastava, Yintao Tai, Sida I. Wang, Wen-tau Yih, and Ziyu Yao. Learning to simulate natural language feedback for interactive semantic parsing. In Anna Rogers, Jordan Boyd-Graber, and Naoaki Okazaki, editors, *Proceedings of the 61st Annual Meeting of the Association for Computational Linguistics (Volume 1: Long Papers)*, pages 3149–3170, Toronto, Canada, July 2023. Association for Computational Linguistics.
27. Ziyu Yao, Yu Su, Huan Sun, and Wen-tau Yih. Model-based interactive semantic parsing: A unified framework and a text-to-SQL case study. In Kentaro Inui, Jing Jiang, Vincent Ng, and Xiaojun Wan, editors, *Proceedings of the 2019 Conference on Empirical Methods in Natural Language Processing and the 9th International Joint Conference on Natural Language Processing (EMNLP-IJCNLP)*, pages 5447–5458, Hong Kong, China, November 2019. Association for Computational Linguistics.
28. Pengcheng Yin and Graham Neubig. A syntactic neural model for general-purpose code generation, 2017.
29. Tao Yu, Rui Zhang, He Yang Er, Suyi Li, Eric Xue, Bo Pang, Xi Victoria Lin, Yi Chern Tan, Tianze Shi, Zihan Li, Youxuan Jiang, Michihiro Yasunaga, Sungrok Shim, Tao Chen, Alexander Fabbri, Zifan Li, Luyao Chen, Yuwen Zhang, Shreya Dixit, Vincent Zhang, Caiming Xiong, Richard Socher, Walter S Lasecki, and Dragomir Radev. Cosql: A conversational text-to-sql challenge towards cross-domain natural language interfaces to databases, 2019.
30. Tao Yu, Rui Zhang, Alex Polozov, Christopher Meek, and Ahmed Hassan Awadallah. Score: Pre-training for context representation in conversational semantic parsing. In *International Conference on Learning Representations*, 2021.
31. Tao Yu, Rui Zhang, Kai Yang, Michihiro Yasunaga, Dongxu Wang, Zifan Li, James Ma, Irene Li, Qingning Yao, Shanelle Roman, Zilin Zhang, and Dragomir Radev. Spider: A large-scale human-labeled dataset for complex and cross-domain semantic parsing and text-to-SQL task. In Ellen Riloff, David Chiang, Julia Hockenmaier, and Jun'ichi Tsujii, editors, *Proceedings of the 2018 Conference on Empirical Methods in Natural Language Processing*, pages 3911–3921, Brussels, Belgium, October-November 2018. Association for Computational Linguistics.
32. Tao Yu, Rui Zhang, Michihiro Yasunaga, Yi Chern Tan, Xi Victoria Lin, Suyi Li, Heyang Er, Irene Li, Bo Pang, Tao Chen, Emily Ji, Shreya Dixit, David Proctor, Sungrok Shim, Jonathan Kraft, Vincent Zhang, Caiming Xiong, Richard Socher, and Dragomir Radev. Sparc: Cross-domain semantic parsing in context, 2019.
33. Hanchong Zhang, Ruisheng Cao, Lu Chen, Hongshen Xu, and Kai Yu. Act-sql: In-context learning for text-to-sql with automatically-generated chain-of-thought. *arXiv preprint arXiv:2310.17342*, 2023.
34. Hanchong Zhang, Ruisheng Cao, Lu Chen, Hongshen Xu, and Kai Yu. ACT-SQL: In-context learning for text-to-SQL with automatically-generated chain-of-thought. In Houda Bouamor, Juan Pino, and Kalika Bali, editors, *Findings of the Association for Computational Linguistics: EMNLP 2023*, pages 3501–3532, Singapore, December 2023. Association for Computational Linguistics.
35. Hanchong Zhang, Ruisheng Cao, Hongshen Xu, Lu Chen, and Kai Yu. Coe-sql: In-context learning for multi-turn text-to-sql with chain-of-editions. *arXiv preprint arXiv:2405.02712*, 2024.

36. Rui Zhang, Tao Yu, Heyang Er, Sungrok Shim, Eric Xue, Xi Victoria Lin, Tianze Shi, Caiming Xiong, Richard Socher, and Dragomir Radev. Editing-based SQL query generation for cross-domain context-dependent questions. In *Proceedings of the 2019 Conference on Empirical Methods in Natural Language Processing and the 9th International Joint Conference on Natural Language Processing (EMNLP-IJCNLP)*, pages 5338–5349, Hong Kong, China, November 2019. Association for Computational Linguistics.
37. Yiyun Zhang, Gengsheng Huang, et al. Se-hcl: Schema enhanced hybrid curriculum learning for multi-turn text-to-sql. *IEEE Access*, 2024.
38. Yanzhao Zheng, Haibin Wang, Baohua Dong, Xingjun Wang, and Changshan Li. HIE-SQL: History information enhanced network for context-dependent text-to-SQL semantic parsing. In Smaranda Muresan, Preslav Nakov, and Aline Villavicencio, editors, *Findings of the Association for Computational Linguistics: ACL 2022*, pages 2997–3007, Dublin, Ireland, May 2022. Association for Computational Linguistics.

Chapter 7
The Code Generation & Summarization Problems

Abstract To gain a broader perspective on the Text-to-SQL and SQL-to-Text tasks discussed in previous chapters, it is useful to examine how similar tasks are addressed in the wider field of generating natural language to and from code. This perspective helps highlight both the shared challenges and the unique characteristics that have motivated the development of systems specifically tailored to SQL. This chapter aims to provide a concise but comprehensive overview of the Code Generation and the Code Summarization problems. It presents the tasks, provides an overview of the most widely used datasets and evaluation metrics and describes representative systems in the field.

7.1 Introduction

The rapid advancements in technology and its integration into nearly every aspect of modern life have significantly increased the demand for programming expertise. As a result, automating software engineering tasks has become an area of great interest, offering the potential to streamline development, accelerate innovation, and even enable users without coding knowledge to create their own applications and systems.

The creation of systems capable of performing various software engineering tasks intensified following the introduction of the Transformer architecture [36]. These tasks span various aspects of software engineering, from software development tasks, such as code completion, which provides real-time code suggestions to developers, to software quality assurance through tasks like vulnerability detection [14]. Among these tasks, we will focus on two software development tasks due to their conceptual similarities with Text-to-SQL and SQL-to-Text tasks discussed in previous chapters. These tasks are: (1) the *Code generation* task, the automatic generation of code from natural language descriptions, and (2) the *Code summarization* task, the inverse problem, the generation of natural language descriptions from code segments.

Both Code Generation and Code Summarization play a crucial role in software engineering, improving productivity by automating repetitive tasks. Code generation

G. Katsogiannis-Meimarakis et al., *Natural Language Interfaces for Databases with Deep Learning*, Data-Centric Systems and Applications,
https://doi.org/10.1007/978-3-032-06905-4_7

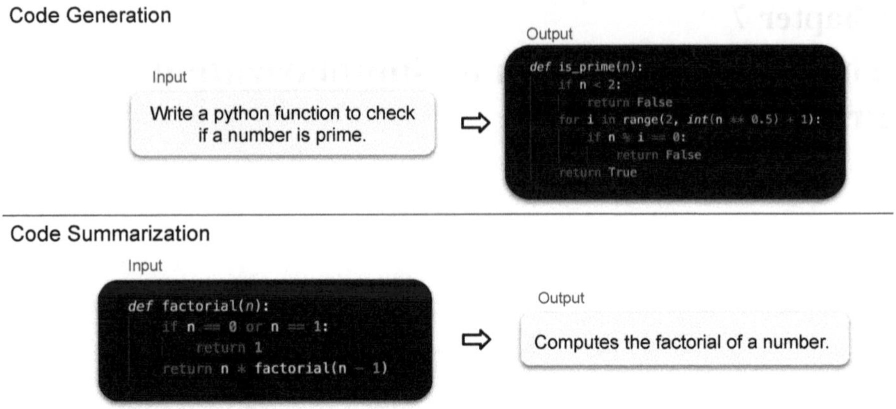

Fig. 7.1: Examples for the tasks of Code Generation and Code Summarization.

has been the most extensively researched software engineering task [14] as it has the potential to significantly accelerate software development while also enabling individuals with little to no programming experience to build applications. Meanwhile, code summarization is among the most popular tasks [14], as it facilitates the documentation process, a fundamental best practice in software development.

This chapter explores these two problems in depth, analyzing their challenges, their distinctions from the Text-to-SQL and SQL-to-Text, and the approaches developed to address them. Additionally, it explores the datasets and evaluation metrics commonly used in this research area, providing a comprehensive overview of the field.

7.2 The Code Generation & Summarization Problems

Since SQL is a programming language, the Code Generation and Code Summarization problems can be viewed as a generalization of the SQL-related problems (Text-to-SQL and SQL-to-Text) discussed in Chapters 3 and 6, respectively. Figure 7.1 provides examples of the Code Generation and Code Summarization tasks. Given a natural language description, the objective of Code Generation is (a) to create a code snippet with the intended functionality and (b) ensure that the generated code is not only syntactically correct but also adheres to best practices and conventions of the target programming language. The Code Summarization task addresses the reverse problem. The task consists of two primary objectives: (a) capturing the core logic and intent of the given code snippet, and (b) generating a fluent and informative natural language description.

7.2.1 Differentiating Code Tasks from SQL Tasks

Despite their conceptual similarities, Code Generation and Code Summarization differ significantly from Text-to-SQL and SQL-to-Text in two key aspects:

Natural language intent. The natural language in the code-related tasks describes the logic and structure of a computational process, aiming to produce executable code that implements the requested functionality. In contrast, in the SQL-related tasks the natural language question is data-oriented—its primary goal is to retrieve or manipulate specific data from a database.

Database dependence. Another major difference between the two sets of tasks is that the SQL-related tasks have a high dependence with the underlying database. This affects the Text-to-SQL task as the natural language question can be highly influenced by the domain of the database, requiring domain-specific knowledge and elaborate reasoning to map with the requested database. Additionally, the SQL query must comply with the underlying database, resulting in database-specific translations. For example, the same natural language question may result in a different SQL query based on the database schema. Similarly, the SQL-to-Text task is affected by the database dependence as the process of explaining a query depends on database-specific table and column names. In contrast, while Code Summarization can benefit from descriptive variable names, the generated code descriptions are generally less constrained by them.

The above differences lead to distinct methodological approaches for tackling the two sets of tasks. However, successful techniques from Code Generation and Summarization can still provide valuable insights for improving SQL-related tasks.

7.2.2 Challenges

There are multiple challenges in Code Generation and Code Summarization tasks. Many of these challenges are similar to those found in SQL-related tasks, such as ambiguities in natural language descriptions and the complexity of code segments, which can make their translation into natural language particularly difficult. However, while database-related challenges are absent in this domain, new challenges arise.

One significant challenge is handling **multiple programming languages**. Since most of the created systems are not language-specific, an important issue is ensuring task performance for programming languages with limited training data. Additionally, many programming languages, such as Python, rely heavily on **external libraries and frameworks**, which introduces another difficulty—implement the requested functionality that may require built-in methods or third-party libraries. Similarly, when summarising or analysing a code snippet, the model may struggle if it encounters function calls or methods that are not defined within the provided snippet, making it harder to generate meaningful outputs.

7.3 Architecture

Both Code Generation and Code Summarization have been formulated as neural translation problems, leveraging advancements in language models. Rather than designing specialized architectures explicitly for these two tasks, research has primarily focused on developing *code language models*, that can be adapted to multiple code-related tasks. Therefore, the architecture of the systems is not so elaborate. Figure 7.2 shows an overview of the systems' architecture. It consists of three main components: (1) Input Construction, (2) Neural Model and (3) Neural Learning. Input Construction is responsible for transforming the input into a numerical representation suitable for model processing. The Neural Model takes this numerical representation and produces the final output. The Neural Learning is the procedure followed in order for the model to learn to perform the downstream tasks, i.e. Code Summarization and/or Code Generation.

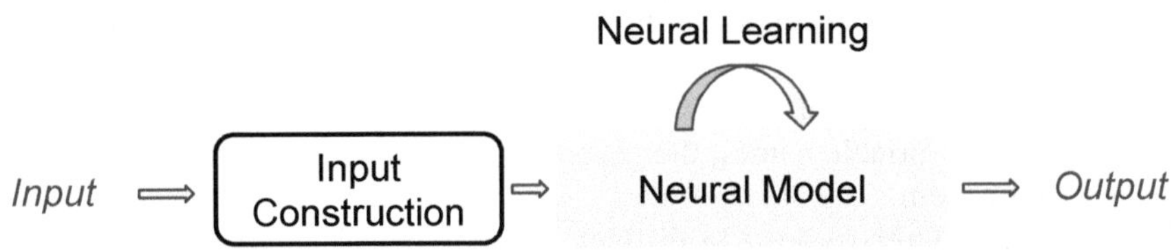

Fig. 7.2: Code language models system architecture.

The overall architecture shares similarities with Text-to-SQL and SQL-to-Text models, particularly in its core components. The key distinction lies in the absence of the pre-processing and post-processing components, which are crucial in the SQL-related tasks.

7.3.1 Input Construction

In this section we are going to elaborate on what type of information is given to the model, how it is represented and how it is tokenized in order to be passed and processed by the neural model.

Since most of the created systems can be utilized for both the Code Summarization and Code Generation tasks, the input can contain both natural language and code. While the representation of natural language is straightforward, the code segments have been represented: (1) as plain text or (2) with the use of the code's Abstract Syntax Tree (AST). The predominant approach is to treat code as plain text [9, 20, 34], allowing the model to learn their syntactic and semantic properties during training. Alternatively, the code's AST has been used to represent the code [11] as it can clearly depict the syntax of the code and therefore help the model to better understand the code segments. Furthermore, additional information about the code can be included in the input, such as the code's data-flow. The code's data-flow is a graph in which nodes represent the variables and edges represent the relation of "where-the-value-comes-from" between variables, has been used [12, 40] to add explicit information for the semantic structure of the code.

In contrast with the Text-to-SQL task, in which multiple methods of the input structuring have been proposed, in this field, the predominant approach is to serialize all the input information, that is then tokenized and passed to a single encoder.

For the tokenization of the input most systems utilize Byte Pair Encoding (BPE) [33], which iteratively merges the most frequent pairs of characters, producing a vocabulary of subwords for the encoding of the input. Some approaches [6, 37] refine tokenization further by filtering the produced tokens or enhancing the final vocabulary (e.g., tokens for representing whitespace runs of different lengths). Lastly, there are efforts to create code-specific tokenizers that will consider the characteristics of code [7] or can be used to properly encode structures like the AST [40].

7.3.2 Neural Model

In most systems, both the encoder and the decoder are implemented using the Transformer architecture. Earlier models [1, 11, 37] predominantly utilized the Transformer encoder-decoder architecture, as it provides a balanced approach to both understanding and generation. However, with the rapid advancements in large language models, decoder-only architectures [20, 32] have become increasingly popular due to their strong generative capabilities. Additionally, there are efforts [18, 34] that explored enhancing the Transformer decoder by integrating techniques such as diffusion or reinforcement learning, to improve the model's performance.

7.3.3 Neural Learning

The neural learning methods adopted by code language models are well established techniques that have been widely used in the literature for the creation of powerful language models.

Pre-training. A common decision across models is to use pre-training as the method that will enable a neural model to learn about code. Earlier systems [1, 9, 37] train the model from scratch, as the first language models [8, 28, 30] that were available at that time did not contain a large amount of code data in their training corpora and therefore their knowledge was related mostly to the natural language. This is not always the case as the power of language models increases and the training data are more diverse. More specifically, there are cases which leverage the pre-trained weights of a language model and continue pre-training to obtain better understanding of the code characteristics [32].

The objectives used for the pre-training are objectives that have been commonly used for pre-training generic language models, while there are works that combine them with objectives specifically applied to code segments aiming to better understand the characteristics of programming languages.

The most popular natural language objectives are the masked language modeling (MLM) [8, 30] and the language modeling objective [28]. In the first, a part of the input is masked and the task of the model is to denoise these masked tokens. The second objective trains the model to predict the next token, based on the preceding text sequence.

Code-specific objectives with varying goals have been introduced from multiple systems [9, 37]. There are no universally adopted code-specific objectives and most of the time their usage is limited to the system that defined them. For example, CodeT5 [37] introduces the identifier tagging objective, that aims to infuse the knowledge of which parts are the identifiers (e.g., function names and variables). More specifically, the hidden states of the encoder are mapped into a sequence of probabilities and compute a binary cross-entropy loss for sequence labeling. Another example is GraphCodeBert [12], in which the edge prediction objective is introduced. This objective trains the model to predict edges existing in the data-flow, to encourage the model to learn structure-aware representations.

Adaptation to Code Generation & Summarization tasks. To adapt the model to downstream tasks, in our case the Code Generation and Summarization tasks, earlier systems fine-tuned the generic-model, created with pre-training, to the downstream tasks. As neural models have become more powerful, the need for fine-tuning has been minimized and most state of the art systems use in-context learning [5], which allows the model to understand task specifications directly from the input prompt.

Comparison with SQL-related tasks. A key distinction between code-related tasks and SQL-related tasks lies in the training paradigm. While code models rely heavily on unsupervised pre-training to develop an understanding of programming languages, most SQL-related systems are trained directly on the downstream task. This highlights a fundamental difference in the way these models learn and generalize across different domains.

7.4 Datasets

One of the most important factors for the creation of code language models are the datasets used for training and evaluation. Multiple code datasets have been created for several different tasks. In the following section, we will give an overview of the datasets used for Code Generation and Summarization.

7.4.1 Training datasets

Pre-training datasets. pre-training of code language models requires a huge amount of data. The data used for pre-training are mostly gathered from GitHub repositories and StackOverflow. Since the quality of the resulting dataset plays a crucial role in the produced model, there are efforts to create datasets that can contribute toward that direction, while in many cases in-situ pipelines were created to construct a training dataset in an effort to ensure its quality [1, 6, 32, 34, 40].

One of the first widely used dataset in the pre-training process is *CodeSearchNet* [15]. The corpus for the creation of CodeSearchNet was collected from publicly available open-source non-fork GitHub repositories. The Go, Java, JavaScript, Python, PHP and Ruby functions and their respective documentation text were tokenized using a heuristic regular expression. Pairs with very short descriptions and functions that were very small or had 'test' in their name were filtered out. Additionally, constructors and standard extension methods were removed. From a function's documentation, only the first paragraph was kept. Lastly, duplicates were removed. The final dataset contains about two million pairs of function-documentation pairs and four million functions without documentation.

Another popular dataset for training models with code understanding and generation capabilities is *The Stack* [17]. For the creation of the dataset, a set of active repositories were collected, from which binary files and files larger than 1 MB were excluded. After deduplication, the final dataset contains 92.36 TB of stored files.

Finally, datasets containing natural language texts, such as *The Pile* [10] or in-situ datasets, have been used [26, 32] to complement the pre-training dataset to enhance the model's natural language understanding capabilities. By increasing the proportion of natural language text during training, these datasets help strengthen the natural language proficiency, which is essential for many downstream code-related tasks, including Code Generation.

Overall, we can see a pool of large-scale datasets for pre-training in this research area. This is another way in which the Text-to-SQL and SQL-to-Text problems differ from this similar line of research.

Fine-tuning datasets. The most widely used dataset for fine-tuning is *CodeXGlue* [24]. Similar to *XGlue* [21], which is designed for natural language tasks, CodeXGlue is a collection of datasets tailored for various code understanding and generation tasks. The dataset includes 14 curated datasets covering a broad spectrum of code-related tasks, including Code Generation and Code Summarization. Each task-specific dataset is split into training, validation (dev), and test sets, making it easy to fine-tune models and evaluate their performance on specific tasks. In 2024, *xCodeEval* [16] was released, as another effort to create a complete benchmark. The benchmark includes datasets for two classification tasks, three generative tasks, among which Code Generation, and two retrieval tasks. It supports 11 different programming languages, and it was created from 25M openly available samples from codeforces.com for a total of 7514 distinct algorithmic problems. Similar to CodexGlue, each task-specific dataset is split in train, validation and test sets.

7.4.2 Evaluation datasets

Code Generation and Summarization have several benchmarks containing pairs of code and natural language descriptions that are used for their evaluation [38], except from the CodexGlue and xCodeEval mentioned in the previous section. The most popular among them are HumanEval [6], MBPP [3] and APPS [13].

The *HumanEval* dataset contains 164 handwritten programming problems in Python. Each problem includes a function signature, docstring, body, and several unit tests, with an average of 7.7 tests per problem. The problems of the dataset require language comprehension, reasoning, algorithms, and simple mathematics.

The *Mostly Basic Programming Problems (MBPP)* dataset contains 974 programming tasks constructed by crowd workers with basic knowledge of Python. Each problem contains a short description, a Python function of maximum 50 lines, that solves the problem and three test cases that check the semantic correctness of the function. The dataset was manually verified, resulting in an edited version, that contains 426 problems. The problems existing in the dataset range from simple numerical manipulations to tasks that require non-trivial external knowledge.

For the creation of the *APPS* dataset, problems from open-source coding websites that range in difficulty from introductory to collegiate competition level were collected. Then, these problems were refined to ensure their quality and standardize the format of the test cases. The problems were categorized based on their difficulty into Introductory, Interview and Competition level. Additionally, the problems come in two formats, the call-based format and the standard input format. In the call-based format, the problems provide an initial starter code (e.g., the function header), while in the standard input format only the problem statement is provided.

7.5 Evaluation metrics

7.5.1 Code Generation metrics

All the tasks that have code as their output (e.g., code generation, code refinement, code translation) require a metric capable of comparing two fragments of code. This is not a trivial task if we consider the equivalences that may exist due to different variable naming and the different ways of implementing a method. For that reason, there are several metrics that have been used. There are metrics considering lexical similarity, task-specific metrics that consider the characteristics of the code, and finally metrics that are mainly focused on the output of the code.

7.5.1.1 Lexical comparison metrics

The metrics that were used in the earlier systems were metrics based on text lexical comparison.

BLEU (BiLingual Evaluation Understudy) [27] score is a metric that was originally proposed for machine translation evaluation. It compares the segments by calculating the overlapping n-grams and returns a value from 0 to 1.

ROUGE (Recall-Oriented Understudy for Gisting Evaluation) [22] is a metric proposed for summarization evaluation. Unlike BLEU, which is a precision-based measure, ROUGE is the n-gram recall between the two segments.

Exact match is a binary metric that checks if two fragments of code are the same.

Although these metrics can give an estimate of a model's performance, they fall short in several scenarios. They do not consider code equivalences, even the ones that can be pretty common, for example the naming conventions of a code snippet. For example, consider the code functions "*def sum(x, y): return x+y*" and "*def total(a, b): return a+b*". Even though these functions do exactly the same thing, they are not similar in a lexical level. Additionally, metrics that calculate similarity based only on the lexical features can boost predictions with serious logical errors.

7.5.1.2 Code-specific metrics

A result of the advancements in this research field is the creation of metrics that can more accurately compare code fragments by considering the characteristics of the programming languages that differentiate them from natural language texts.

CodeBLEU [31] is an evaluation metric created specifically for code. It is calculated by the weighted summation of BLEU, the weighted n-gram match, the syntactic AST match and the semantic data-flow match. The weighted n-gram match assigns weights to n-grams, so that the code keywords may have higher weights. The syntactic AST match is calculated as the overlap of all the sub-trees of the code's abstract syntax trees in the referenced and generated code segment. The leaves are removed from the compared sub-trees, since they represent the names of the functions and the variables. Finally, the semantic data-flow match considers code as a graph, where nodes represent variables and edges represent the origin of the variable's value. Its value is calculated as the overlap of the data-flows in the referenced and generated code segments.

CodeBERTScore [39] computes the pairwise cosine similarities between the encoded tokens of the referenced and generated code. The description of the code is encoded along with the code snippet to get the encoded tokens. Then, the maximum similarity of each referenced code token is considered to compute the precision and the maximum similarity for every generated code token to calculate recall. The model used for the creation of the embeddings is based on CodeBERT [9].

7.5.1.3 Execution-based metrics

As already mentioned in the Text-to-SQL chapter, another way to compare the code is by comparing its functionality. For that reason, many systems validate the correctness of their predictions by **executing unit tests** created to test the functionality of the referenced code snippet. The problem with this approach is the manual and labor-intensive effort required to create the tests, as well as, the security risks that arise with their execution. Thus, this evaluation is limited to benchmarks that already include unit tests. As a solution to the security risks, researchers have proposed a secure and scalable framework for executing the unit tests [16].

7.5.2 Code Summarization metrics

For the task of Code Summarization, the most used metric is smoothed-BLEU [23]. The smoothed-BLEU is a variation of the BLEU [27] metric, so that it can calculate the similarity in a sentence level. Their difference is that one count is added to the n-gram hit and total n-gram count for $n > 1$. As noted in prior work [9], smoothed-BLEU is more appropriate for the evaluation of Code Summarization, since the summaries are mostly short.

Despite its broad usage, smoothed-BLEU, like other n-gram based metrics, has several limitations, such as in capturing semantic similarities (see Sections 5.5.1, 7.5.1.1). These shortcomings underscore the need for alternative evaluation methods that can provide more accurate evaluation of the generated summaries.

7.6 Systems

This section provides descriptions of a wide variety of code language models in an effort to create a better understanding of the methods used in this research field. More specifically, we have created sections that represent important lines of research in this field, in which we included the descriptions of selected representative systems. As already mentioned, the main focus of the work in this research field is the creation of code language models that can be adjusted to perform multiple code-related tasks and for that reason the systems are not divided to the ones for Code Summarization and Code Generation. Table 7.1 summarizes the main characteristics of the systems that are going to be described in this section.

System	Model Type	Input Content	Objectives	Evaluated Tasks
CodeBERT [9]	Encoder	Code, NL	NL	Summarization
CodeT5 [37]	Encoder-Decoder	Code, NL	NL, Code-specific	Both
PLBart [1]	Encoder-Decoder	Code, NL	NL	Both
GraphCodeBERT [12]	Encoder	Code, NL, Data-flow	NL, Code-specific	None
UnixCoder [11]	Encoder-Decoder	NL, AST	NL, Code-specific	Both
GrammarT5 [40]	Encoder-Decoder	Code, NL, Data-flow	NL	Both
CodeFusion [34]	Custom	Code, NL	NL	Generation
CodeRL [18]	Custom	Code, NL	NL	Generation
CodeLlama [32]	Decoder	Code, NL	NL	Generation
CodeGEN [25]	Decoder	Code, NL	NL	Generation
StarCoder [20]	Decoder	Code, NL	NL	Both

Table 7.1: Sampled Systems for Code Generation and Summarization. Evaluation tasks: reports which of the tasks studied (code summarization and generation) have been evaluated with the model.

7.6.1 The Dawn of an Era

Following the development of the Transformer model and its widespread success across various tasks, the first models with code understanding and generation capabilities emerged as a popular research area. These models mainly used a pattern similar to existing language models [8, 29, 30]. They used a transformer-based architecture that was trained from scratch on a large corpus of code. The pre-training objectives were mainly the ones that were used by most language models at the time, with efforts to define code-specific objectives. The pre-training datasets were collected mostly from Github repositories and StackOverflow posts, with CodeSearchNet [15] being one of the first large datasets that was used for training.

CodeBERT [9] is one of the first efforts of creating a system that can perform code-related tasks. It is an encoder pre-trained with the CodeSearchNet dataset. The training objectives that were used are the masked language objective and the replaced token detection objective. The second objective is adapted to the use case with the use of an NL and a Programming Language (PL) generator that generate plausible alternatives for randomly selected positions. Then, the CodeBERT model is requested to predict whether a word is original or not. The model was evaluated in the tasks of Code search, which aims at finding similar code snippets with the one provided, and Code Summarization, referred as Code2NL. For the Code Summarization task, a Transformer decoder was added to the trained CodeBERT encoder, and the model was trained to the downstream task of Code Summarization.

CodeT5 [37] builds on the T5 model [30], using an encoder-decoder architecture. In its training, except for the masking objective, two identifier-aware objectives were defined to capture the code-specific characteristics. In more detail, identifier tagging is introduced, in which the model is requested to predict whether a token is an identifier or not, and masked identifier prediction where all identifiers in the input code are masked, and the model is trained to predict the value of each unique identifier. Its evaluation contains several tasks, including Code Generation and Summarization.

PLBART [2] is based on the encoder-decoder model BART [19], pre-trained with three denoising objectives, (1) token masking, (2) token deletion, and (3) token infilling [19]. In the first task, tokens are randomly masked, and the model has to produce the input without the masks. In token deletion, random tokens are deleted, and the model must reconstruct the input with the deleted tokens. Finally, in token infilling, several text spans are sampled and replaced with a single mask token, that the model has to reconstruct.

7.6.2 Code-specific input representation

Programming languages follow strict syntax rules and have a more constrained output space than natural languages. To better align the models with these properties, several efforts introduce code-specific objectives or use code representations that can explicitly capture some of the code characteristics. The following systems are representative examples of such efforts.

GraphCodeBERT [12] is a model that tries to utilize the information from the code structure. The input of the model contains the comments, the code, and the variables sequence from the code's data flow. The model was trained with (1) the masked language objective (MLM) applied to the source code and comments, (2) the edge prediction objective, in which edges in the data flow are masked and the model is trained to predict whether the edge exists, and (3) the node alignment objective, in which model is trained to predict edges between code tokens and nodes.

UniXcoder [11] is a unified cross-modal pre-trained model. Mask attention matrices with prefix adapters are utilized to enable encoder-only, decoder-only, and encoder-decoder attention. The input includes cross-modal contents, i.e. the AST and code comments, to provide the model with an rich information regarding the code. The model is pre-trained with three natual language objectives, namely (1) Masked language modeling, (2) Unidirectional language modeling and (3) Denoising. Additionally, two code-specific objectives were introduced, (1) multi-modal constructive learning and (2) cross-modal generation, to aid the model in understanding the AST semantic embeddings. In multi-modal constructive learning, the same input was forwarded, using different hidden dropout masks, as positive examples and other representations of codes in the same batch as negative examples. With cross-modal generation, the model was trained to generate the input comment, to understand the code semantics, and to align representations among different programming languages.

GrammarT5 [40] is a T5-based [30] model that introduces Tokenized Grammar Rule Sequence (TGRS), a grammar-integrated code representation. The defined grammar describes the programming language and assigns a unique identifier to each rule. TGRS parses the code into an AST and obtains the grammar rules sequence that describes the AST. Then, each grammar terminal is tokenized, and they construct the final tokenized AST via the grammar, extended with the new rules for the tokenized terminals. The model is pre-trained with the use of five self-supervised tasks, (1) Masked Span Prediction (MSP), which masks segments of the input and trains the model to predict the values of the masks, (2) Generation Masked Prediction, which trains the model to predict a sequence, given the preceding sequence, (3) Edge prediction, which trains the model to predict the location of a grammar parent rule, given the parent rule sequence, (4) Identifier Prediction, which masks each identifier in the code with a unique mask token and trains the model to predict the value of each mask, and (5) sub-tree prediction, which masks sub-trees of the AST and trains the model to retrieve the mask values.

7.6.3 Unique architectures

As previously mentioned, the most common approach for creating a model with code generation and understanding capabilities is the use of a Transformer-based architecture, which are pre-trained in code data. However, there are efforts that explore alternative methods, leveraging techniques such as reinforcement learning or diffusion models.

CodeFusion [34] is a pre-trained diffusion code generation model that tries to tackle the limitation of auto-regressive models, which do not reconsider earlier generated tokens. It consists of four components, an encoder, a denoiser, a decoder, and a classification head. The encoder produces the embeddings of the natural language utterance and is implemented using the CodeT5 [37] model. The denoiser iteratively removes noise and predicts the code embedding, given the natural language embedding and a time step. The Transformer decoder produces the final code embedding, given the denoising embedding and the natural language embedding. Finally, the classification head produces the actual code, given the denoised code embedding and the natural language embedding. The model is trained in 2 phases. In the first phase, the denoiser and the decoder are pre-trained in an unsupervised manner, while in the second phase, supervised fine-tuning is used to adjust the model in the downstream task.

CodeRL [18] uses CodeT5, with an enlarged pre-training dataset and an additional pre-training task of next-token prediction, as an actor model that produces the sequence of the program tokens. Additionally, a critic model is trained to assign a reward to each token based on its likelihood of passing unit tests. For the creation of CodeRL, the weights of the actor model are considered as the policy and fine-tuning is applied to maximize the rewards provided by the critic model.

7.6.4 The Rise of LLMs

The dominance of LLMs in several natural language tasks, has led to a growing trend of using LLMs for code language models, as well. Unlike Pre-trained Language Models (PLMs), LLMs benefit from their significantly larger scale, which enables them to perform a variety of tasks in a zero-shot or few-shot setting, without requiring additional training. This characteristic makes them particularly suitable for tackling multiple code-related tasks, including Code Generation and Summarization.

CodeLlama [32] is a family of open-source models based on Llama2 [35] created for code generation. Three model variants are provided, CodeLlama, for general-purpose code generation, CodeLlama-Python, a model specialized for Python code generation and CodeLlama-Instruct, that better follows human instructions. All models are initialized with Llama2 and further trained in a dataset mostly containing code, with a multitask objective consisting of both autoregressive and causal infilling prediction. Additionally, a fine-tuning stage is introduced, that extends the maximum context length to 100000 tokens to unlock repository-level reasoning. For the creation of the Python version, the model is trained with a dataset containing mostly Python code, after the training in the general-code dataset. Lastly, for the instruct version, a final instruction fine-tuning is applied.

CodeGen [26] is a family of models, all trained in The Pile dataset [10], while some are further trained in additional corpora (BigQuery, BigPython), with the next-token prediction objective. the fragmentation of problems into simpler ones with the use of multi-turn prompts, each of which will solve a subproblem.

Another approach trained a decoder-only model in a curated dataset based on the Stack dataset [17], containing over 80 programming languages and one trillion tokens, resulting in the StarCoderBase model [20]. The objective that was used is the fill-in-the-middle [4] objective. Furthermore, the BPE tokenizer [33] was used, in which additional sentinel tokens were included. Finally, a Python-focused variance was created, named *StarCoder*, by further fine-tuning in a Python subset of the training dataset.

References

1. Wasi Ahmad, Saikat Chakraborty, Baishakhi Ray, and Kai-Wei Chang. Unified pre-training for program understanding and generation. In *Proceedings of the 2021 Conference of the North American Chapter of the Association for Computational Linguistics: Human Language Technologies*, pages 2655–2668, Online, June 2021. Association for Computational Linguistics.
2. Wasi Uddin Ahmad, Saikat Chakraborty, Baishakhi Ray, and Kai-Wei Chang. Unified pre-training for program understanding and generation. *arXiv preprint arXiv:2103.06333*, 2021.
3. Jacob Austin, Augustus Odena, Maxwell Nye, Maarten Bosma, Henryk Michalewski, David Dohan, Ellen Jiang, Carrie Cai, Michael Terry, Quoc Le, et al. Program synthesis with large language models. *arXiv preprint arXiv:2108.07732*, 2021.
4. Mohammad Bavarian, Heewoo Jun, Nikolas Tezak, John Schulman, Christine McLeavey, Jerry Tworek, and Mark Chen. Efficient training of language models to fill in the middle. *arXiv preprint arXiv:2207.14255*, 2022.

5. Tom Brown, Benjamin Mann, Nick Ryder, Melanie Subbiah, Jared D Kaplan, Prafulla Dhariwal, Arvind Neelakantan, Pranav Shyam, Girish Sastry, Amanda Askell, et al. Language models are few-shot learners. *Advances in neural information processing systems*, 33:1877–1901, 2020.
6. Mark Chen, Jerry Tworek, Heewoo Jun, Qiming Yuan, Henrique Ponde De Oliveira Pinto, Jared Kaplan, Harri Edwards, Yuri Burda, Nicholas Joseph, Greg Brockman, et al. Evaluating large language models trained on code. *arXiv preprint arXiv:2107.03374*, 2021.
7. Nadezhda Chirkova and Sergey Troshin. Codebpe: Investigating subtokenization options for large language model pretraining on source code. *arXiv preprint arXiv:2308.00683*, 2023.
8. Jacob Devlin, Ming-Wei Chang, Kenton Lee, and Kristina Toutanova. BERT: pre-training of deep bidirectional transformers for language understanding. *CoRR*, abs/1810.04805, 2018.
9. Zhangyin Feng, Daya Guo, Duyu Tang, Nan Duan, Xiaocheng Feng, Ming Gong, Linjun Shou, Bing Qin, Ting Liu, Daxin Jiang, and Ming Zhou. CodeBERT: A pre-trained model for programming and natural languages. In *Findings of the Association for Computational Linguistics: EMNLP 2020*, pages 1536–1547, Online, November 2020. Association for Computational Linguistics.
10. Leo Gao, Stella Biderman, Sid Black, Laurence Golding, Travis Hoppe, Charles Foster, Jason Phang, Horace He, Anish Thite, Noa Nabeshima, et al. The pile: An 800gb dataset of diverse text for language modeling. *arXiv preprint arXiv:2101.00027*, 2020.
11. Daya Guo, Shuai Lu, Nan Duan, Yanlin Wang, Ming Zhou, and Jian Yin. Unixcoder: Unified cross-modal pre-training for code representation. *arXiv preprint arXiv:2203.03850*, 2022.
12. Daya Guo, Shuo Ren, Shuai Lu, Zhangyin Feng, Duyu Tang, Shujie Liu, Long Zhou, Nan Duan, Alexey Svyatkovskiy, Shengyu Fu, et al. Graphcodebert: Pre-training code representations with data flow. *arXiv preprint arXiv:2009.08366*, 2020.
13. Dan Hendrycks, Steven Basart, Saurav Kadavath, Mantas Mazeika, Akul Arora, Ethan Guo, Collin Burns, Samir Puranik, Horace He, Dawn Song, et al. Measuring coding challenge competence with apps. *arXiv preprint arXiv:2105.09938*, 2021.
14. Xinyi Hou, Yanjie Zhao, Yue Liu, Zhou Yang, Kailong Wang, Li Li, Xiapu Luo, David Lo, John Grundy, and Haoyu Wang. Large language models for software engineering: A systematic literature review. *ACM Transactions on Software Engineering and Methodology*, 2023.
15. Hamel Husain, Ho-Hsiang Wu, Tiferet Gazit, Miltiadis Allamanis, and Marc Brockschmidt. Codesearchnet challenge: Evaluating the state of semantic code search. *arXiv preprint arXiv:1909.09436*, 2019.
16. Mohammad Abdullah Matin Khan, M Saiful Bari, Do Long, Weishi Wang, Md Rizwan Parvez, and Shafiq Joty. Xcodeeval: An execution-based large scale multilingual multitask benchmark for code understanding, generation, translation and retrieval. In *Proceedings of the 62nd Annual Meeting of the Association for Computational Linguistics (Volume 1: Long Papers)*, pages 6766–6805, 2024.
17. Denis Kocetkov, Raymond Li, Loubna Ben Allal, Jia Li, Chenghao Mou, Carlos Muñoz Ferrandis, Yacine Jernite, Margaret Mitchell, Sean Hughes, Thomas Wolf, et al. The stack: 3 tb of permissively licensed source code. *arXiv preprint arXiv:2211.15533*, 2022.
18. Hung Le, Yue Wang, Akhilesh Deepak Gotmare, Silvio Savarese, and Steven Chu Hong Hoi. Coderl: Mastering code generation through pretrained models and deep reinforcement learning. *Advances in Neural Information Processing Systems*, 35:21314–21328, 2022.
19. Mike Lewis, Yinhan Liu, Naman Goyal, Marjan Ghazvininejad, Abdelrahman Mohamed, Omer Levy, Veselin Stoyanov, and Luke Zettlemoyer. BART: denoising sequence-to-sequence pre-training for natural language generation, translation, and comprehension. *CoRR*, abs/1910.13461, 2019.
20. Raymond Li, Loubna Ben Allal, Yangtian Zi, Niklas Muennighoff, Denis Kocetkov, Chenghao Mou, Marc Marone, Christopher Akiki, Jia Li, Jenny Chim, et al. Starcoder: may the source be with you! *arXiv preprint arXiv:2305.06161*, 2023.
21. Yaobo Liang, Nan Duan, Yeyun Gong, Ning Wu, Fenfei Guo, Weizhen Qi, Ming Gong, Linjun Shou, Daxin Jiang, Guihong Cao, et al. Xglue: A new benchmark dataset for cross-lingual pre-training, understanding and generation. *arXiv preprint arXiv:2004.01401*, 2020.

22. Chin-Yew Lin. ROUGE: A package for automatic evaluation of summaries. In *Text Summarization Branches Out*, pages 74–81, Barcelona, Spain, July 2004. Association for Computational Linguistics.
23. Chin-Yew Lin and Franz Josef Och. Orange: a method for evaluating automatic evaluation metrics for machine translation. In *COLING 2004: Proceedings of the 20th International Conference on Computational Linguistics*, pages 501–507, 2004.
24. Shuai Lu, Daya Guo, Shuo Ren, Junjie Huang, Alexey Svyatkovskiy, Ambrosio Blanco, Colin Clement, Dawn Drain, Daxin Jiang, Duyu Tang, et al. Codexglue: A machine learning benchmark dataset for code understanding and generation. *arXiv preprint arXiv:2102.04664*, 2021.
25. Erik Nijkamp, Hiroaki Hayashi, Caiming Xiong, Silvio Savarese, and Yingbo Zhou. Codegen2: Lessons for training llms on programming and natural languages. *arXiv preprint arXiv:2305.02309*, 2023.
26. Erik Nijkamp, Bo Pang, Hiroaki Hayashi, Lifu Tu, Huan Wang, Yingbo Zhou, Silvio Savarese, and Caiming Xiong. Codegen: An open large language model for code with multi-turn program synthesis. *arXiv preprint arXiv:2203.13474*, 2022.
27. Kishore Papineni, Salim Roukos, Todd Ward, and Wei-Jing Zhu. Bleu: a method for automatic evaluation of machine translation. In *Proceedings of the 40th annual meeting of the Association for Computational Linguistics*, pages 311–318, 2002.
28. Alec Radford. Improving language understanding by generative pre-training. 2018.
29. Alec Radford, Jeffrey Wu, Rewon Child, David Luan, Dario Amodei, Ilya Sutskever, et al. Language models are unsupervised multitask learners. *OpenAI blog*, 1(8):9, 2019.
30. Colin Raffel, Noam Shazeer, Adam Roberts, Katherine Lee, Sharan Narang, Michael Matena, Yanqi Zhou, Wei Li, and Peter J. Liu. Exploring the limits of transfer learning with a unified text-to-text transformer. *CoRR*, abs/1910.10683, 2019.
31. Shuo Ren, Daya Guo, Shuai Lu, Long Zhou, Shujie Liu, Duyu Tang, Neel Sundaresan, Ming Zhou, Ambrosio Blanco, and Shuai Ma. Codebleu: a method for automatic evaluation of code synthesis. *arXiv preprint arXiv:2009.10297*, 2020.
32. Baptiste Roziere, Jonas Gehring, Fabian Gloeckle, Sten Sootla, Itai Gat, Xiaoqing Ellen Tan, Yossi Adi, Jingyu Liu, Romain Sauvestre, Tal Remez, et al. Code llama: Open foundation models for code. *arXiv preprint arXiv:2308.12950*, 2023.
33. Rico Sennrich, Barry Haddow, and Alexandra Birch. Neural machine translation of rare words with subword units. *arXiv preprint arXiv:1508.07909*, 2015.
34. Mukul Singh, José Cambronero, Sumit Gulwani, Vu Le, Carina Negreanu, and Gust Verbruggen. Codefusion: A pre-trained diffusion model for code generation. *arXiv preprint arXiv:2310.17680*, 2023.
35. Hugo Touvron, Louis Martin, Kevin Stone, Peter Albert, Amjad Almahairi, Yasmine Babaei, Nikolay Bashlykov, Soumya Batra, Prajjwal Bhargava, Shruti Bhosale, et al. Llama 2: Open foundation and fine-tuned chat models. *arXiv preprint arXiv:2307.09288*, 2023.
36. Ashish Vaswani, Noam Shazeer, Niki Parmar, Jakob Uszkoreit, Llion Jones, Aidan N Gomez, L ukasz Kaiser, and Illia Polosukhin. Attention is all you need. In I. Guyon, U. Von Luxburg, S. Bengio, H. Wallach, R. Fergus, S. Vishwanathan, and R. Garnett, editors, *Advances in Neural Information Processing Systems*, volume 30. Curran Associates, Inc., 2017.
37. Yue Wang, Weishi Wang, Shafiq Joty, and Steven C.H. Hoi. CodeT5: Identifier-aware unified pre-trained encoder-decoder models for code understanding and generation. In *Proceedings of the 2021 Conference on Empirical Methods in Natural Language Processing*, pages 8696–8708, Online and Punta Cana, Dominican Republic, November 2021. Association for Computational Linguistics.
38. Daoguang Zan, Bei Chen, Fengji Zhang, Dianjie Lu, Bingchao Wu, Bei Guan, Yongji Wang, and Jian-Guang Lou. Large language models meet nl2code: A survey. *arXiv preprint arXiv:2212.09420*, 2022.
39. Shuyan Zhou, Uri Alon, Sumit Agarwal, and Graham Neubig. Codebertscore: Evaluating code generation with pretrained models of code. *arXiv preprint arXiv:2302.05527*, 2023.
40. Qihao Zhu, Qingyuan Liang, Zeyu Sun, Yingfei Xiong, Lu Zhang, and Shengyu Cheng. Grammart5: Grammar-integrated pretrained encoder-decoder neural model for code. In *Proceedings of the IEEE/ACM 46th International Conference on Software Engineering*, pages 1–13, 2024.

Chapter 8
The Data-to-Text Problem

Abstract Data-to-Text refers to the process of generating natural language descriptions from structured data (e.g., tables, graphs, query outputs) or unstructured data (e.g., images, video, audio). This capability is especially valuable in contexts where data needs to be explained, where large volumes of information exceed human processing capacity, or where users expect natural language responses—an increasingly common expectation in modern interfaces. This chapter begins by defining the Data-to-Text task and highlighting key use cases. It then explores the main challenges, focusing on two core subfields: Table-to-Text and Graph-to-Text and examining how earlier non Deep Learning approaches addressed them. The chapter concludes with a review of datasets and benchmarks relevant to Table-to-Text and Graph-to-Text tasks, providing a foundation for evaluating the solutions presented in the following chapter.

8.1 Introduction

In today's data-driven world, individuals are exposed to vast amounts of information presented in a variety of formats. Yet, our ability to interpret and act on this information is often constrained by two key factors: domain knowledge and time. First, understanding complex data frequently requires specialized expertise. For example, interpreting the health implications of chemical compounds in food may only be accessible to a chemist. Second, the sheer volume of available data can overwhelm users, who may not have the time or capacity to analyze extensive datasets, such as hundreds of weather indicators, to make a simple decision like whether to carry an umbrella. Data-to-Text systems aim to bridge this gap by automatically translating structured data (e.g., tables, graphs, query results) and unstructured data (e.g., images, text collections) into coherent, contextually appropriate natural language. This transformation not only enhances accessibility but also aligns with the growing demand for natural language interfaces that simplify human-data interaction.

G. Katsogiannis-Meimarakis et al., *Natural Language Interfaces for Databases with Deep Learning*, Data-Centric Systems and Applications,
https://doi.org/10.1007/978-3-032-06905-4_8

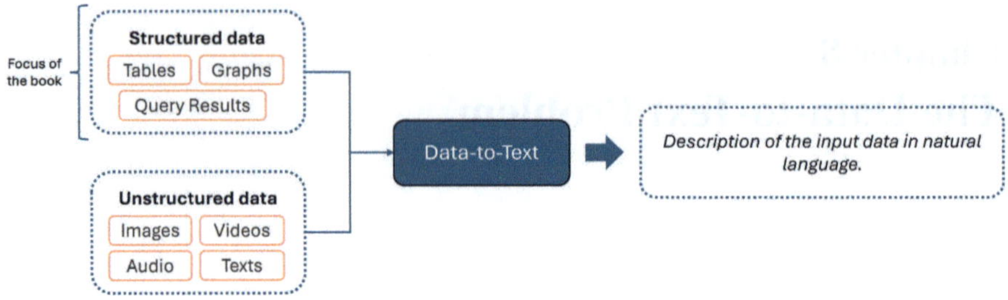

Fig. 8.1: The Data-to-Text pipeline.

This chapter introduces the Data-to-Text task by first clarifying what constitutes "data" in this context. We then explore the motivations behind the development of such systems. We examine the challenges of Data-to-Text generation, and review early rule-based approaches. We also present key datasets, benchmarks, and evaluation strategies that underpin current research and applications.

8.2 The Data-to-Text Problem

Data-to-Text solutions have emerged in the past years due to two main reasons.

Data size. As data volumes grow, users increasingly prefer concise summaries or the ability to query specific aspects of the data in natural language. For example, instead of analyzing numerous weather indicators (Figure 8.2), a user planning a trip to Athens would benefit from a simple summary like: "*Expect hot weather in Athens with an air temperature of 37°C.*"

Data complexity. Some data require domain-specific interpretation. A contour wind map, for example, may be difficult for a layperson to understand. A Data-to-Text system can simplify this by generating a statement such as "*The winds in the general area of Athens are low and should not affect your traveling.*" (Figure 8.2, right).

The objective of Data-to-Text systems (Figure 8.1) extends beyond simply describing data. They aim to produce natural language explanations that make complex or large-scale information more accessible, actionable, and human-centric. By translating data into coherent narratives, these systems help users derive meaning, make informed decisions, and interact with data more intuitively.

A fundamental question in this context is: *What types of input data are suitable for Data-to-Text generation*? In general, data can be either structured—such as tables, graphs, and query results—or unstructured, including free-form text, image collections, or multimedia content. While both types are relevant to the broader field, this book focuses specifically on structured data. More precisely, we concentrate on three widely studied modalities: tables, graphs, and query outputs defining respectively the Table-to-Text, Graph-to-Text, and Query Results-to-Text subfields (Figure 8.3).

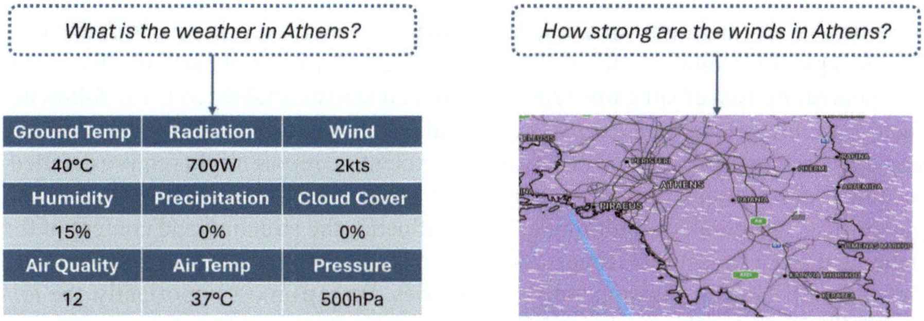

Fig. 8.2: (Left) Weather variables of Athens. (Rights) Contour wind map of Athens. Both examples showcase the need for a Data-to-Text system to accelerate data interpretation.

Table-to-Text involves generating descriptive or analytical text from tabular data. Tables are ubiquitous across domains—from spreadsheets and financial reports to sports statistics and scientific datasets. The challenge lies in identifying relevant rows, columns, or patterns and verbalizing them in a coherent and contextually appropriate manner. Systems must decide what information to include, how to aggregate or summarize it, and how to express it fluently in natural language.

Graph-to-Text focuses on generating text from graph-structured data, such as knowledge graphs, dependency trees, or network diagrams. These structures encode entities and their relationships, often in a non-linear format. The task requires understanding the semantics of nodes and edges, traversing the graph meaningfully, and producing text that captures both the structure and the content.

The third subfield we explore is **Query Results-to-Text**, where the input is the result of a specific database query, and the goal is to produce a natural language description of that output. Since query results are often presented in tabular form, this task shares similarities with Table-to-Text. However, a key distinction lies in the contextual dependency of the data. In Table-to-Text, it is generally assumed that the table can be interpreted independently—that is, all necessary information for generating a description is contained within the table itself. In contrast, Query Results-to-Text often requires additional contextual information to be meaningful. For example, interpreting a query result that includes a column labeled *COUNT(*)* necessitates understanding what is being counted—information that may only be available in the original SQL query or the database schema. This dependency on external context introduces unique challenges in content selection and verbalization. Systems must not only verbalize the data but also infer or retrieve the missing semantic links that make the output intelligible to the user. A detailed discussion of this subfield is provided in Chapter 10.

A second fundamental question is: *What is a natural language explanation (verbalization)* The form and quality of natural language explanations generated by Data-to-Text systems can vary widely depending on several key factors. There are various options ranging from a quick sentence focusing on specific parts of the data, for example, highlighted cells of Wikipedia tables [20] to whole articles, for example, generating basketball game reports from their statistics table [31]. The following factors are important. *Context* plays a crucial role: a weather summary for a mobile app may prioritize brevity and clarity, while a scientific report might require detailed, technical descriptions. Similarly, the *nature of the data*—whether it is numerical, categorical, temporal, or multimodal—can influence the structure and content of the generated text. For instance, time-series data may call for trend analysis, while tabular data might benefit from comparative summaries. Perhaps most importantly, the *target audience* shapes the tone, vocabulary, and depth of explanation. A layperson may need simplified, jargon-free language, whereas a domain expert might expect precise terminology and in-depth insights. Effective Data-to-Text systems must therefore be adaptable, capable of tailoring their outputs to meet the informational needs and expectations of diverse users across varying contexts.

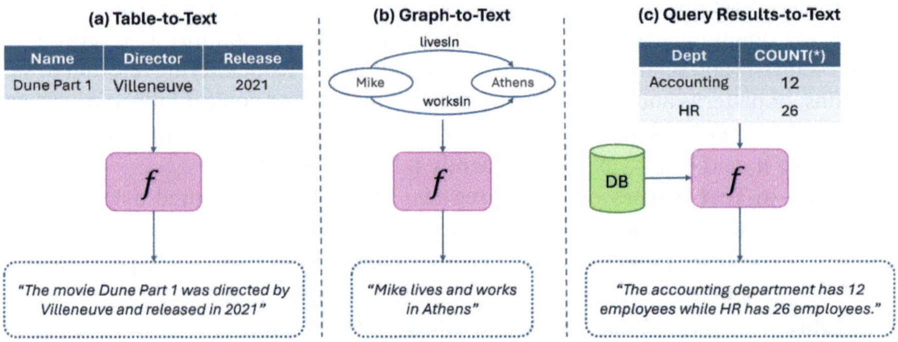

Fig. 8.3: The three different sub-fields of Data-to-Text that we are going to cover in detail.

8.3 The Table-to-Text Problem

Table-to-Text is the task of generating natural language descriptions from tabular data, often accompanied by metadata such as table titles or column headers. The goal is to produce coherent and contextually appropriate text that conveys the most relevant information contained in the table. Depending on the domain and the communicative intent, the generated description may summarize the entire table or focus selectively on specific parts. For example, suppose we want to write a short article about a basketball game based on box score statistics [31], where hundreds of statistics are kept for a single game. In such cases, the system must identify the most salient information, such as top scorers or standout performances, rather than exhaustively listing every statistic. This requires not only content selection and aggregation but also an understanding of what constitutes "interesting" information in a given context.

8.3.1 Challenges

To be effective, a Table-to-Text system must satisfy the following key criteria. First, the verbalization must be faithful to the input table, accurately reflecting the underlying data without introducing errors or hallucinations. Second, it must be informative, conveying information that is relevant and valuable to the end user. This involves avoiding the omission of important details while also excluding trivial or redundant content. Determining which parts of a table are considered "interesting" is inherently subjective and often depends on both the table's contents and the user's specific goals or context. Finally, the generated text must be fluent, meaning it can be easily understood while remaining engaging for the end user. As a result, Table-to-Text generation requires a careful balance between *faithfulness*, *informativeness*, and *fluency*, adapting its outputs to the needs of the target audience, the data, and the communicative goals (context) of the application. The Table-to-Text challenges are:

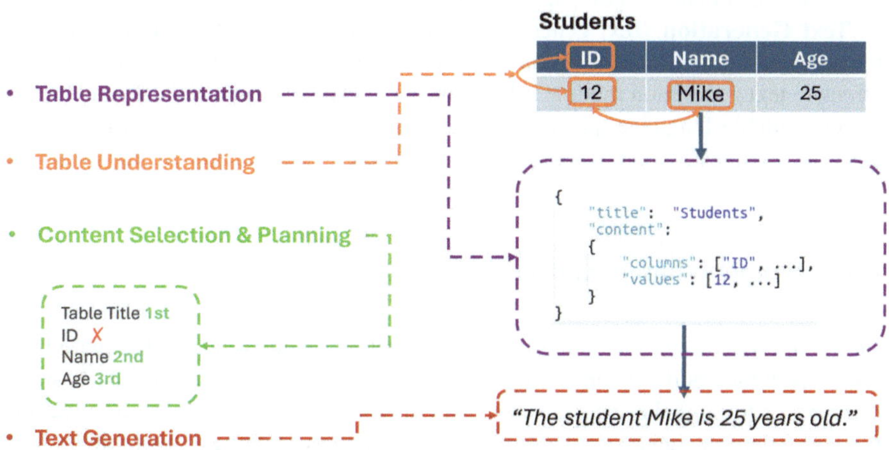

Fig. 8.4: Table-to-Text Challenges.

Table Representation. A typical table consists of several key components: a title that provides context, column headers that define the attributes or dimensions of the data, and a set of rows that contain the actual data entries, often in the form of numerical values or natural language text. For a Table-to-Text system to process this information, it must convert the table into a machine-readable format. This involves encoding the content (e.g., column names, cell values) into representations that can be consumed by computational systems such as neural models.

Table Understanding. Beyond raw representation, a Table-to-Text system must also infer and reason over the relationships that exist within the table. A human, by visually observing a table will immediately understand the relations between columns and rows. For example, in Figure 8.4, we can easily understand column-row relations - *"The student has the id 12"*, column-column relations - *"The ID and the Name refer to the same student entity"*, row-row relations - *"Mike has the ID 12 and is 25 years old"*. These inferences are made effortlessly by humans, but for a Table-to-Text system, they must be explicitly modeled. This requires the system to capture and represent inter-column, inter-row, and cross-dimensional relationships in a way that supports accurate and coherent text generation.

Content Selection & Planning. Tables may be large depending on their domain and often not all columns are important when we want to describe the table in natural language. Content selection is the choice of which parts of the table should be part of the final descriptions and which ones should be omitted. In our student example, we did not include the column ID since this does not offer any information on our downstream users. Notice that content selection highly depends on the use case and the same table might require different ways of being described. On the other hand, content planning poses the challenge of finding the correct order of describing these columns. The plan should facilitate a fluent description for the next step, text generation. For example, the description *"The student aged 25 is named Mike"* comes unnatural compared to *The student Mike is 25 years old.*

Text Generation. Text generation will take as input the table representations, the selected content, and the plan and will produce the final table description. An effective text generation module bridges the gap between structured data and human-understandable language, presenting information in a way that is both informative and easy to digest.

8.3.2 Template-based Approaches

Earlier approaches for the Table-to-Text task predominantly relied on template-based methods, which address the challenges above with deterministic and rule-based algorithms. Although these approaches do not incorporate deep learning architectures, they have demonstrated strong empirical performance, offering a favorable trade-off between computational efficiency (i.e., low latency) and output fluency. In specific application contexts, such methods remain the most appropriate choice due to their deterministic behavior and high-quality verbalizations [25].

These approaches start with an offline phase, where two steps take place. The first step involves the construction of templates. This process typically begins with a detailed examination of the target corpus, encompassing both the structured input data and the corresponding textual outputs. The objective is to derive a set of mapping rules that align data fields with their linguistic realizations. This step often necessitates the involvement of domain experts, who provide insights into which data attributes are important for the verbalization and how they should be accurately verbalized. To facilitate and partially automate template creation, unsupervised techniques such as clustering can be employed. These methods are used to group similar text outputs together based on surface-level features such as lexical similarity. By organizing the corpus into clusters of similar sentences or descriptions, common patterns can be identified. Each cluster can then be examined to extract a shared template that generalizes the structure of the text.

The second step is the definition of an intermediary language. Generating text directly from structured input via sequential rule application often results in disjointed or repetitive sentences, which can compromise textual coherence and naturalness. For instance, a naive verbalization such as 'The train to Aberdeen leaves in 5 minutes. The train to Aberdeen leaves from platform 5.' lacks fluency and cohesion. A more natural rendering would be: 'The train to Aberdeen leaves in 5 minutes from platform 5.' An intermediary language enables higher-level operations, such as sentence aggregation, clause restructuring, and discourse-level planning, that facilitate the generation of more cohesive and contextually appropriate text. This abstraction layer serves as a bridge between raw data and verbalization, enhancing the overall readability and fluency of the output. Figure 8.5 shows an example of such intermediary representation [25].

Moving on to the online phase, given a table, the Table-to-Text system will instantiate the templates with the input data, and then map them to an intermediate representation and translate them to the final text. The rules are manually defined through observation of the corpus.

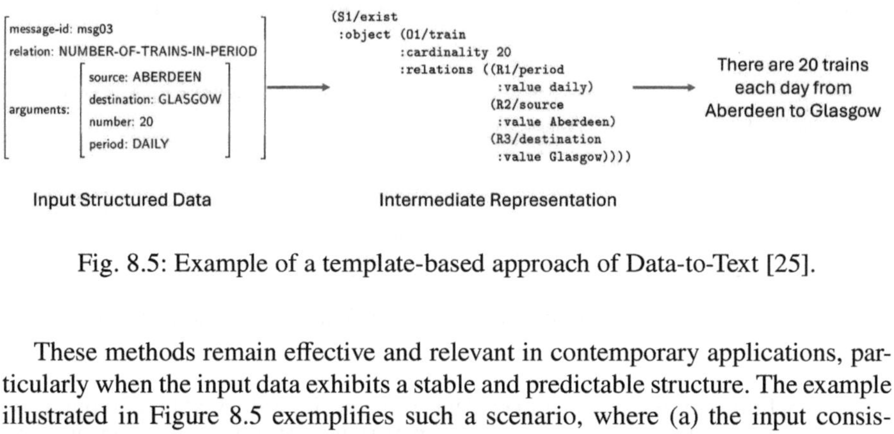

Fig. 8.5: Example of a template-based approach of Data-to-Text [25].

These methods remain effective and relevant in contemporary applications, particularly when the input data exhibits a stable and predictable structure. The example illustrated in Figure 8.5 exemplifies such a scenario, where (a) the input consistently adheres to a fixed schema, and (b) the communicative intent remains invariant—specifically, to express *the quantity of trains X departing from location Y.* Furthermore, due to their deterministic behavior and minimal computational overhead, these approaches offer a cost-efficient and interpretable solution when applicable.

However, a primary limitation of template-based approaches in Table-to-Text generation lies in their poor generalizability across unseen tables, whether within the same domain or across different domains. Sustaining such systems necessitates (a) frequent modification of existing templates to reflect changes in the underlying data schema, and (b) the continual addition of new templates to accommodate emerging data formats and content types. This results in high maintenance overhead and reduced scalability in dynamic data environments posing the need for more generalizable approaches powered by Neural Networks which are explored in the next chapter.

8.3.3 Benchmarks

Having examined the challenges of Table-to-Text, we continue with presenting benchmarks to get a better idea of the task and which problems Table-to-Text systems (more in Chapter 9) must be able to address. Benchmarks play a major role in the advancement of Table-to-Text solutions. There are various axes that we can observe to assess the quality and usefulness of benchmarks. Firstly, *size*, since small benchmarks are less qualified to train a model and evaluate it in a representative enough test split. A second axis is *diversity of tables*, since benchmarks with diverse table characteristics, such as different number of rows or columns, and variety in the domain of the tables are harder to solve. Finally, *quality*, which mainly depends on whether the descriptions of the tables were gathered automatically or annotated by humans. For example, in WIKIBIO, a dataset of Wikipedia biography info-boxes (tables), the description of the table is automatically set as the first sentence of the page, which probably does not use the whole info-box but also presents information not covered by the info-box, making it impossible to produce a correct description.

Dataset	Size	Collection	Domain	Avg. Cells	Avg. Description Len	Tokens
WEATHERGOV [17] (2009)	22K	Human	Weather	-	-	-
WikiBio [16] (2015)	728K	Auto	Wikipedia Biographies	19.7	26.1	19M
ROTOWIRE [31] (2017)	4.8K	Human	Basketball	628.0	337.1	1.6M
ToTTo [20] (2020)	136K	Human	Wikipedia	32.7	17.4	1.3M
LogicNLG [5] (2020)	37K	Human	Wikipedia	13.5	14.2	52.7K
WIKITABLET [4] (2021)	1.5M	Auto	Wikipedia	51.9	115.9	169M
Hitab [9] (2022)	11K	Human	Wikipedia/Stat Reports	-	-	-

Table 8.1: List of influential Table-to-Text Benchmarks and Datasets.

Table 8.1 presents a selection of key datasets in the Table-to-Text field, though it is not exhaustive. Early datasets, such as WEATHERGOV, WikiBio, and ROTOWIRE, are more domain-specific, reflecting the limitations of the neural architectures at the time—mainly recurrent neural networks (LSTMs, GRUs) with attention mechanisms. These models performed well in specific domains but struggled with generalization. Later, as transformer-based models and pre-trained language models emerged, they could handle datasets spanning diverse domains, such as ToTTo, which includes Wikipedia articles on sports, movies, politics, and more. We explore the architectures in detail in later sections.

WEATHERGOV is a weather dataset containing information from 22K weather forecasts in a structured format and the goal descriptions we want to generate are short forecast reports. The forecasts were obtained from US cities over a period of 3 days. The info covered in the tables includes hour-by-hour weather indicators such as temperature, wind speed, sky cover, chance of rain, etc.

Wikibio [16] gathers 728,321 biographies from English Wikipedia. For each article, they provide the first paragraph and the infobox. The input infobox and the expected text output have a length of 26 and 53 words on average respectively. Its small input and output length, its big size, and the simplicity of the task make it a relatively easy dataset to solve.

On the other hand, *ROTOWIRE* [31], considered one of the most challenging datasets, consisting of (human-written) NBA basketball game summaries aligned with their corresponding statistics. There are 4,853 distinct summaries, covering NBA games played between 1/1/2014 and 3/29/2017 with some games having multiple summaries. The summaries have been randomly split into training, validation, and test sets consisting of 3,398, 727, and 728 summaries, respectively. The input statistics have on average 628 records and the output has an average length of 805 words. As a result, the model not only has to pick the most interesting insights from the statistics that a journalist would report but also generate an article with multiple sentences.

ToTTo [20] is an open-domain English table-to-text dataset with over 135,000 datapoints, which proposes a controlled generation task: given a Wikipedia table and a set of highlighted table cells, produce a one-sentence description. During the dataset creation process, tables from English Wikipedia are matched with (noisy) descriptions. Each table cell mentioned in the description is highlighted and the descriptions are iteratively cleaned and corrected to faithfully reflect the content of the highlighted cells. ToTTo is an impactful dataset in Table-to-Text since it is big (135K), diverse (having tables from multiple Wikipedia domains such as politics and entertainment), and of high quality since the verbalisations were manually created and corrected.

LogicNLG [5] is derived from TabFact [6], a table-based fact-checking dataset built using Wikipedia tables. In table-based fact-checking, the model evaluates whether a series of facts are supported by the table. For LogicNLG, the authors selected tables from TabFact and retained only the correct facts as descriptions. The dataset contains 37,000 table-description pairs. Unlike other datasets, LogicNLG requires logical inferences, such as arithmetic reasoning, rather than providing shallow descriptions of the tables.

WIKITABLET [4] is the biggest dataset in the list with 1.5M pairs of tables and descriptions. It uses information from a knowledge base called Wikidata, which provides support for Wikimedia [1] including Wikipedia. In this dataset, each pair consists of multiple tables covering article data, title data, and section data needed to generate a full Wikipedia section. In comparison with other Wikipedia datasets,

[1] `https://www.wikimedia.org/`

the tables and consequently the descriptions are longer requiring multiple sentences (on average 116 words).

Finally, *Hitab* [9] is one of the most recent Table-to-Text dataset and emphasizes hierarchical tables. A table is considered hierarchical *if its header exhibits a multi-level structure* (Table 8.2). The dataset is cross-domain with tables obtained from Wikipedia and statistical reports from Statistics Canada[2] and National Science Foundations[3]. The two sources of hierarchical tables are mixed producing a Table-to-Text dataset of 11K table-description pairs. The descriptions of the pairs are manually created by human annotators.

Table 8.2: Example of a hierarchical table

Model	Price	
	Euro	USD
ModelA	23K	27K
ModelB	30K	35K

8.4 The Graph-to-Text Problem

Graph-to-text is the process of generating natural language descriptions or explanations from graph-structured data. In this task, the input is a graph, which consists of nodes (representing entities) and edges (representing relationships or interactions between those entities), and the goal is to automatically convert this structured information into coherent, readable text.

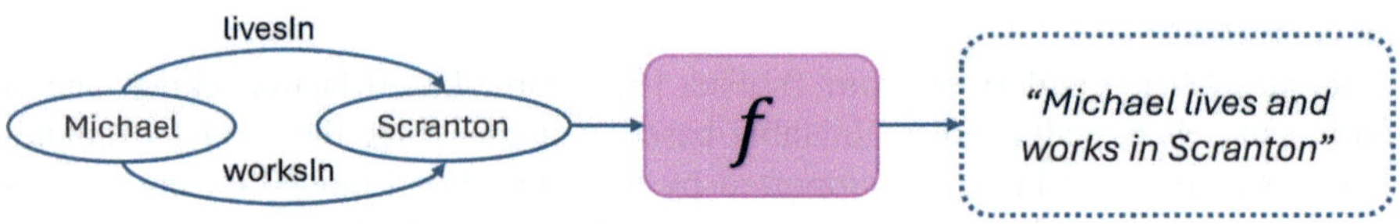

Fig. 8.6: Graph-to-Text example.

Graphs can be observed in many cases as the preferred structure of representing knowledge such as social networks where the users are nodes and the interactions between them (eg. follow, message, etc.) are the edges. Via representation as a graph, data analysis insights can be extracted that were not possible by just having a table of users and a table of interactions. Such insights include neighborhood discovery or discovery of the influential nodes.

[2] `https://www.statcan.gc.ca`

[3] `https://www.nsf.gov`

Graphs are not easily understood by humans, especially non-experts, and they tend to be large and complex. Even when focusing on specific parts of a graph, generating clear descriptions and useful insights is challenging. This is where Graph-to-Text comes in. It takes a graph as input and produces a natural language description that humans can quickly read to understand the graph's contents. This approach simplifies the interpretation of complex graph data.

8.4.1 Challenges

Graph-to-Text, being under the Data-to-Text umbrella, shares common challenges with Table-to-Text. Content Selection & Planning and Text Generation (Figure 8.4) need addressing in Graph-to-Text too, and as we are going to see in later sections share common solutions in both cases. However, due to the underlying structure being a graph, two new challenges are introduced:

- **Representation of a Graph** A graph consists of nodes and edges that connect them. Typically, graphs are represented programmatically using adjacency matrices, adjacency lists, or edge lists. However, deep learning models require vector inputs, making it necessary to use embedding methods. These methods need to account for both nodes and edges, which adds complexity.
- **Graph Understanding** For a Graph-to-Text model to generate meaningful text, it must encode not only direct connections between nodes but also indirect ones, where nodes are linked through multiple other nodes.

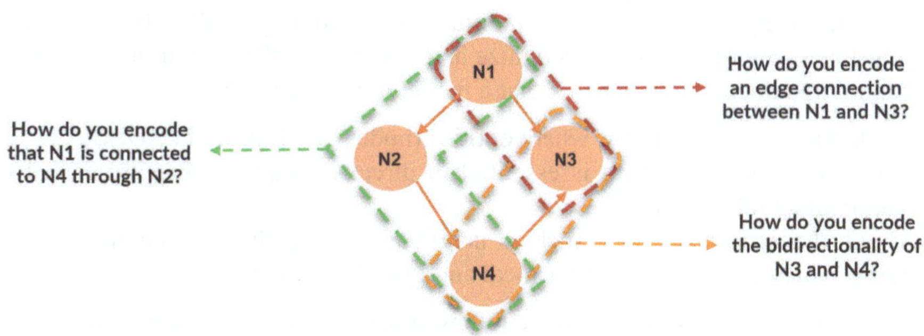

Fig. 8.7: The challenge of encoding relationships between nodes in Graph-to-Text.

8.4.1.1 Representation of a Graph

Representing a graph or more specifically serializing it into a continuous string poses a greater challenge than in Table-to-Text. In Table-to-Text, there are various ways to represent a table that are easy to understand such as Markdown, json, or XML. However, graphs have a more diverse structure compared to tables and that complexity must included in the serialization.

One solution is to sequentially list all the triplets that appear in the graph such as *":H: Apollo 12 :R: backup pilot :T: Alfred Worden"* where the :H: token is the head, :R: the relation, and :T: the tail. An example of this technique is shown in Figure .

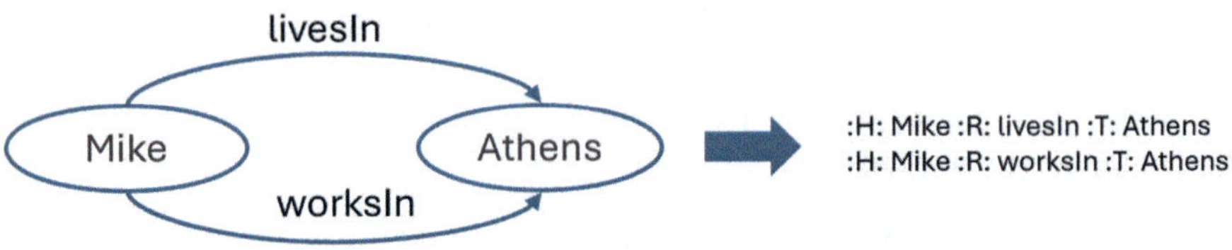

Fig. 8.8: Example of graph serialization.

8.4.1.2 Graph Understanding

Another key challenge that distinguishes Graph-to-Text from Table-to-Text generation is the requirement for graph understanding. While humans can often interpret graphs intuitively—especially when familiar with the domain—deep learning models must be explicitly taught to recognize and reason over the structural elements of a graph. Fundamental components that a model must learn include:

- Node-to-node connectivity, where entities (nodes) are linked via edges.
- Edge directionality, which is essential in directed graphs to capture causal or hierarchical relationships.
- Graph-theoretic properties, such as neighborhoods, paths, and subgraph structures, which provide context for local and global reasoning

There are 2 main solutions that are followed in Graph-to-Text solution that utilize deep learning, enhancing the self-attention mechanism of the transformer architecture and unsupervised pretraining over a corpus of graphs.

Graph Transformer. Traditional transformers perform pairwise attention calculations of a token with all the others and itself. However, in the graph case we have to also encode that two nodes might be explicitly connected with each other via a path [3].

To achieve that a new term r in the self-attention calculation of the transformer equations is introduced as shown below. Between 2 nodes i, j the term $r_{i \to j}$ describes their graph relationship (path).

$$a_{i \to j} = x_i W_q^T W_k x_j + x_i W_q^T W_k r_{j \to i} + r_{i \to j} W_q^T W_k x_j + r_{i \to j} W_q^T W_k r_{j \to i}$$

In the above equation, the extra terms introduced are the $r_{i \to j}$ and $r_{j \to i}$. This term is calculated by finding the shortest path between these two nodes if it exists and then passing the embeddings of the edges through an aggregator network which can be a simple SUM or AVG or something more intricate like an RNN or 1D convolution. The idea behind this modification of the transformer equations is that two nodes will be able to be related with each other regardless of the path size that connects them.

Graph Pretraining. Similar to Table-to-Text where Table Pretraining exists, the same framework can be followed in Graph-to-Text. The idea is that by first training the model on more general tasks around graphs that require the model to use all structural parts of a graph (nodes and edges), it will then better transition to the downstream Graph-to-Text task achieving higher performance [1]. The tasks draw inspiration from the Masked Language Modelling technique where parts of text are hidden from the model which is then tasked with retrieving them back. In the Graph-to-Text case, two example tasks proposed are:

- *Node and edge denoising.* Random node and edge values are discarded and the model is tasked with retrieving them back.
- *Sub-graph denoising.* Randomly picked subgraphs of the original graph are discarded an the model has to retrieve them.

These two tasks force the model to capture knowledge about node and edge values along with facilitating general graph-level learning

8.4.2 Benchmarks

High-quality, large-scale benchmarks are essential for developing and evaluating effective deep-learning models. However, creating Graph-to-Text benchmarks is particularly challenging. Unlike Table-to-Text benchmarks, where Wikipedia tables are easily paired with article sections, such combinations are rare in the real world for graphs. As a result, Graph-to-Text benchmarks are often manually created, which is time-consuming and expensive. Nevertheless, considerable efforts have been made to produce high-quality, manually crafted benchmarks.

In Table 8.3, we observe that human-created datasets for Graph-to-Text are generally smaller than those for Table-to-Text. Two notable datasets, WebNLG and LDC, have undergone multiple releases over the past decade, with each update introducing new graph-text pairs and improving existing ones. This highlights the complexity and time investment required to build such high-quality datasets. Below, we examine some of these datasets to better understand their contents and challenges.

The *WebNLG* [13] dataset consists of sets of triplets that describe facts (entities and their relationships) and corresponding natural language descriptions. Each set

Dataset	Size	Collection	Type / Domain
LDC [15] (2020*)	59K	Human	AMR
WebNLG [13] (2020*)	17K	Human	DBpedia
AGENDA [26] (2020)	41K	Human	Knowledge Graphs
LOGIC2TEXT [7] (2020)	11K	Human	Wikipedia
WITA [29] (2020)	55K	Human	Wikipedia
GenWiki [14] (2020)	1.6M	Auto	Wikipedia
ENT-DESC [8] (2020)	110K	Auto	Knowledge Graphs
WikiGraphs [30] (2021)	26K	Human	Wikipedia
Map2Seq [27] (2021)	7K	Human	Open Street Map
DART [18] (2021)	82K	Semi-auto	Wikipedia + Restaurant
EventNarrative [10] (2021)	224K	Auto	EventKG + Wikipedia

Table 8.3: List of influential Graph-to-Text Benchmarks and Datasets.

includes up to seven triplets and one or more reference texts. The test set is divided into two parts: "seen," which contains entities and relations from DBpedia categories that appeared in the training data, and "unseen," which includes entities and relations from five previously unseen categories. Examples of categories include movies, sports, and industry. WebNLG was first introduced in 2017 but had 2 extra releases in 2020 and 2023 adding more categories, improving existing ones and adding new languages for target text.

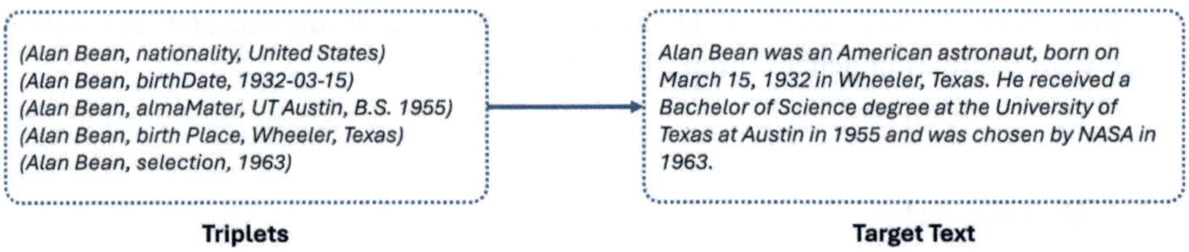

Fig. 8.9: Example of the WebNLG dataset.

The *LDC AMR* [4] dataset is structured to capture "who is doing what to whom" in a sentence. Each sentence is paired with a graph representing its full meaning as a tree structure (Abstract Meaning Representation). In an AMR graph, nodes represent concepts and edges represent semantic relations. These sentences, sourced from journal entries, forum discussions, and blogs, are manually annotated to create their semantic trees. Similarly to WebNLG, LDC has had multiple iterations in 2014, 2017, and finally 2020.

GenWiki [14] is a large-scale and general-domain Graph-to-Text **unsupervised** dataset. The challenges that this dataset addresses are:

[4] `https://catalog.ldc.upenn.edu/LDC2020T02`

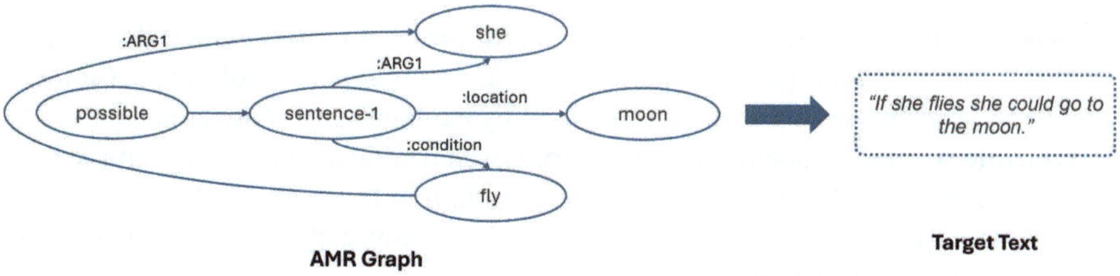

Fig. 8.10: Example of the LDC AMR dataset.

- The lack of large scale dataset compared to the much smaller and much more expensive supervised datasets we have mentioned
- The lack of a general domain dataset with a much broader distribution of edges and nodes

However, in order to achieve a large scale in a cost-effective and automatic way the created dataset of 1.3M graphs and texts is unsupervised, meaning that there are no annotated connections between a graph and a text. GenWiki consists of Wikipedia texts, which had their respective knowledge graphs queried from DBpedia meaning that there is not a necessary connection between the text passages and the graph. For that reason, GenWiki$_{FINE}$ also exists which is smaller with 750K texts and graphs but with more entity constraints enforced between knowledge graphs and Wikipedia text passages.

Then, *Map2Seq* [27] is a much different dataset in terms of domain, graph definition and goal. The goal is to provide navigation instructions in natural language utilising landmarks along the route, like asking a stranger on the street, instead of using turns and distances like map navigation applications. In this context, the graph is composed of road segments and nearby landmarks such as shops, parks, and hotels. These elements are represented as nodes, while the edges capture spatial relationships by linking road segments to one another and to adjacent landmarks. The resulting graph structure reflects both the physical layout of the environment and the contextual cues that make human navigation intuitive. The dataset consists of 7,672 such pairs of graphs and natural language navigation instructions, which were manually created and manually validated to ensure high quality.

8.5 Evaluation

The evaluation of Data-to-Text models aims to quantify how close the predicted natural language description is to the ground truth, which was created by annotators or obtained automatically. An ideal metric or evaluation method would return a value of 0 to 1 with 1 being a perfect description of the input structured data and 0 a completely wrong one. However, a "perfect" description of data is subjective and depends on multiple variables:

- **Expertise of the user.** An expert user might prefer a more detailed description and of more specific parts of the data, while a non-expert would expect a more general description possibly accompanied by explanations of specific terms.
- **Multiple ways to describe information.** Given a table, even if it is a simple one, there are many and different ways of describing it in terms of syntax, vocabulary. In some cases two verbalisations that focus on completely different parts of the data might be both valid.
- **Size of the data.** If the data required to be described increase in size a lot, for example a table with 10+ columns and 5+ rows, a description covering all pieces of information would end up being an unhelpful wall of text. Instead, a summary that focuses on key insights would be more interesting but in turn "interestingness" is again a subjective term.

As a consequence of the above challenges, it becomes apparent that the correct verbalisation does not only depend on the unstructured data that the models take as input, but on external variables too such as the user, and the use case which existing datasets lack in covering.

8.5.1 Evaluation Metrics

Metrics are needed in Data-to-Text to have a quantitative indicator of the system performance. The metrics in Data-to-Text will compare two texts, the ground truth one and the predicted one, and output a number usually from 0 to 1 indicating if the generated description matches the ground truth. Some of the metrics described below were also described in SQL-to-Text (Section 5.4.2) since in this case as well, the output is text. However, Data-to-Text has different structured input such as a table, allowing for specialized metrics that take into account the contents of the data, specifically PARENT [12] and Data-QuestEval [23].

8.5.1.1 Deterministic Metrics

BLEU score [19] is a widely used text comparison metric used in various tasks such as machine translation, question answering and text summarization. BLEU calculates the n-gram precision of different sized n-grams between the two texts. BLEU has been one of the most widely used Data-to-Text metrics despite its shortcomings, of not being able to capture semantic similarities.

chrF [21] and **chrF++** [22] are automatic metrics similar to BLEU but take into account character n-grams as well.

METEOR [2], is again based on n-gram matching but takes into account the ordering of the words.

PARENT [12] on the other hand, is Table-to-Text metric since it takes into account that our goal is to verbalize a table. At its core, it uses the BLEU formula for calculating n-gram similarity. However, it penalizes the model less if our reference text contains information not included in the input table or if our predicted text includes information that is in the table but not in the reference text.

8.5.1.2 Learned Metrics

Sentence Transformers [24] is a training technique of siamese encoder models such as BERT, specifically fine-tuned to generate embeddings of a text that captures similarities and differences with other text embeddings generated with the same model. The similarity value ends up being the cosine similarity between the two generated embeddings.

BLEURT [28] use the BERT's [CLS] token and a linear layer to predict a score. The main difference to Sentence Transformers above is that BLEURT, processes the two inputs (i.e., reference and candidate) at the same time, and not separately. The output [CLS] token contains a contextualised representation based on both inputs, which is then used to predict a score through a linear layer.

Bertscore [32] instead of using n-gram comparisons like BLEU and PARENT, compares embeddings generated by a BERT [11] model. This way we are comparing the semantic meaning of the reference and the predicted sentences. For example, the two sentences "The lake is beautiful", "The lake is magnificent", will have a low BLEU score but a high Bertscore, since BERT will generate similar embeddings for the words "beautiful" and "magnificent".

Data-QuestEval [23] is a method based on QuestEval which was used to evaluate purely textual tasks such as text summarization. In QuestEval, a set of synthetic questions is created from the input source document and ground truth summarization. Then another model is tasked to answer these questions using the ground truth output first and the predicted output second. It then compares the generated answers using n-gram overlap. However, since QuestEval require purely textual tasks, Data-QuestEval was proposed which is multi-modal taking into account structured data, while the main idea of evaluation the prediction through question remains the same.

References

1. Xuefeng Bai, Yulong Chen, and Yue Zhang. Graph pre-training for amr parsing and generation. *arXiv preprint arXiv:2203.07836*, 2022.
2. Satanjeev Banerjee and Alon Lavie. METEOR: An automatic metric for MT evaluation with improved correlation with human judgments. In *Proceedings of the ACL Workshop on Intrinsic and Extrinsic Evaluation Measures for Machine Translation and/or Summarization*, pages 65–72, Ann Arbor, Michigan, June 2005. Association for Computational Linguistics.
3. Deng Cai and Wai Lam. Graph transformer for graph-to-sequence learning. In *Proceedings of the AAAI conference on artificial intelligence*, volume 34, pages 7464–7471, 2020.
4. Mingda Chen, Sam Wiseman, and Kevin Gimpel. Wikitablet: A large-scale data-to-text dataset for generating wikipedia article sections. *arXiv preprint arXiv:2012.14919*, 2020.
5. Wenhu Chen, Jianshu Chen, Yu Su, Zhiyu Chen, and William Yang Wang. Logical natural language generation from open-domain tables. *arXiv preprint arXiv:2004.10404*, 2020.

6. Wenhu Chen, Hongmin Wang, Jianshu Chen, Yunkai Zhang, Hong Wang, Shiyang Li, Xiyou Zhou, and William Yang Wang. Tabfact: A large-scale dataset for table-based fact verification. *arXiv preprint arXiv:1909.02164*, 2019.
7. Zhiyu Chen, Wenhu Chen, Hanwen Zha, Xiyou Zhou, Yunkai Zhang, Sairam Sundaresan, and William Yang Wang. Logic2Text: High-fidelity natural language generation from logical forms. In Trevor Cohn, Yulan He, and Yang Liu, editors, *Findings of the Association for Computational Linguistics: EMNLP 2020*, pages 2096–2111, Online, November 2020. Association for Computational Linguistics.
8. Liying Cheng, Dekun Wu, Lidong Bing, Yan Zhang, Zhanming Jie, Wei Lu, and Luo Si. ENT-DESC: Entity description generation by exploring knowledge graph. In Bonnie Webber, Trevor Cohn, Yulan He, and Yang Liu, editors, *Proceedings of the 2020 Conference on Empirical Methods in Natural Language Processing (EMNLP)*, pages 1187–1197, Online, November 2020. Association for Computational Linguistics.
9. Zhoujun Cheng, Haoyu Dong, Zhiruo Wang, Ran Jia, Jiaqi Guo, Yan Gao, Shi Han, Jian-Guang Lou, and Dongmei Zhang. Hitab: A hierarchical table dataset for question answering and natural language generation. *arXiv preprint arXiv:2108.06712*, 2021.
10. Anthony M. Colas, Ali Sadeghian, Yue Wang, and Daisy Zhe Wang. Eventnarrative: A large-scale event-centric dataset for knowledge graph-to-text generation. *CoRR*, abs/2111.00276, 2021.
11. Jacob Devlin, Ming-Wei Chang, Kenton Lee, and Kristina Toutanova. BERT: pre-training of deep bidirectional transformers for language understanding. *CoRR*, abs/1810.04805, 2018.
12. Bhuwan Dhingra, Manaal Faruqui, Ankur P. Parikh, Ming-Wei Chang, Dipanjan Das, and William W. Cohen. Handling divergent reference texts when evaluating table-to-text generation. *CoRR*, abs/1906.01081, 2019.
13. Claire Gardent, Anastasia Shimorina, Shashi Narayan, and Laura Perez-Beltrachini. Creating training corpora for nlg micro-planning. In *55th annual meeting of the Association for Computational Linguistics (ACL)*, 2017.
14. Zhijing Jin, Qipeng Guo, Xipeng Qiu, and Zheng Zhang. GenWiki: A dataset of 1.3 million content-sharing text and graphs for unsupervised graph-to-text generation. In *Proceedings of the 28th International Conference on Computational Linguistics*, pages 2398–2409, Barcelona, Spain (Online), December 2020. International Committee on Computational Linguistics.
15. Kevin Knight, Bianca Badarau, Laura Baranescu, Claire Bonial, Madalina Bardocz, Kira Griffitt, Ulf Hermjakob, Daniel Marcu, Martha Palmer, Tim O'Gorman, et al. Abstract meaning representation (amr) annotation release 3.0. 2021.
16. Rémi Lebret, David Grangier, and Michael Auli. Neural text generation from structured data with application to the biography domain. *arXiv preprint arXiv:1603.07771*, 2016.
17. Percy Liang, Michael Jordan, and Dan Klein. Learning semantic correspondences with less supervision. In Keh-Yih Su, Jian Su, Janyce Wiebe, and Haizhou Li, editors, *Proceedings of the Joint Conference of the 47th Annual Meeting of the ACL and the 4th International Joint Conference on Natural Language Processing of the AFNLP*, pages 91–99, Suntec, Singapore, August 2009. Association for Computational Linguistics.
18. Linyong Nan, Dragomir Radev, Rui Zhang, Amrit Rau, Abhinand Sivaprasad, Chiachun Hsieh, Xiangru Tang, Aadit Vyas, Neha Verma, Pranav Krishna, Yangxiaokang Liu, Nadia Irwanto, Jessica Pan, Faiaz Rahman, Ahmad Zaidi, Mutethia Mutuma, Yasin Tarabar, Ankit Gupta, Tao Yu, Yi Chern Tan, Xi Victoria Lin, Caiming Xiong, Richard Socher, and Nazneen Fatema Rajani. DART: Open-domain structured data record to text generation. In *Proceedings of the 2021 Conference of the North American Chapter of the Association for Computational Linguistics: Human Language Technologies*, pages 432–447, Online, June 2021. Association for Computational Linguistics.
19. Kishore Papineni, Salim Roukos, Todd Ward, and Wei-Jing Zhu. Bleu: a method for automatic evaluation of machine translation. In *Proceedings of the 40th annual meeting of the Association for Computational Linguistics*, pages 311–318, 2002.
20. Ankur P. Parikh, Xuezhi Wang, Sebastian Gehrmann, Manaal Faruqui, Bhuwan Dhingra, Diyi Yang, and Dipanjan Das. Totto: A controlled table-to-text generation dataset. *CoRR*, abs/2004.14373, 2020.

21. Maja Popović. chrF: character n-gram F-score for automatic MT evaluation. In *Proceedings of the Tenth Workshop on Statistical Machine Translation*, pages 392–395, Lisbon, Portugal, September 2015. Association for Computational Linguistics.
22. Maja Popović. chrF++: words helping character n-grams. In *Proceedings of the Second Conference on Machine Translation*, pages 612–618, Copenhagen, Denmark, September 2017. Association for Computational Linguistics.
23. Clement Rebuffel, Thomas Scialom, Laure Soulier, Benjamin Piwowarski, Sylvain Lamprier, Jacopo Staiano, Geoffrey Scoutheeten, and Patrick Gallinari. Data-QuestEval: A referenceless metric for data-to-text semantic evaluation. In Marie-Francine Moens, Xuanjing Huang, Lucia Specia, and Scott Wen-tau Yih, editors, *Proceedings of the 2021 Conference on Empirical Methods in Natural Language Processing*, pages 8029–8036, Online and Punta Cana, Dominican Republic, November 2021. Association for Computational Linguistics.
24. Nils Reimers and Iryna Gurevych. Sentence-bert: Sentence embeddings using siamese bert-networks. In *Proceedings of the 2019 Conference on Empirical Methods in Natural Language Processing*. Association for Computational Linguistics, 11 2019.
25. Ehud Reiter and Robert Dale. Building applied natural language generation systems. *Natural Language Engineering*, 3(1):57–87, 1997.
26. Yi Luan Mirella Lapata Rik Koncel-Kedziorski, Dhanush Bekal and Hannaneh Hajishirzi. Text Generation from Knowledge Graphs with Graph Transformers. In *NAACL*, 2019.
27. Raphael Schumann and Stefan Riezler. Generating landmark navigation instructions from maps as a graph-to-text problem. *arXiv preprint arXiv:2012.15329*, 2020.
28. Thibault Sellam, Dipanjan Das, and Ankur Parikh. BLEURT: Learning robust metrics for text generation. In *Proceedings of the 58th Annual Meeting of the Association for Computational Linguistics*, pages 7881–7892, Online, July 2020. Association for Computational Linguistics.
29. Sun-Kyung Lee Ue-Hwan Kim*, Yewon Hwang* and Jong-Hwan Kim. Writing in the air: Unconstrained text recognition from finger movement using spatio-temporal convolution. 2021.
30. Luyu Wang, Yujia Li, Ozlem Aslan, and Oriol Vinyals. WikiGraphs: A Wikipedia text - knowledge graph paired dataset. In Alexander Panchenko, Fragkiskos D. Malliaros, Varvara Logacheva, Abhik Jana, Dmitry Ustalov, and Peter Jansen, editors, *Proceedings of the Fifteenth Workshop on Graph-Based Methods for Natural Language Processing (TextGraphs-15)*, Mexico City, Mexico, June 2021. Association for Computational Linguistics.
31. Sam Wiseman, Stuart M Shieber, and Alexander M Rush. Challenges in data-to-document generation. *arXiv preprint arXiv:1707.08052*, 2017.
32. Tianyi Zhang, Varsha Kishore, Felix Wu, Kilian Q Weinberger, and Yoav Artzi. Bertscore: Evaluating text generation with bert. *arXiv preprint arXiv:1904.09675*, 2019.

Chapter 9
Table-to-Text Neural Architecture and Systems

Abstract This chapter will present solutions to the main challenges of Table-to-Text listed in Chapter 8. It focuses on Deep Learning Table-to-Text architectures, which integrate various of these solutions into a unified framework. This chapter focuses specifically on Table-to-Text systems, as in a Natural Language Interface to Databases (NLIDB), the result of an executed query is typically returned in the form of a table, meaning that there is some alignment between Table-to-Text and an NLIDB

9.1 Introduction

A *Table-to-Text* system takes structured data as input and, through a series of processing steps, transforms it into coherent natural language text. These steps typically include representing the input data in a format suitable for the model being used (*Table Representation*), analyzing and interpreting the structure and semantics of the data (*Table Understanding*), identifying which parts of the data should be expressed in text (*Content Selection*), determining the most appropriate order in which to present the selected content (*Planning*), and finally, generating the textual output in a way that remains faithful to the selected content and intended plan(*Guided Generation*).

9.1.1 Neural Approaches

With the advent of deep learning, particularly with advancements in Natural Language Processing, novel generative approaches have emerged that significantly reduce or eliminate manual intervention, aside from the potential requirement of curating a training dataset. These models have expanded the capabilities of Table-to-Text generation beyond rigid, domain-specific templates to systems capable of

G. Katsogiannis-Meimarakis et al., *Natural Language Interfaces for Databases with Deep Learning*, Data-Centric Systems and Applications,
https://doi.org/10.1007/978-3-032-06905-4_9

interpreting arbitrary tabular structures and producing fluent, diverse, and syntactically coherent textual descriptions.

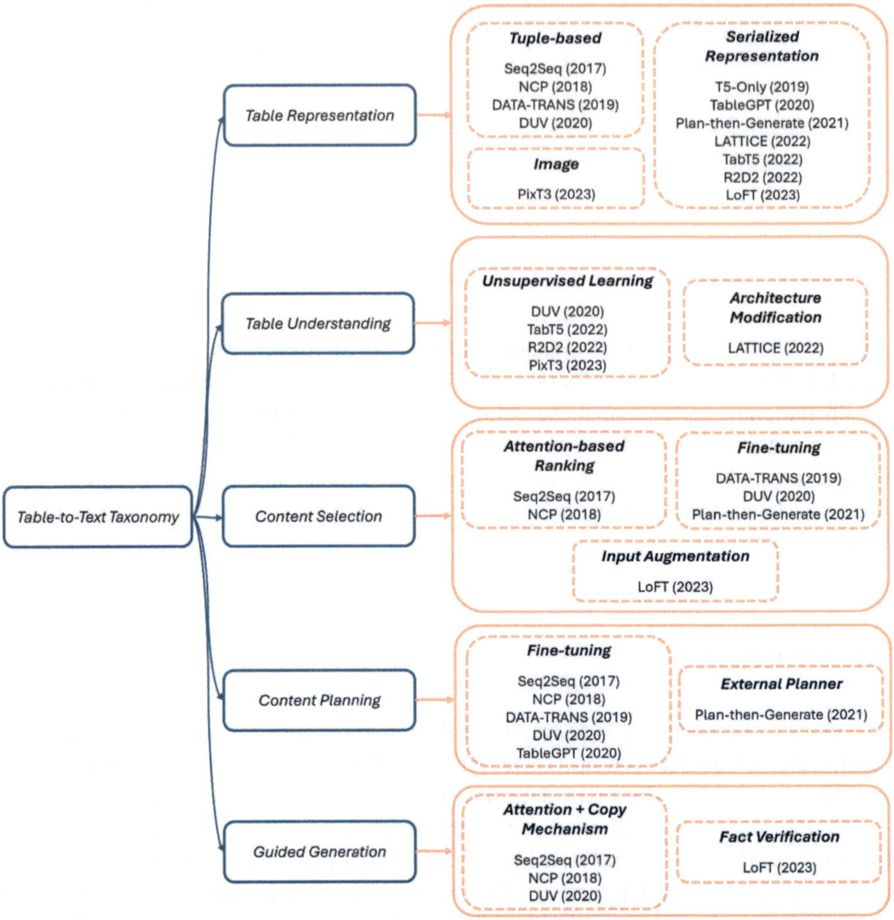

Fig. 9.1: Table-to-Text taxonomy with existing solutions.

In Section 8.3.1, we outlined the key challenges inherent to Table-to-Text generation. To systematically organize deep learning-based solutions, we introduce a taxonomy that groups methods according to the specific challenges they address. This framework enables a structured analysis of the methodologies behind each approach, setting the stage for this chapter, to examine Table-to-Text systems.

9.1.1.1 Table Representation

Table Representation refers to the process of transforming a table into a machine-readable format, specifically one that can be effectively processed by neural network architectures. We distinguish three primary representation strategies: (*a*) tuple-based (*b*) serialized and (*c*) image.

Tuple-based Representation. In this approach, tabular data is decomposed into structured records or tuples, which are then embedded into vector representations using neural networks. These embedding networks are typically trained from scratch and can be tailored to the specific characteristics of the task.

For example, in the ROTOWIRE benchmark, focused on basketball game statistics, records may take the form of tuples such as `[Points, Thomas, 18, Home Game]` or `[Assists, Thomas, 5, Home Game]` [13]. Embedding architectures can vary: one strategy involves using separate fully connected networks for each statistic type (e.g., E_{points}, $E_{assists}$, ...), while another applies a shared network across all types. In both cases, the embedding weights are optimized jointly with the downstream Table-to-Text generation model. However, training embeddings end-to-end can introduce challenges such as the vanishing gradient problem, where gradients diminish as they propagate through deep layers, potentially hindering effective learning.

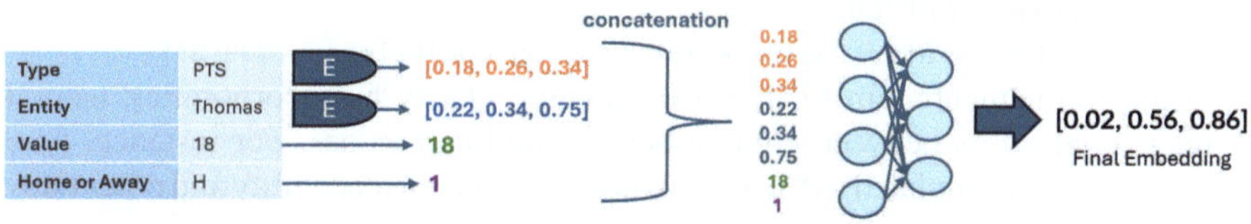

Fig. 9.2: The embedding creation process for a single record of the ROTOWIRE dataset as described in NCP [13].

One key positive of custom embeddings, is that they allow for architecture designs that emphasize semantically important aspects of the data. For instance, in basketball statistics, the interpretation of a value like "10" depends on the context—10 assists is notable, while 10 points may be average. To address such nuances, the DUV architecture [5] incorporates additional embedding networks that model the quality of numerical values relative to their statistic type. While the example here focuses on basketball game statistics, embedding architectures can be highly customized for other applications where different parts of the data may require specific emphasis.

Serialized Representation. With the rise of large language models, a newer approach to table representation involves converting the table into a continuous string of text. While this may seem counterintuitive due to the loss of the table's structured format, it allows LLMs—designed to process text—to understand table content and generate fluent, accurate descriptions.

Various methods exist for serializing a table into text, each balancing detail and token efficiency. One approach is to serialize the table into an XML-like format with tags such as <table>, <row>, <cell>,<col_header> to preserve the table structure [12]. As illustrated in Figure 9.3, this format captures the full content and structure of the table and can be extended with additional tags to encode metadata such as titles or descriptions.

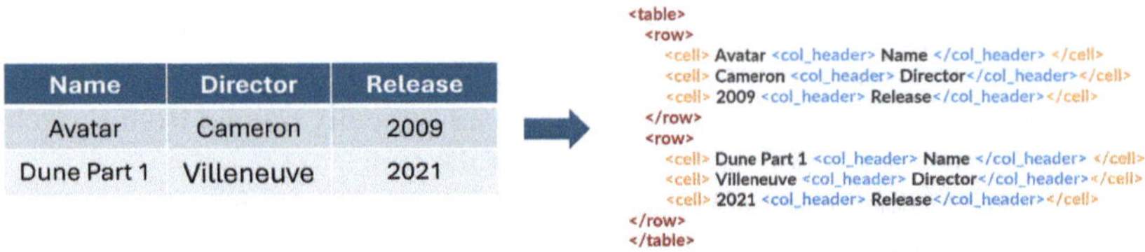

Fig. 9.3: Serializing a table into an XML continuous string.

However, XML serialization is verbose with repeated opening and closing tags for every row, cell, and column. As table size increases, this verbosity can quickly exhaust token limits, truncating the model's input. To mitigate this, more compact serialization schemes have been proposed. One such approach replaces structural tags with special separator tokens like `[SEP]` for rows and `[COL]` for columns, reducing token usage [14]. For instance:

```
[SEP][COL]Name Avatar[COL]Director Cameron[COL]Release 2009[SEP] ...
```

Further refinements aim to improve semantic clarity by incorporating natural language connectors between column headers and cell values. For instance, `Name Avatar` may be reformulated as `Name is Avatar`, enhancing readability and potentially aiding model comprehension [6].

These serialization methods have been used with earlier pretrained models like T5 and BART, which are fine-tuned to understand specific tag-based formats. In contrast, modern LLMs, like GPT-4 and Llama3.1, often rely on prompt engineering rather than fine-tuning. For these models, tables are typically serialized using widely recognized formats such as HTML, JSON, or Markdown—formats frequently encountered during pretraining.

A key limitation of text-based serialization is the *loss of spatial relationships* inherent to tabular data. In natural language, nearby words are often related, while distant words contribute to broader context. However, serialized tables may separate semantically linked elements, such as values from the same column but different rows, by large token distances. This disrupts the model's ability to capture intra-column or intra-row dependencies effectively. This limitation has motivated the development of image-based representations, which aim to preserve the visual and spatial structure of tables, and more crucially, table understanding techniques studied in Section 9.1.1.2.

Image Representation. A more recent approach involves rendering tables as images (e.g., in PNG format) by converting them into HTML tables first [1]. This preserves structural elements like rows and columns in a two-dimensional layout. Using image-based models, especially those with text-recognition capabilities, enables models to interpret both the layout and content of tables effectively.

Unlike text serialization, images naturally maintain spatial relationships: horizontally aligned values belong to the same row, while vertically aligned values belong to the same column. This spatial proximity in 2D formats addresses challenges faced by the linear (1D) nature of text serialization.

9.1.1.2 Table Understanding

Most humans intuitively understand the structure of a table, its rows, columns, and headers, and can effortlessly interpret the relationships between its elements. In contrast, deep learning models lack any inherent understanding of tabular structure, necessitating techniques that explicitly teach them the relational patterns that humans take for granted.

Employee Name	Salary
Mike	2,500
Dwight	5,000

Table 9.1: Employee Table

Tables typically encode three primary types of relationships:

- A *column-to-row* relationship refers to the association between a column and the corresponding cell value in a specific row. For example, the value in the `Employee Name` column for a given row is Mike.
- A *column-to-column* relationship captures the semantic dependency or correlation between two columns within the same row. For example, the `Salary` column indicates how much the employee named in the `Employee Name` column is paid.
- A *row-to-row* relationship refers to comparisons or patterns across different rows, often involving the same columns. For instance, the employee earning 5,000 is paid twice as much as the one earning 2,500 in another row.

In this section, we explore methods for modeling these relationships, grouped into two broad categories: (*a*) unsupervised learning techniques and (*b*) architectural modifications. While pretrained language models (PLMs) such as GPT and BERT have been exposed to tabular data during training and may exhibit some implicit understanding of these relationships, the volume of table data in their training corpora is negligible compared to natural text. As a result, additional mechanisms are often required to enhance their tabular reasoning capabilities.

Unsupervised Learning. By definition, unsupervised training is a framework where models are trained on unlabeled datasets, which are larger and much less expensive to create than manually labeled ones. A well-known example of models that utilize unsupervised learning are LLMs such as T5, BART, GPT4o. These models are trained on terabytes of text, often sourced from the internet, using *tasks* like *masked language modeling* to learn vocabulary, grammar, syntax, and semantics. Subsequently, they are fine-tuned for downstream Text-to-Text tasks, such as summarization or question answering.

In Table-to-Text, the goal now instead of just teaching the model language understanding, which is still needed due to the text generation part of the task, the model also needs to be taught the structure of a table. When using a pre-trained LLM, we typically initialize the model with its existing weights—which already encode strong language understanding—and then adapt it to tabular data using unsupervised techniques like table denoising.

Table denoising is an unsupervised pretraining task designed to teach models how to interpret and reason over tables [6]. In this approach, tokens from random cells or columns in a table are either removed or corrupted, and the model is required to reconstruct them. To make accurate predictions, the model must focus on different parts of the table, such as other values in the same row or column, as well as the overall table context, which are the main targets of table understanding.

Description perturbation [11] is a technique closely related to denoising, but instead of corrupting the table itself, it modifies the natural language description associated with the table. The model is then trained to classify table-description pairs as either faithful (accurate) or unfaithful (perturbed). This binary classification task encourages the model to develop a deeper understanding of the alignment between structured data and its textual representation. To ensure the perturbed descriptions are challenging yet informative, they must remain semantically close to the original. If the perturbations are too obvious or nonsensical, the model can easily detect them without learning meaningful reasoning skills relevant to Table-to-Text generation.

Perturbations can be generated using two approaches:

- *Knowledge-based perturbation.* This approach replaces values in the description with similar ones from other rows or columns in the table, excluding the correct value.
- *Model-based perturbation.* A teacher model is used to generate descriptions from the table. Among its outputs, the incorrect predictions with high confidence are selected as perturbations.

One aspect of the table not covered by the above techniques is numerical values. Especially in use cases that have a high amount of numerical values compared to text values the model must understand the semantics behind a number value. For instance, in generating a basketball game report from statistics, the model must differentiate the significance of the same value in different contexts. Scoring 10 points might indicate an average performance, whereas making 10 assists is impressive. Similarly, scoring 20 points is notable if no teammate scored as much, but less so if all teammates scored 20 or more.

To achieve *numerical understanding* in the DUV system [5], a separate neural network is trained for each type of value (e.g., points, assists, blocks). The core of this module is a transformer encoder that generates embedding vectors for all values of the same type within the table. During training, a fully connected neural network with a sigmoid output is added on top of the encoder. The network is trained to output a value close to 1 for statistically impressive performances and a low value for below-average ones. After training, only the encoders are retained and integrated as embedding layers for numerical values in the downstream task.

When the input table is provided as an image [1], the neural network must be trained to identify which pixels correspond to columns, values, and the dividing lines between them. For this task, a large dataset of synthetic table images is generated. The model is then trained to parse these images and convert their contents into text. This approach helps bridge the gap between models pre-trained for general image understanding and those designed specifically for table parsing.

Architecture Modification. The unsupervised techniques discussed earlier focus on guiding the model to understand tables without altering its architecture. Instead, they use tasks that encourage the model to implicitly learn table structure. A more direct approach, however, involves modifying the model's architecture, specifically the attention mechanism in the transformer, to better suit table inputs.

The core insight behind these modifications is that values within the same row or column are more likely to be semantically related, whereas values across unrelated rows and columns typically have weaker associations. However, the standard transformer architecture, originally designed for unstructured text, applies full self-attention—computing interactions between all token pairs—regardless of their structural relevance.

The attention-pruning modification [15] restricts the model's attention mechanism by removing attention edges between tokens from different columns and rows. It retains only the attention between values within the same column or row, as well as the edges connecting values to their respective column headers. While this adjustment aligns the architecture more closely with the structure of the Table-to-Text problem, it may negatively impact the performance of a model pre-trained with all attention edges intact. As a result, this approach requires a larger volume of Table-to-Text data to ensure effective fine-tuning and avoid potential performance issues.

9.1.1.3 Content Selection

In Table-to-Text tasks, not all rows and columns in a table are relevant for generating meaningful and concise descriptions. A table might include non-informative content, such as row numbers or unique identifiers, which, if included, could make the output text cluttered and harder to read. For instance, when generating a description of the next day's weather based on a table of indicators (e.g., humidity, temperature), the output should highlight only the most significant details, such as *"high chance of thunderstorms"*, rather than listing all indicators and their values. The methods described below aim to help the model prioritize the most relevant parts of the table while ignoring unnecessary data and are divided into: (*a*) attention-based ranking, (*b*) finetuning, and (*c*) input augmentation.

Attention-based Ranking. One approach for implicit content selection in neural networks leverages the attention mechanism over all table values. These methods typically pair attention modules with recurrent neural networks (RNNs), such as LSTMs, to generate text iteratively token by token. At each time step t_i, the attention module processes table encodings for all values along with the sequence of tokens generated so far. For the next time step t_{i+1}, the attention mechanism outputs a score between 0 and 1 for each table value. A score close to 1 indicates that the next token should focus on the corresponding table value, while a score near 0 means the value can be ignored.

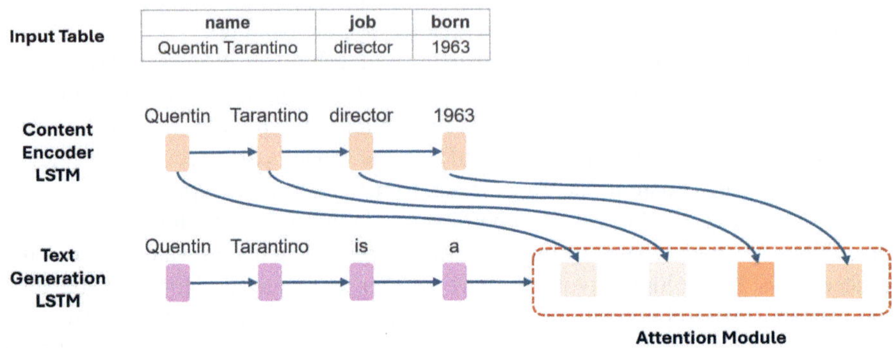

Fig. 9.4: Example of attention-based content selection for the next token prediction.

As illustrated in Figure 9.4, the model, at generation step i, has already produced the partial phrase "*Quentin Tarantino is a.*" At this point, the attention mechanism plays a crucial role in guiding the next word prediction. Specifically, the model scans the input table and assigns higher attention weights to the most relevant field—in this case, the director token—indicating that this field is likely to influence the next word. These attention weights are then passed into the LSTM decoder, which integrates this contextual signal to generate the subsequent token. Notably, when the next word to be generated is not directly tied to a specific table value, such as function words like "*is*" or "*a*", the attention distribution tends to be more uniform across the table. This balanced weighting reflects the model's reliance on general language modeling rather than specific table content for such tokens. This attention-based technique effectively prioritizes table values, significantly improving performance, especially with large tables containing more than 100 values [13].

A more advanced approach, known as dual attention [10], attends over the column names along with the table values, and then the attention between columns and values is summed up to form the final attention vector over the table.

Fine-tuning. Fine-tuning is another effective technique for addressing the content selection task. This approach involves training the model specifically to identify which table values should or should not be included in the generated description. Fine-tuning requires three key components: (*a*) Tables sourced from Table-to-Text datasets, (*b*) Annotations that label each table value as relevant (to be included in the description) or irrelevant, (*c*) a loss function, typically cross-entropy loss, which is minimized when the model correctly predicts 1 for values that appear in the description and 0 for those that do not. Annotations are automatically extracted from table descriptions using methods like those illustrated in Figure 9.5.

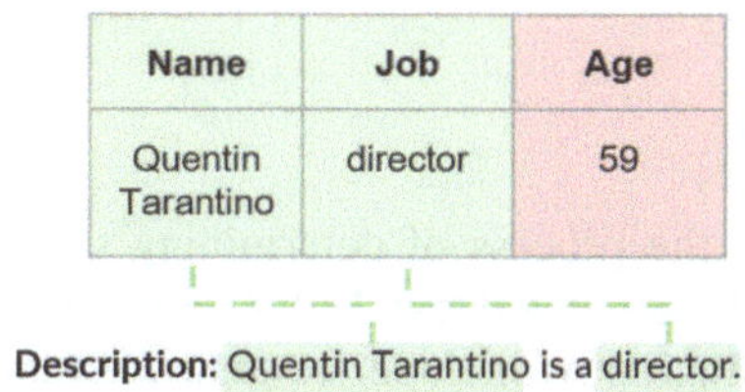

Fig. 9.5: Example of extracting which values appear in the description of a table.

This fine-tuning technique is typically applied to transformer-based architectures such as T5 and BART. A fully connected neural network followed by a sigmoid activation function is added on top of the embeddings produced by the model's encoder. The network is trained to output a score for each value, where scores closer to 1 indicate relevance and scores closer to 0 indicate irrelevance. To prevent overfitting on the content selection task, the model is trained for content selection in parallel with the primary Table-to-Text task. This joint training approach ensures the model maintains its overall performance while effectively learning to prioritize relevant table values.

Input Augmentation. In Table-to-Text tasks, the model is typically provided with the table and any accompanying metadata, such as its title. While this suffices for generating simple descriptions, it can be challenging when the task requires reasoning or deriving insights from the data. In such cases, content selection becomes more complex, as the relevant information may not be explicitly present in the table but instead requires additional logical steps to uncover.

To address this, the model's input can be augmented with the results of various operations applied to the table, such as calculating the maximum, average, or minimum values. By including these pre-computed insights, the model is explicitly presented with key information that can guide content selection and enable the generation of more meaningful descriptions.

These additional insights can be generated automatically using a template-based approach [17], formatted into logical representations. For example, the reference text *"Hale Irwin is the only player that has more than 40 wins"* is described in logic form as shown below.

```
and {
 only{filter_greater{all_rows;
Wins; 40}};
 eq{hop{filter_greater{all_rows;
Wins; 40}; Player}; Hale Irwin}
}
```

During inference, since the reference text is unavailable, templates of logic-based operations are used to generate multiple forms of these insights. This augmentation ensures the model has access to key derived information, improving its ability to select relevant content and produce insightful, human-like descriptions.

9.1.1.4 Content Planning

Content planning refers to the process of determining the optimal sequencing of selected table elements in the generated text. Unlike content selection, which focuses on identifying what information to include, content planning addresses how that information should be organized to enhance fluency, coherence, and readability. This task is crucial for improving the fluency and readability of the output, as human descriptions often follow a logical or intuitive order rather than strictly sticking to the table's structure (e.g., moving from the left-most column to the right).

Finetuning. The fine-tuning process for content planning is similar to that used for content selection. However, instead of predicting binary relevance labels (0 for non-relevant, 1 for relevant), the model is trained to predict an ordered sequence (e.g., *1, 2, 3*), as illustrated in Figure 9.6. The data for fine-tuning is extracted from reference texts in existing datasets.

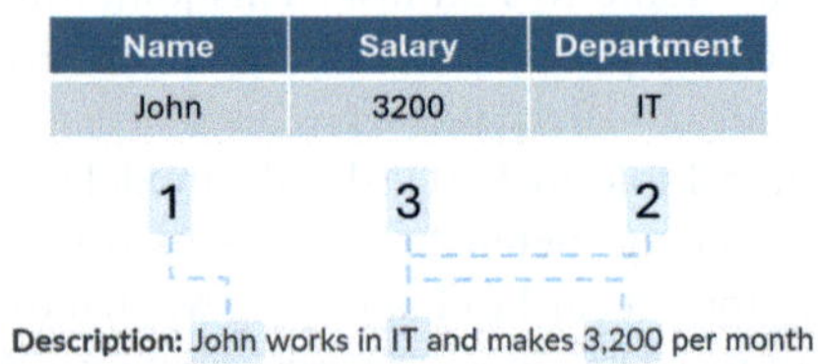

Fig. 9.6: Example of extracting the order in which values appear in a table.

Some solutions treat content selection and content planning as separate tasks, fine-tuning models for each independently. Another approach combines the two tasks into a single objective [5]. In this combined setup, the content planner is also capable of outputting a special *null* value to indicate that a column should be ignored. This combination allows the model to simultaneously decide what to include and in what order, streamlining the content generation process and ensuring better coherence in the output.

External Planner. An alternative approach to content planning is using a separate neural network dedicated to generating the optimal plan. Often, this external planner also performs content selection as part of its process. The external planner is trained independently using fine-tuning methods, as described earlier. Once trained, the generated plan is passed to the Table-to-Text model alongside the table contents, providing explicit guidance on the order in which selected elements should appear in the description.

Specifically for planning a conditional random field model (CRF) has been used which takes as input the embeddings of the table contents and finds their optimal order [14]. CRFs are particularly powerful for predicting the optimal order because they are designed to model sequential and contextual dependencies in data. This stems from their ability to make predictions based on the global context of the entire sequence, rather than making independent predictions for each element.

9.1.1.5 Guided Generation

The final stage of the Table-to-Text pipeline is generating the description. At this point, the model integrates the insights gained from earlier stages—table understanding, content selection, and content planning—to produce a fluent, coherent text. Despite these preparations, deep learning models, including large language models (LLMs), can sometimes generate "hallucinations," or fabricated information that does not correspond to the input table. The mechanisms below aim to address these challenges by grounding the generation process in the table content.

Attention and Copy Mechanism. One early solution to handle the limitations of neural networks, particularly Recurrent Neural Networks (RNNs) with attention mechanisms, was the introduction of a copy mechanism [7]. Early neural text generation models relied on a fixed vocabulary of tokens, which often excluded domain-specific or infrequent words that appeared in tables. This limitation was especially problematic when dealing with specialized terminology or rare entities, increasing the likelihood of generating errors.

The copy mechanism enables the model to directly use words from the input table, even if they are not part of its vocabulary. For each token generation step, the model determines whether to generate a word from its predefined vocabulary or copy a word directly from the input table. A neural network component predicts a "copy weight," a value between 0 and 1 that balances these two options. During the token generation process if the copy mechanism is activated (high copy weight), the model selects the word from the table that has the highest attention score at that step. If not, the model selects a word from its vocabulary.

For example, consider a table describing weather data with unique column headers like "UV Index" or "Dew Point." Without the copy mechanism, the model might skip or replace these terms with generic equivalents. With the mechanism, it can directly reference the precise terms, ensuring the description reflects the original data accurately.

Fact Verification. Fact verification is another effective method to guide text generation by ensuring the output remains grounded in the table's content. This approach relies on using verified facts that can either be extracted from text surrounding the table, such as accompanying descriptions or captions, or generated through deterministic operations directly applied to the table, like calculating maximum, minimum, or average values. These facts serve as a reference for evaluating the accuracy of the generated descriptions.

In practice, the model first generates multiple candidate descriptions for the table. Each of these candidates is then evaluated using a fact-checking model, such as TABFACT [4], which assesses the alignment of the generated text with the set of verified facts. Candidates that contradict any of these truths are filtered out, leaving only factually consistent descriptions.

This approach enhances the accuracy and reliability of the generated text by ensuring that it aligns with verified information, reducing the likelihood of hallucinations.

9.2 Table-to-Text Systems

In the previous section, we examined specific mechanisms designed to address the core challenges of Table-to-Text generation. In this section, we focus on how these mechanisms are integrated into complete end-to-end systems, highlighting how different architectures combine data representation, content selection, planning, and text generation to produce coherent and faithful descriptions from structured tables.

The following sections describe various Table-to-Text systems, organized into four main categories based on their design and methodology:

1. Content Selection & Planning Focus. These systems utilize dedicated mechanisms to identify and select the most relevant parts of the input table while omitting less important content. Additionally, they prioritize generating the description in a coherent order by planning the sequence in which the selected content is verbalized.

2. Use of Unsupervised Learning. Several systems adopt unsupervised deep learning techniques, primarily to enhance table understanding. The growth of this category has been driven by the increasing scale of models and hardware resources, enabling pretraining on large corpora of tables, such as WIKITABLET [3].

3. Specialized Architectures. Some systems move beyond the conventional pipeline of Table Representation, followed by Table Understanding, followed by Content Selection & Planning and finally, Output Generation. These systems often implement more complex pipelines or directly modify the neural components themselves to better address the unique characteristics of the Table-to-Text task.

4. Table as Images. An alternative approach involves rendering the table as an image and processing it using a visual model. In this case, the table is treated as a visual object, and Table-to-Text generation is approached as an Image-to-Text problem.

9.2.1 Content Selection & Planning Focus

The *Field-gating Seq2Seq* system [10] was introduced based on the observation that when humans write a short biography using a Wikipedia infobox, they typically first decide which fields to include and in what order (a process known as global addressing), and only then choose how to phrase or copy individual values (local addressing). To address this, the Field-gating Seq2Seq model introduces the dual attention mechanism that attends separately to row values and column names. At each timestep *t*, the input to the row value encoder is augmented with the output of the column name encoder from the previous timestep $t-1$. This allows the model to maintain alignment between row values and their associated fields. The use of two separate encoders enables a more nuanced dual attention: a word-level attention that captures intra-record detail by focusing on the content within each field, and a field-level attention that models inter-record importance across the entire table. This structure helps the decoder make more informed decisions, both in terms of which data to include and how to present it, thereby improving the overall coherence and relevance of the generated text.

The word-level and field-level attention mechanisms are subsequently aggregated to produce a unified context vector, guiding the decoder LSTM to focus on the most relevant part of the table during the prediction of the next token. This aggregated attention helps the model dynamically determine which field and corresponding value should influence the current decoding step. To handle cases where the decoder generates an unknown token (*UNK*), the following technique is employed: the *UNK* token is replaced with the input token from the table that received the highest attention weight. This strategy mitigates the out-of-vocabulary problem by allowing the model to directly copy uncommon or unseen tokens from the input table, thus improving both fluency and factual accuracy in the generated text.

NCP [13] (Neural Content Planning) diverges from the traditional encoder-decoder structure of Seq2Seq models by introducing intermediate stages dedicated to content selection and planning. This separation of stages proves especially effective when verbalizing long, information-dense tables, such as those found in sports statistics or report generation. For instance, NCP has shown strong performance in generating summaries of basketball games [16], where the input tables contain a large number of detailed and interrelated statistics. Without dedicated mechanisms for selecting and organizing content, models may struggle to maintain focus, even when the full input fits within the context window.

In the first stage, NCP encodes each record in the table and computes attention scores over them. The objective is to direct attention toward data points that are both significant and semantically coherent. The second stage involves constructing a content plan, determining the order in which the selected records should be verbalized. This is implemented using a pointer network, which at each timestep *t* selects a record to generate based on both the input table and the sequence of previously chosen records. The pointer network uses an LSTM whose hidden state is initialized with the average of the record embeddings. At each step, attention is applied over the input records in combination with the current hidden state to compute the probability distribution over candidate records, guiding the generation order in a content-aware and contextually consistent manner.

The *Plan-then-Generate* system [14] approaches Table-to-Text generation as a two-step process. In the first step, a content plan is created to determine which records from the table should be included in the output and in what order. In the second step, this plan is provided as input, along with the serialized table contents, to a language model, which generates the final textual description by following the specified plan. The generated plan, consisting of an ordered sequence of column-value pairs, is serialized as a structured string and prepended to the serialized table before being passed as input to the language model.

In the original implementation, T5 was used as the text generation model. However, it was found that T5 often struggled to consistently follow the generated plan. To address this, the model was further trained using reinforcement learning, where it was rewarded for adhering to the plan and penalized for deviating from it. This additional training helped improve the faithfulness of the generation with respect to the predefined structure, producing more coherent and controllable outputs. However, recent LLM models would not have a hard time following the plan without further training required.

9.2.2 Use of Unsupervised Learning

DUV [5] is a system designed for report generation, particularly in the context of basketball game summaries. Like NCP, it targets the verbalization of structured statistics from the ROTOWIRE dataset [16]. While DUV builds upon a similar base architecture to NCP, it introduces a key enhancement: a dedicated *value encoder* that captures the semantic significance of numerical values. This addition addresses an important limitation of prior models—namely, their inability to discern when a statistic is noteworthy based solely on end-to-end training. DUV includes a value encoder that is pretrained to estimate the importance of a record based on both its value and its type (e.g., points, assists, rebounds). This targeted training helps the model better prioritize high-impact statistics during content selection, ultimately producing more informative and relevant textual summaries.

TabT5 [2] builds upon the T5 architecture by introducing an intermediate pretraining phase designed to better adapt the model to Table-to-Text tasks. While T5 is originally trained on general text generation objectives, TabT5 narrows the domain gap by pretraining on tabular data. The source of tables used in pretraining consists of 6.2M Wikipedia tables and 2.9M Wikipedia infoboxes [8].

After this domain-adaptive pretraining, the model can be fine-tuned on specific downstream Table-to-Text tasks. This two-phase approach, starting from a general-purpose pretrained model and then specializing it for structured data, helps improve both the fluency and factual accuracy of the generated text, especially in settings where training data is limited.

9.2.3 Specialized Architectures

The *R2D2* system [11] addresses a critical challenge in Table-to-Text generation: ensuring that the generated text remains faithful to the source table. Neural models often hallucinate values or become confused by similar entries, leading to inaccurate outputs. To mitigate this, R2D2 uses the technique called *description perturbation*, which frames the task as a form of textual entailment, determining whether a given description is logically entailed by the contents of the table.

LATTICE [15] is a technique designed to adapt transformer-based models for structured data by pruning their attention mechanisms to better align with the inherent structure of tables. In addition to pruning attention edges, LATTICE modifies the model's positional embeddings. Traditional transformers encode the relative position of tokens, which is crucial in natural language but less meaningful in tabular data, where row and column orderings often do not carry semantic weight. To avoid misleading the model with irrelevant positional signals, LATTICE discards most positional embeddings, retaining only those within the same table cell, where token order may influence meaning, such as in multi-word entries.

The LATTICE technique is architecture-agnostic and can be applied to any transformer-based model, including T5, which was used as the base model in its original evaluation. The primary requirement for applying LATTICE is access to the model's architecture and weights, as the pruning of attention edges and the replacement of standard positional embeddings with structure-aware, transformation-invariant ones must be done at the architectural level. Once these modifications are applied, the model must be fine-tuned on the downstream Table-to-Text task. This is essential because the pretrained weights were optimized under the assumption of a fully connected attention mechanism. Pruning attention edges alters the information flow in the network, making it incompatible with the original pretraining setup unless additional fine-tuning is performed to adapt the model to the new, table-aware configuration.

9.2.4 Tables as Images

PixT3 [1] introduces a novel perspective on the Table-to-Text task by reframing it as an Image-to-Text problem. Traditional Text-to-Text approaches, while effective, can lose structural cues inherent to table, such as alignment, grouping, or spatial relationship, that are readily apparent to humans through their eyes. By treating the table as an image, PixT3 aims to capture this visual structure and more closely mimic how humans interpret tabular data.

The PixT3 pipeline begins by initializing the model with the pretrained weights of Pix2Struct [9], a general-purpose visual language model trained on image-text pairs. To help the model learn the visual patterns of tabular data, tables populated with random row and column values are rendered as HTML and converted into images. The model is then pretrained on these synthetic tables to learn how to parse visual layouts and infer semantic relationships across rows and columns. After this visual pretraining stage, PixT3 is fine-tuned on a standard Table-to-Text dataset, such as ToTTo, where real-world table-description pairs are available.

References

1. Iñigo Alonso, Eneko Agirre, and Mirella Lapata. Pixt3: Pixel-based table to text generation. *arXiv preprint arXiv:2311.09808*, 2023.
2. Ewa Andrejczuk, Julian Martin Eisenschlos, Francesco Piccinno, Syrine Krichene, and Yasemin Altun. Table-to-text generation and pre-training with tabt5. *arXiv preprint arXiv:2210.09162*, 2022.
3. Mingda Chen, Sam Wiseman, and Kevin Gimpel. Wikitablet: A large-scale data-to-text dataset for generating wikipedia article sections. *arXiv preprint arXiv:2012.14919*, 2020.
4. Wenhu Chen, Hongmin Wang, Jianshu Chen, Yunkai Zhang, Hong Wang, Shiyang Li, Xiyou Zhou, and William Yang Wang. Tabfact: A large-scale dataset for table-based fact verification. *arXiv preprint arXiv:1909.02164*, 2019.
5. Heng Gong, Wei Bi, Xiaocheng Feng, Bing Qin, Xiaojiang Liu, and Ting Liu. Enhancing content planning for table-to-text generation with data understanding and verification. In *Findings of the Association for Computational Linguistics: EMNLP 2020*, pages 2905–2914, 2020.
6. Heng Gong, Yawei Sun, Xiaocheng Feng, Bing Qin, Wei Bi, Xiaojiang Liu, and Ting Liu. TableGPT: Few-shot table-to-text generation with table structure reconstruction and content matching. In *Proceedings of the 28th International Conference on Computational Linguistics*, pages 1978–1988, Barcelona, Spain (Online), December 2020. International Committee on Computational Linguistics.
7. Jiatao Gu, Zhengdong Lu, Hang Li, and Victor OK Li. Incorporating copying mechanism in sequence-to-sequence learning. *arXiv preprint arXiv:1603.06393*, 2016.
8. Jonathan Herzig, Pawel Krzysztof Nowak, Thomas Müller, Francesco Piccinno, and Julian Eisenschlos. TaPas: Weakly supervised table parsing via pre-training. In Dan Jurafsky, Joyce Chai, Natalie Schluter, and Joel Tetreault, editors, *Proceedings of the 58th Annual Meeting of the Association for Computational Linguistics*, pages 4320–4333, Online, July 2020. Association for Computational Linguistics.
9. Kenton Lee, Mandar Joshi, Iulia Raluca Turc, Hexiang Hu, Fangyu Liu, Julian Martin Eisenschlos, Urvashi Khandelwal, Peter Shaw, Ming-Wei Chang, and Kristina Toutanova. Pix2struct: Screenshot parsing as pretraining for visual language understanding. In *International Conference on Machine Learning*, pages 18893–18912. PMLR, 2023.
10. Tianyu Liu, Kexiang Wang, Lei Sha, Baobao Chang, and Zhifang Sui. Table-to-text generation by structure-aware seq2seq learning. In *Thirty-Second AAAI Conference on Artificial Intelligence*, 2018.
11. Linyong Nan, Lorenzo Jaime Yu Flores, Yilun Zhao, Yixin Liu, Luke Benson, Weijin Zou, and Dragomir Radev. R2d2: Robust data-to-text with replacement detection. *arXiv preprint arXiv:2205.12467*, 2022.
12. Ankur P. Parikh, Xuezhi Wang, Sebastian Gehrmann, Manaal Faruqui, Bhuwan Dhingra, Diyi Yang, and Dipanjan Das. Totto: A controlled table-to-text generation dataset. *CoRR*, abs/2004.14373, 2020.
13. Ratish Puduppully, Li Dong, and Mirella Lapata. Data-to-text generation with content selection and planning. *CoRR*, abs/1809.00582, 2018.
14. Yixuan Su, David Vandyke, Sihui Wang, Yimai Fang, and Nigel Collier. Plan-then-generate: Controlled data-to-text generation via planning. *arXiv preprint arXiv:2108.13740*, 2021.
15. Fei Wang, Zhewei Xu, Pedro Szekely, and Muhao Chen. Robust (controlled) table-to-text generation with structure-aware equivariance learning. *arXiv preprint arXiv:2205.03972*, 2022.

16. Sam Wiseman, Stuart M Shieber, and Alexander M Rush. Challenges in data-to-document generation. *arXiv preprint arXiv:1707.08052*, 2017.
17. Yilun Zhao, Zhenting Qi, Linyong Nan, Lorenzo Jaime Yu Flores, and Dragomir Radev. Loft: enhancing faithfulness and diversity for table-to-text generation via logic form control. *arXiv preprint arXiv:2302.02962*, 2023.

Chapter 10
The Results-to-Text Problem and Systems

Abstract (Query) Results-to-Text focuses on turning query results into natural language. When users engage with a database using a natural language interface, they expect a seamless text-based interaction, including how results are presented. In this chapter, we'll dive into the hurdles of Results-to-Text, drawing parallels and distinctions with other Data-to-Text areas, particularly Table-to-Text. We'll also showcase current solutions and highlight research opportunities in this largely unexplored domain.

10.1 Introduction

Results-to-Text is the task of converting the structured results of a database query, typically presented in tabular format, into natural language descriptions. The motivation for this task parallels the objectives of Data-to-Text, addressing scenarios where users may lack the expertise to interpret raw tabular data or where the sheer volume of rows in the results makes quick comprehension difficult. This challenge is especially prevalent in Results-to-Text, where result tables are often significantly larger than those encountered in domains like Wikipedia. By translating query results into descriptive text, Results-to-Text aims to streamline data interpretation, helping users analyze and derive insights more efficiently.

Consider a relational database of publications of various domains containing their metadata and abstracts. A user leverages the natural language interface on top of the database and asks the question "Bring me a list of papers along with their abstracts on text summarization published in the last 3 years". Text-to-SQL generates the appropriate query and retrieves a list of papers along with their abstracts. Now, gaining insights into the contents of the papers would require the user to sequentially read each one of the abstracts, a time-consuming process. Instead, a Results-to-Text model would return a summary of the abstracts focusing on the most important parts and letting the user quickly pick which papers should look into more detail.

G. Katsogiannis-Meimarakis et al., *Natural Language Interfaces for Databases with Deep Learning*, Data-Centric Systems and Applications,
https://doi.org/10.1007/978-3-032-06905-4_10

Figure 10.1 depicts a user asking a database of companies some analytical questions in natural language and getting back an answer. Without Results-to-Text the system displays a raw table containing the results of the query. In this example, the table shows averages and a count but lacks context or explanation, requiring the user to interpret the values manually. With Results-to-Text the system generates a natural language summary of the same query results, translating the table into a coherent sentence. This approach provides a more user-friendly and accessible way to understand the data, especially for non-technical users who may find raw tables challenging to interpret.

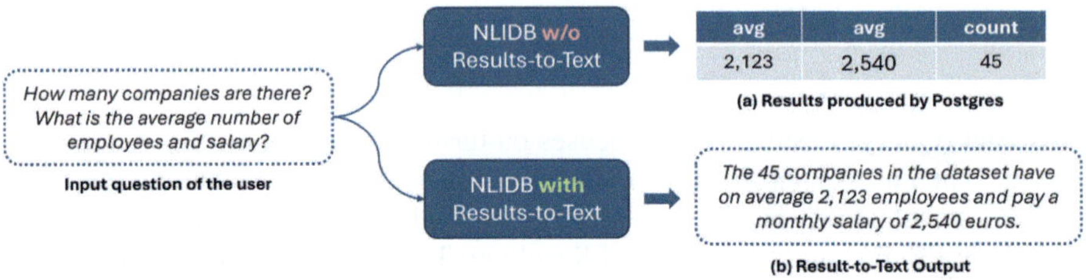

Fig. 10.1: An example of a user asking a question about a dataset of companies and retrieving back the results as a table (a) and in text (b).

This chapter uses query results obtained from relational databases as running examples. However, the challenges remain fairly similar across other types of databases such as document stores or graph databases, and alternative result formats like JSON or XML.

10.2 Challenges

Given that query results are also structured in a tabular format, there are some common challenges with the Table-to-Text problem. Despite their similarities however, Results-to-Text poses distinct challenges that set it apart from traditional Table-to-Text tasks. These challenges, discussed in detail below, highlight the complexities of transforming structured query results into meaningful, context-aware natural language descriptions tailored to user intent and database context.

Incorporating Database Context. Unlike standalone data tables such as those found on Wikipedia, result tables in Results-to-Text are deeply tied to their database context. The columns and rows of a result table often lack sufficient information to provide a meaningful natural language description without additional context from the database schema or other data not present in the result.

For instance, consider a result table with a column labeled "title" containing the value "*The Wizard of Oz*". Without further context, it is ambiguous whether the table refers to books, movies, or another domain. The verbalizations "*A book titled The*

Wizard of Oz" and "*A movie titled The Wizard of Oz*" are both plausible. However, if the database schema explicitly identifies the table as belonging to a "books" database, the Results-to-Text model can confidently generate the correct description.

Similarly, a table containing a column labeled "Grade" with a value of 3.9 could imply different things depending on the dataset. Is 3.9 a high grade, indicating strong performance, or is it below average? The answer depends on the broader dataset context, such as the distribution of grades among other students. While these examples are relatively straightforward, the importance of database context becomes even more apparent as the database grows in size and complexity.

Understanding and incorporating this database context is essential to generating accurate, coherent, and contextually appropriate natural language descriptions. This remains a core challenge in Results-to-Text, requiring sophisticated modeling approaches that can effectively integrate schema-level information and dataset-wide patterns.

Incorporating User Intent. In the Results-to-Text task, the generated description must address the specific query posed by the user, whether it was expressed in SQL or natural language which was then translated into SQL. This requirement distinguishes Results-to-Text from traditional Table-to-Text, where the goal is typically a general translation of the table's contents. In Results-to-Text, the verbalization must not only be accurate but also directly aligned with the user's intent, ensuring the output provides a clear and relevant answer to the query.

Extracting and incorporating user intent introduces new challenges that demand novel solutions and architectures. However, this focus on intent also mitigates a key issue in Data-to-Text tasks: the ambiguity of multiple valid descriptions. In traditional Table-to-Text, evaluating the generated text can be difficult because there may be many equally correct outputs depending on which parts of the table are emphasized. By contrast, Results-to-Text benefits from the clear objective defined by the user query, simplifying evaluation by narrowing the scope of valid descriptions.

For example, consider a table containing numerous meteorological indicators, such as temperature, humidity, and precipitation. Without user intent, a Table-to-Text model might either describe the indicators it deems most interesting —an inherently subjective choice— or attempt to cover all of them, resulting in long and potentially unhelpful descriptions. However, if the user's query is known e.g., "How hot will it be tomorrow and will it rain?" the model can focus exclusively on the relevant indicators: temperature and precipitation.

The Many Rows Problem. While incorporating user intent helps narrow the focus to specific columns of query results, the challenge of handling multiple rows remains significant. A naive approach might involve processing each row individually through the Results-to-Text model and concatenating the resulting descriptions. However, this method is impractical for several reasons. First, generating a lengthy, text-heavy output is unlikely to be helpful, as users would often prefer even a small number of rows (e.g., three) to remain in a table format. Second, treating each row independently misses opportunities to derive meaningful insights across rows, which could provide a more valuable summary of the data.

Adaptation to User Expertise. Adapting to user epxertise is a crucial aspect of Results-to-Text, as it allows for tailoring natural language descriptions to match the user's familiarity with the domain. While an SQL query always returns the same result table regardless of who executes it, the flexibility of natural language descriptions enables a more user-centered approach. This adaptability is essential for ensuring that the descriptions are both accessible to novices and sufficiently detailed for experts.

For instance, consider a query about weather data that returns a field like *"Barometric pressure"*. For an expert in meteorology, the generated description could be something like, *"The barometric pressure is 29.27 inHg"* as this technical term is meaningful to them. Conversely, a novice user with no specialized knowledge would benefit more from a simplified interpretation, such as, *"Expect clear skies and low winds"* derived from the same data point.

10.3 Steps Towards a Solution

Results-to-Text remains a relatively underexplored task, presenting significant opportunities for future research to address the challenges outlined above. This section proposes potential research directions that could guide the development of novel solutions. While these approaches have not yet been extensively examined or defined in detail, they serve as recommendations for areas where future work could focus in advancing the state of Results-to-Text systems.

10.3.1 Incorporating Database Context

To effectively leverage LLMs for verbalizing query results, preprocessing plays a crucial role in optimizing the input fed into the model. The first step involves processing the SQL query itself. While SQL queries return results in a tabular format, these tables often lack important contextual information that could enhance the quality of the generated text. Given that LLMs are pretrained with text and for natural language generation, it is beneficial to ensure that both column names and table contents are as interpretable and natural as possible.

Figure 10.3 illustrates key preprocessing techniques applied to SQL queries before generating natural language descriptions. Each technique addresses common challenges in database querying and improves the interpretability of results:

JOIN Aliasing, which ensures that column names in the result table remain unambiguous. Without aliasing, a query that retrieves both employee and manager ages could return two columns simply labeled "age," forcing the model to infer which value belongs to whom. By explicitly incorporating table names into column headers (e.g., "employee_age" and "manager_age"), the model can more accurately associate values with their respective entities.

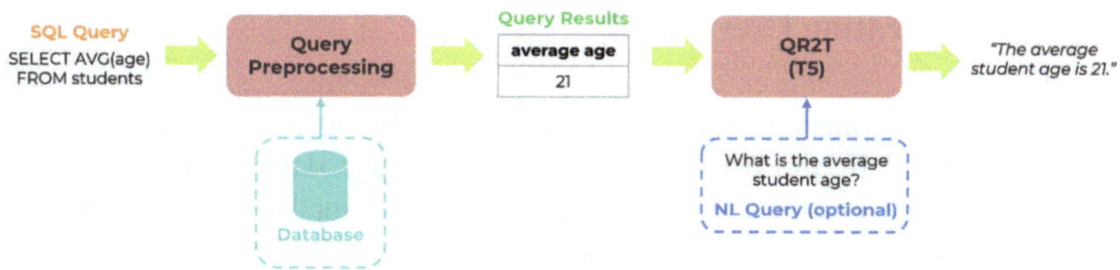

Fig. 10.2: A Results-to-Text pipeline that first preprocesses the executed query and during the generation by the LLM the NL Query is also incorporated if it exists.

SQL Verbalization, which replaces SQL-specific notation with its natural language equivalent based on predefined mapping rules. This step enhances the readability of query results and aligns them more closely with the training data of LLMs. Verbalization is particularly useful when working with smaller models with less than 10B parameters [1], where reducing appearances of complex database syntax can improve output quality. Examples of such mappings can be seen in Figure 10.3(b).

Finally, SELECT Injections help improve verbalization quality by enriching query results with additional contextual information. By default, SQL queries only return the columns explicitly requested by the user. However, incorporating extra attributes such as WHERE clause attributes can provide the LLM with a richer understanding of the retrieved data, leading to more informative and context-aware descriptions.

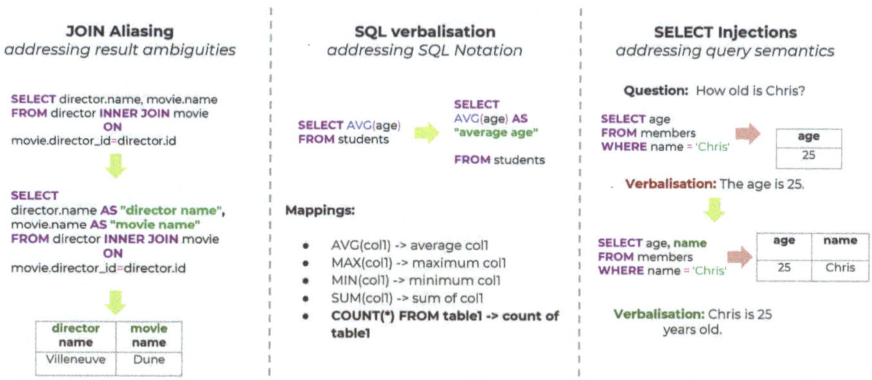

Fig. 10.3: Preprocessing steps applied to the query.

10.3.2 Incorporating User Intent

A verbalization of query results should not be too broad and adapt to what the questions is asked by the user. One idea is to leverage data provenance, which captures how data is derived within a query [2]. The methodology begins with provenance tracking that aligns with natural language queries. When the query is executed, provenance data is collected at the value level, ensuring fine-grained tracking of how specific data points contribute to the result. Rather than relying on traditional tuple-based provenance, which records only the source tuples involved in a query result, the system adopts a value-based model that preserves the exact values assigned to each query variable. This model allows the provenance to be translated more precisely into a natural language explanation. This value-based tracking can be seen in the orange boxes in Figure 10.4(b).

Once provenance is tracked, the next step is its transformation into natural language. A query tree is first generated from the original natural language query, providing a structured representation of its grammatical composition, obtained by its Part-of-Speech tags (Figure 10.4(b)). Afterward, the query tree is brought closer to natural language by generating the answer tree Figure 10.4(c). The answer tree is then used to guide the construction of an explanation that maintains the sentence structure of the input query.

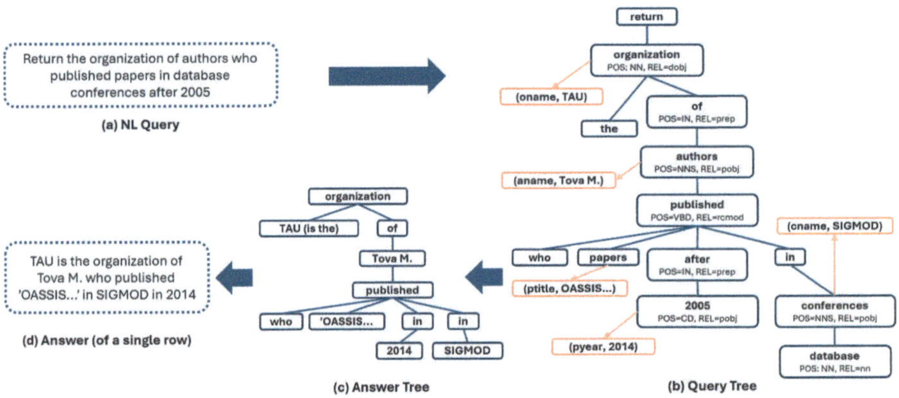

Fig. 10.4: The intermediate tree-based representations that combine both the part of speech analysis and provenance values.

10.3.3 The Many Rows Problem

This challenge underlines the need for result summarization techniques tailored to large query outputs. These techniques aim to prioritize the most interesting or relevant rows and, when appropriate, perform aggregations to distill the data into a concise and informative summary. The objective is not to exhaustively describe every detail in the result table but to highlight key insights that guide the user toward deeper exploration, enabling further queries or drilling down into the original table for additional context. By focusing on summarization, Results-to-Text systems can provide users with actionable and digestible information, even when dealing with extensive query results.

One other idea is to deterministically factorize the generated output reducing its length. This method groups the same values together, reducing repetition while maintaining completeness. Unlike conventional algebraic factorization, which optimizes for minimal expression size, this approach is constrained by the structural relationships in the original query, ensuring that explanations follow a natural order that reflects how users originally formulated their queries. The possible factorizations are greedily discovered by traversing the query tree in BFS order, keeping the factorization that has the minimum length without altering the order of entities in the user query. An example of factorization can be seen in Figure 10.5(b).

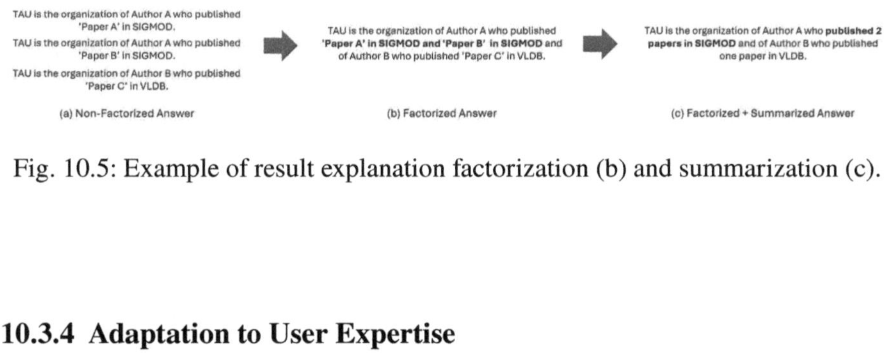

Fig. 10.5: Example of result explanation factorization (b) and summarization (c).

10.3.4 Adaptation to User Expertise

To address this challenge, it is first necessary to assess the expertise of the user. This step is particularly critical in Results-to-Text, as it operates within domain-specific databases where understanding the data often requires specialized knowledge. Estimating user expertise can be approached in several ways:

- **Explicitly Asking the User.** The system could include an initial setup step where users are asked about their familiarity with the domain.
- **Assuming a Default Expertise Level.** For instance, the system might assume that only meteorology professionals access a weather database, defaulting to expert-level descriptions unless otherwise specified.
- **Inferring Expertise from User Queries.** The language and specificity of the user's query can provide clues. For example, a novice might ask, *"Will it rain*

today?" while an expert might pose a more detailed question like, *"What are the humidity and dew point values?"*

By combining these methods, Results-to-Text systems can dynamically adjust their output to align with the user's knowledge level, making the descriptions both relevant and comprehensible. This user-centric approach enhances accessibility and usability, distinguishing Results-to-Text from more generic Data-to-Text solutions.

10.4 Conclusion

Despite significant advancements in the general field of Data-to-Text, Results-to-Text remains underexplored. The lack of a standardized methodology for integrating database context, user intent, and user expertise into a coherent text output highlights the need for further research in this area. Developing robust Results-to-Text frameworks is crucial for enhancing database accessibility, particularly for non-expert users who rely on natural language explanations to interpret complex query results.

Also, Results-to-Text should not be considered as an *always on* feature of NLIDBs that is called on every user query. While text can provide valuable insights and make query results more accessible, it is not always the optimal format for presenting tabular data. In some situations, and for certain users, the table itself may remain the most effective representation, especially for those accustomed to interpreting specific tables regularly. Results-to-Text should be viewed as a complementary tool rather than a replacement, facilitating database accessibility for users with varying levels of expertise, much like Text-to-SQL or SQL-to-Text.

References

1. Abdelrahman Abouelenin, Atabak Ashfaq, Adam Atkinson, Hany Awadalla, Nguyen Bach, Jianmin Bao, Alon Benhaim, Martin Cai, Vishrav Chaudhary, Congcong Chen, et al. Phi-4-mini technical report: Compact yet powerful multimodal language models via mixture-of-loras. *arXiv preprint arXiv:2503.01743*, 2025.
2. Jonathan Berant, Daniel Deutch, Amir Globerson, Tova Milo, and Tomer Wolfson. Explaining queries over web tables to non-experts. In *2019 IEEE 35th International Conference on Data Engineering (ICDE)*, pages 1570–1573. IEEE, 2019.

Chapter 11
Conclusions

Abstract Throughout this book, we have explored the main components of Natural Language Interface to Databases (NLIDB) systems, namely Text-to-SQL, SQL-to-Text, and Results-to-Text, examining each in isolation. In this final chapter, we discuss the challenges involved in combining these components into a unified system. Additionally, we highlight important challenges that arise when such systems are deployed in real-world scenarios. Finally, we outline additional research areas, whose incorporation could further enhance the functionality and impact of NLIDB systems.

11.1 Building a NLIDB

Building a NLIDB that enables non-technical users to access relational data, requires three fundamental properties: (a) the ability for users to interact with the system using natural language, (b) the system's ability to communicate its actions, and (c) a comprehensive representation of the query results.

Throughout this book, we have explored how these three properties can be addressed through specific tasks. First, we examined the task of Text-to-SQL, the foundational component of a NLIDB that enables user interaction by allowing users to express their information needs in natural language. Next, we discussed SQL-to-Text, which contributes to feedback communication by enabling systems to verbalize the logic of the generated queries, thereby enhancing user trust and interpretability. Finally, we studied Results-to-Text, a key task for supporting result presentation, by helping users understand the query results through natural language.

In this final chapter, we briefly discuss the challenges towards building a fully operational NLIDB and its deployment in real-world scenarios. Additionally, we touch upon auxiliary capabilities that can further enhance the usability and value of such systems.

G. Katsogiannis-Meimarakis et al., *Natural Language Interfaces for Databases with Deep Learning*, Data-Centric Systems and Applications,
https://doi.org/10.1007/978-3-032-06905-4_11

11.2 Challenges toward a unified solution

A complete NLIDB can be constructed by selecting the best-performing systems for each of the core tasks. The challenge that arises is how to orchestrate communications between these components, establish their connection to the underlying database, and deploy them in a manner that satisfies performance and resource constraints.

Integrating these components into a single system introduces several practical challenges that must be addressed to evaluate the feasibility and applicability of the solution in real-world scenarios.

Evaluation of NLIDBs. While each component of an NLIDB has established separate evaluation frameworks and metrics, these component-wise evaluations do not directly reflect the overall performance of a full NLIDB. In a pipeline setting, an error in any single component can propagate through the system, ultimately rendering the entire user interaction unsuccessful. For instance, a highly accurate Text-to-SQL model may generate a correct query, but if the SQL-to-Text component produces misleading or incorrect explanations, the user may lose trust in the results and misinterpret the output. Similarly, a faithful Data-to-Text component cannot compensate for an incorrect query interpretation.

Therefore, for an NLIDB interaction to be considered successful, all three components must operate correctly and coherently. This dependence underscores the need for holistic evaluation approaches that assess the system as a whole. Currently, the lack of unified benchmarks, where each component is typically evaluated on separate datasets using task-specific metrics, makes it difficult to estimate how well a system will perform in an end-to-end NLIDB setting. Developing standardized, integrated benchmarks specifically designed for evaluating complete NLIDB pipelines is essential for measuring real-world performance and enabling fair comparisons between systems.

Intuitive UI/UX Design. A critical factor in the success of an NLIDB is the design of its user interface. Even the most accurate and advanced underlying systems may fail to deliver value if the user interface is unintuitive, cluttered, or difficult to navigate. An overly complex UI can hinder user engagement and lead to frustration, ultimately discouraging users from relying on the system, regardless of the correctness of the results it produces.

In recent years, non-technical users have become increasingly familiar with chat-based AI assistants, which offer a natural and accessible mode of interaction. The design principles employed in these systems—such as minimalism, conversational flow, and feedback, serve as a strong foundation for NLIDB interfaces as well. Adopting such user-centric design can significantly enhance usability and increase user trust.

11.3 Challenges toward real-world deployment

Deploying a NLIDB in real-world scenarios introduces a range of concerns that are often overlooked in research systems. While traditional metrics, such as accuracy, remain essential, they alone are insufficient to guarantee the system's readiness for real-world adoption. In practical applications, NLIDBs must not only deliver correct answers but, among others, remain cost effective, have low latency, ensure compliance with legal and ethical standards, maintain data security and privacy, and provide mechanisms to assess the trustworthiness of generated responses. In this section, we briefly examine key factors that are critical for increasing the usability NLIDBs in real-world scenarios.

11.3.1 Latency & Cost

We consider the combination of the three main tasks discussed in this book, Text-to-SQL, SQL-to-Text and Results-to-Text, shown in Figure 11.1, as our running example of a NLIDB to discuss the challenges regarding latency and cost.

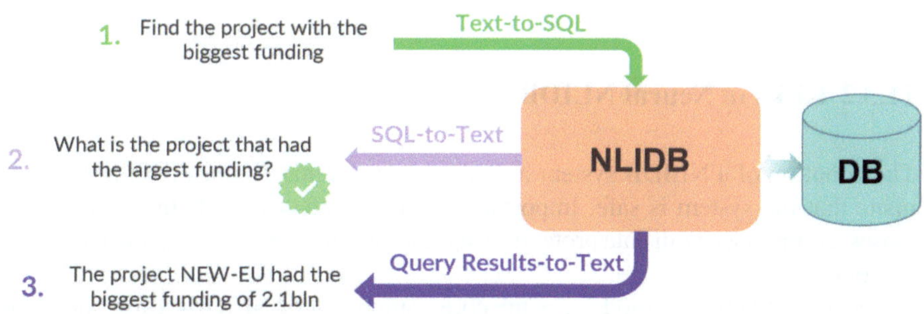

Fig. 11.1: Example pipeline of a Natural Language Interface of Databases.

Each of the three components—Text-to-SQL, SQL-to-Text, and Results-to-Text—is powered by deep learning models, often large language models, which require significant computational resources. From a usability perspective, users may be discouraged if the interface introduces significant delays. Similarly, stakeholders may hesitate to adopt such solutions if the benefits are marginal relative to their computational expense. To address these concerns, optimization techniques are not just desirable, but essential for any complete NLIDB solution. These optimizations span the entire NLIDB pipeline.

For instance, it is common for Text-to-SQL systems to focus on query correctness, often overlooking the efficiency of the generated SQL queries. In some cases a Text-to-SQL system might generate inefficient or redundant JOIN clauses that lead to a correct result but take longer to execute. Unfortunately, very few works on Text-to-SQL take this into account. Since inefficient queries can introduce significant delays in execution time, and thus the user waiting time, it should be considered equally important to accuracy.

Additionally, there are many scenarios where user queries are not answerable, for example in case of ambiguities in the NLQ or irrelevance with the underlying database. Proceeding with SQL execution, or other tasks (e.g., Results-to-Text), in such cases is a waste of resources and time. Those cases should be minimized, either through interactive mechanisms (see Section 6.2) or answerability estimation mechanisms (more in Section 11.3.3), to prevent unnecessary executions in the pipeline.

Furthermore, it is important that the value of the execution of each component in the NLIDB is carefully assessed before usage. For example, there are many cases for which a table representation may be the ideal representation of the results. In such cases, the component of Results-to-Text should not be executed as it will introduce unnecessary computational costs.

Lastly, caching mechanisms play a critical role in practical NLIDB deployments. Users frequently pose variations of similar queries, particularly in domain-specific applications. Caching intermediate outputs, such as parsed SQL queries or generated descriptions, can significantly reduce both latency and computational overhead, enabling faster and more cost-effective interactions.

11.3.2 Risks in Neural NLIDBs

The adoption of a NLIDB system in real use-case scenarios must have as a prerequisite that the system is safe. Important factors of safety include the mitigation of biases, compliance with data protection regulations, and robustness against malicious exploitation.

The use of language models, as the core component of NLIDBs, raise significant concerns regarding the introduced biases and stereotypes, that exist in these models [10, 19, 20]. These issues can be carried in the context of NLIDBs [17], posing significant risks, especially in cases where these systems are used as decision-making tools that can impact individuals or whole communities.

Another important aspect is the robustness against data leakage, where users may unintendedly or maliciously gain access to information they are not authorized to see, such as sensitive data or the database schema. Several works identified vulnerabilities in Text-to-SQL models that allow data leakage [14, 28]. This highlights the importance of mechanisms to prevent data leakages in scenarios where restricted access to data must be applied.

Beyond data leakage, systems must be resilient to any kind of malicious usage. It has been shown [22, 23, 31] that systems can be manipulated through prompting to create SQL injection attacks that can compromise the database, making clear the need for strict control over the executable operations.

All of these issues require extensive focus and further work needs to be done if we want to create a NLIDB that can assist the users and enhance data accessibility rather than introducing additional barriers or exploitation of existing data.

11.3.3 Question Answerability and System Reliability

Even though NLIDB systems are continuously evolving and their range of supported questions expands accordingly, there will always be questions that the system can not answer. Consider the scenario where the user asks for information that is not related to the underlying database or ambiguous questions that can have multiple interpretations. This is a common issue, given that the goal of these systems is to enable data accessibility for non-technical users, who may not fully understand the type of questions that such systems can answer.

In this context, several benchmarks [2, 8, 25, 30, 32] have been created, that define taxonomies of unanswerable questions, each with different levels of granularity. Across these works, the primary sources of unanswerability fall into three broad categories: (1) *Ambiguity*, where the NLQ is unclear or can be interpreted in multiple ways, (2) *Incompatibility with the DB*, where the underlying data or data model are not sufficient to answer the NLQ, and (3) *External knowledge dependency*, where an external source of data is necessary in order to answer the NLQ. However, the definition and categorization of unanswerable questions vary across the literature. For example, PRACTIQ [8] and NoisySP [30] include the category of questions that reference to non-existent columns, while TriageSQL [32] defines ambiguous questions that can contain all kinds of ambiguity.

Given an unanswerable question, the system should be able to identify it and respond appropriately. However, achieving this behavior is challenging due to the widespread use of LLMs as core components of NLIDBs. This is because their design and training objectives, in many cases, steer these models to always try to provide "satisfactory" responses and generate an answer even when the question is unanswerable. To address this issue, various strategies have been proposed. One approach is to create detectors that will be able to identify unanswerable questions [15, 30, 32]. Another line of work uses methods for uncertainty estimation, such as considering the output probabilities of the model [15] or internal signals from the model that indicate errors [6]. These methods aim to detect all types of errors, including those due to unanswerable questions. Finally, there are efforts that focus solely in ambiguity and try to deal with these questions by producing all the possible interpretations [2, 25]. However, this approach is limited to certain types of ambiguity. For example, the question "Give me the papers with many citations" has a large set of plausible interpretations, making exhaustive enumeration both difficult and unhelpful.

In summary, the ability to recognize and handle unanswerable questions is a critical requirement for reliable NLIDBs and a necessary step toward their real-world adoption. Building user confidence that the answers they get are what they actually asked for is essential and, in this case, it is also essential to inform them that it is not possible to provide these answers.

11.4 Auxiliary capabilities

While the core goal of a Natural Language Interface to Database (NLIDB) is to enable non-technical users to pose analytical questions using natural language, real-world use cases may require additional functionalities. Users may wish not only to retrieve specific answers, but also to explore the data more freely or perform advanced analytical tasks. To accommodate these broader user needs, modern NLIDB systems must be equipped with auxiliary capabilities, that can further help in utilizing the vast amount of data existing nowadays. In this section, we explore possible directions that can enhance the utility of NLIDBs.

11.4.1 Beyond SQL Capabilities

The built-in functionalities of the SQL language support a wide range of questions. However, as progress in the field of NLIDBs continues, there is a growing research interest on how to extend the expressive capabilities of these systems beyond what standard SQL supports. Consider, for example, the question: "Find the restaurants with the best reviews", posed over a database containing information about restaurants, such as names, locations, and review texts. This query requires the semantic analysis of the reviews' texts, a task that cannot be expressed directly using plain SQL. Similarly, we can think of several scenarios requiring tasks such as text summarization or other data analysis tasks that go beyond SQL's native capabilities.

To address these limitations, several systems [16, 21] have introduced additional operators designed to handle these additional tasks. Although these systems do not focus on enabling natural language interfaces, their advancements offer the foundations upon which NLIDBs can be extended to support a broader range of query types. Additionally, there are systems [3, 11] that start directly from the natural language question with the goal of supporting such advanced tasks.

Although significant work remains to be done, this is an important direction towards the evolution of NLIDBs, as it can substantially expand their applicability and make them more useful in complex, real-world data interaction scenarios.

11.4.2 Incorporating data exploration techniques

Data exploration can address the needs of users who may not know exactly what they are looking for [12]. While NLIDBs are designed to allow users to pose analytical queries in natural language, their value could significantly increase with the incorporation of established data exploration techniques. This section outlines example of data exploration domains that, when incorporated into NLIDBs, can improve usability and engagement.

Query Recommendations. In many scenarios, users may lack specific questions, familiarity with the underlying database, or may not know how to precisely express their information needs. Query recommendations systems can assist the user in crafting or refining queries, making it easier to uncover relevant or insightful parts of the data. There are several systems that can support guiding users toward interesting or previously underexplored areas of the data [5, 9], help interpret partial intents to suggest meaningful completions or transformations [4, 7], or provide suggestions based on user query logs [26, 27].

Entity Recommendations. Recommendation systems are used in a wide range of applications, from e-commerce and streaming platforms to personalized healthcare and educational technologies with an established scientific community and research outputs [1, 24]. The core motivation behind recommendation systems is to assist users in discovering items of interest from large and often overwhelming information spaces. All the entities in a database (e.g., authors, datasets, publications, movies) could be considered as possible recommendation items. This way entities can be recommended based on their similarity to other entities, their usage from users, or any other type of recommendation paradigm. This way users can discover more data that is useful to them, enhancing the utility of a NLIDB system.

Data Visualization. Visualization techniques are the de facto standard for modern business intelligence and data analysis, providing an overview of massive datasets and helping users interpret the results of data analytics [29]. The incorporation of existing approaches of data visualization [13, 18] could be extremely beneficial, especially for non-technical users, as it can offer a more intuitive understanding of data than raw tables or textual summaries.

Overall, incorporating additional functionalities in NLIDBs can help in creating more powerful and holistic systems that can facilitate several user needs and bring us closer to unlock the full value of the data stored in relational databases.

11.5 Closing Remarks

Throughout this book we discussed problems that have been challenging researchers for many decades. Yet still, the quest for database accessibility continues with an ever-increasing interest and a new set of tools to help carve the way. NLIDBs are undoubtedly seeing a new wave of progress, fueled by the rapid advancements in Deep Learning and NLP, with new systems and methods appearing one after the other. However, it becomes evident that focusing on separate tasks and measuring progress by a few specific benchmarks can often impede the overall goal.

In fact, although remarkable progress has been made into each of the problems we studied, a lot of open questions still remain on building complete NLIDBS. While there is no sure way to achieve this goal, current challenges hint that adopting more holistic evaluation and system design practices can serve as a good starting point. Following industry efforts to provide NLIDBS over already existing DB management products, researchers should also approach this problem as a complete solution rather than specific subproblems.

To conclude, half a century after the introduction of NLIDBS, a lot of challenges and opportunities for research remain open. Despite the surge of work that we observe, it is evident that this area will continue to be a point of high interest. After all, in the age of information, where data rules all human activity, the access to it should not be reserved for the few and the experts.

And so the never-ending quest for data accessibility continues.

References

1. Charu C Aggarwal et al. *Recommender systems*, volume 1. Springer, 2016.
2. Adithya Bhaskar, Tushar Tomar, Ashutosh Sathe, and Sunita Sarawagi. Benchmarking and improving text-to-SQL generation under ambiguity. In Houda Bouamor, Juan Pino, and Kalika Bali, editors, *Proceedings of the 2023 Conference on Empirical Methods in Natural Language Processing*, pages 7053–7074, Singapore, December 2023. Association for Computational Linguistics.
3. Asim Biswal, Liana Patel, Siddarth Jha, Amog Kamsetty, Shu Liu, Joseph E. Gonzalez, Carlos Guestrin, and Matei Zaharia. Text2sql is not enough: Unifying ai and databases with tag. *ArXiv*, abs/2408.14717, 2024.
4. Angela Bonifati, Radu Ciucanu, and Slawomir Staworko. Interactive inference of join queries. In *Gestion de Données-Principes, Technologies et Applications (BDA)*, 2014.
5. Gloria Chatzopoulou, Magdalini Eirinaki, and Neoklis Polyzotis. Query recommendations for interactive database exploration. In Marianne Winslett, editor, *Scientific and Statistical Database Management, 21st International Conference, SSDBM 2009, New Orleans, LA, USA, June 2-4, 2009, Proceedings*, volume 5566 of *Lecture Notes in Computer Science*, pages 3–18. Springer, 2009.
6. Kaiwen Chen, Yueting Chen, Nick Koudas, and Xiaohui Yu. Reliable text-to-sql with adaptive abstention. *Proceedings of the ACM on Management of Data*, 3(1):1–30, 2025.
7. Kyriaki Dimitriadou, Olga Papaemmanouil, and Yanlei Diao. Explore-by-example: An automatic query steering framework for interactive data exploration. In *Proceedings of the 2014 ACM SIGMOD international conference on Management of data*, pages 517–528, 2014.
8. Mingwen Dong, Nischal Ashok Kumar, Yiqun Hu, Anuj Chauhan, Chung-Wei Hang, Shuaichen Chang, Lin Pan, Wuwei Lan, Henghui Zhu, Jiarong Jiang, Patrick Ng, and Zhiguo Wang. PRACTIQ: A practical conversational text-to-sql dataset with ambiguous and unanswerable queries. *CoRR*, abs/2410.11076, 2024.
9. Marina Drosou and Evaggelia Pitoura. Ymaldb: exploring relational databases via result-driven recommendations. *VLDB J.*, 22(6):849–874, 2013.
10. Shangbin Feng, Chan Young Park, Yuhan Liu, and Yulia Tsvetkov. From pretraining data to language models to downstream tasks: Tracking the trails of political biases leading to unfair NLP models. In Anna Rogers, Jordan Boyd-Graber, and Naoaki Okazaki, editors, *Proceedings of the 61st Annual Meeting of the Association for Computational Linguistics (Volume 1: Long Papers)*, pages 11737–11762, Toronto, Canada, July 2023. Association for Computational Linguistics.
11. Parker Glenn, Parag Dakle, Liang Wang, and Preethi Raghavan. BlendSQL: A scalable dialect for unifying hybrid question answering in relational algebra. In Lun-Wei Ku, Andre Martins, and Vivek Srikumar, editors, *Findings of the Association for Computational Linguistics:*

ACL 2024, pages 453–466, Bangkok, Thailand, August 2024. Association for Computational Linguistics.
12. Stratos Idreos, Olga Papaemmanouil, and Surajit Chaudhuri. Overview of data exploration techniques. In *Proceedings of the 2015 ACM SIGMOD international conference on management of data*, pages 277–281, 2015.
13. Alicia Key, Bill Howe, Daniel Perry, and Cecilia Aragon. Vizdeck: self-organizing dashboards for visual analytics. In *Proceedings of the 2012 acm sigmod international conference on management of data*, pages 681–684, 2012.
14. ore Klisura and Anthony Rios. Unmasking database vulnerabilities: Zero-knowledge schema inference attacks in text-to-SQL systems. In Luis Chiruzzo, Alan Ritter, and Lu Wang, editors, *Findings of the Association for Computational Linguistics: NAACL 2025*, pages 6954–6976, Albuquerque, New Mexico, April 2025. Association for Computational Linguistics.
15. Gyubok Lee, Woosog Chay, Seonhee Cho, and Edward Choi. Trustsql: Benchmarking text-to-sql reliability with penalty-based scoring. *arXiv preprint arXiv:2403.15879*, 2024.
16. Chunwei Liu, Matthew Russo, Michael J. Cafarella, Lei Cao, Peter Baille Chen, Zui Chen, Michael J. Franklin, Tim Kraska, Samuel Madden, and Gerardo Vitagliano. A declarative system for optimizing ai workloads. *ArXiv*, abs/2405.14696, 2024.
17. Yan Liu, Yan Gao, Zhe Su, Xiaokang Chen, Elliott Ash, and Jian-Guang Lou. Uncovering and categorizing social biases in text-to-SQL. In Anna Rogers, Jordan Boyd-Graber, and Naoaki Okazaki, editors, *Proceedings of the 61st Annual Meeting of the Association for Computational Linguistics (Volume 1: Long Papers)*, pages 13573–13584, Toronto, Canada, July 2023. Association for Computational Linguistics.
18. Yuyu Luo, Xuedi Qin, Nan Tang, and Guoliang Li. Deepeye: Towards automatic data visualization. In *2018 IEEE 34th international conference on data engineering (ICDE)*, pages 101–112. IEEE, 2018.
19. Marta Marchiori Manerba, Karolina Stańczak, Riccardo Guidotti, and Isabelle Augenstein. Social bias probing: Fairness benchmarking for language models. *ArXiv*, abs/2311.09090, 2023.
20. Chandler May, Alex Wang, Shikha Bordia, Samuel R. Bowman, and Rachel Rudinger. On measuring social biases in sentence encoders. In Jill Burstein, Christy Doran, and Thamar Solorio, editors, *Proceedings of the 2019 Conference of the North American Chapter of the Association for Computational Linguistics: Human Language Technologies, Volume 1 (Long and Short Papers)*, pages 622–628, Minneapolis, Minnesota, June 2019. Association for Computational Linguistics.
21. Liana Patel, Siddharth Jha, Melissa Pan, Harshit Gupta, Parth Asawa, Carlos Guestrin, and Matei Zaharia. Semantic operators: A declarative model for rich, ai-based data processing. 2024.
22. Rodrigo Pedro, Daniel Castro, Paulo Carreira, and Nuno Santos. From prompt injections to sql injection attacks: How protected is your llm-integrated web application? *ArXiv*, abs/2308.01990, 2023.
23. Xutan Peng, Yipeng Zhang, Jingfeng Yang, and Mark Stevenson. On the vulnerabilities of text-to-sql models. *2023 IEEE 34th International Symposium on Software Reliability Engineering (ISSRE)*, pages 1–12, 2022.
24. Francesco Ricci, Lior Rokach, and Bracha Shapira. Introduction to recommender systems handbook. In *Recommender systems handbook*, pages 1–35. Springer, 2010.
25. Irina Saparina and Mirella Lapata. Ambrosia: A benchmark for parsing ambiguous questions into database queries. *Advances in Neural Information Processing Systems*, 37:90600–90628, 2024.
26. Thibault Sellam and Martin Kersten. Cluster-driven navigation of the query space. *IEEE Transactions on Knowledge and Data Engineering*, 28(5):1118–1131, 2016.
27. Thibault Sellam, Martin L Kersten, et al. Meet charles, big data query advisor. In *CIDR*, volume 13, pages 1–1, 2013.
28. Yanqi Song, Ruiheng Liu, Shu Chen, Qianhao Ren, Yu Zhang, and Yongqi Yu. SecureSQL: Evaluating data leakage of large language models as natural language interfaces to databases. In

Yaser Al-Onaizan, Mohit Bansal, and Yun-Nung Chen, editors, *Findings of the Association for Computational Linguistics: EMNLP 2024*, pages 5975–5990, Miami, Florida, USA, November 2024. Association for Computational Linguistics.

29. Nan Tang, Eugene Wu, and Guoliang Li. Towards democratizing relational data visualization. In *Proceedings of the 2019 International Conference on Management of Data*, pages 2025–2030, 2019.
30. Bing Wang, Yan Gao, Zhoujun Li, and Jian-Guang Lou. Know what I don't know: Handling ambiguous and unknown questions for text-to-SQL. In Anna Rogers, Jordan Boyd-Graber, and Naoaki Okazaki, editors, *Findings of the Association for Computational Linguistics: ACL 2023*, pages 5701–5714, Toronto, Canada, July 2023. Association for Computational Linguistics.
31. Jinchuan Zhang, Yan Zhou, Binyuan Hui, Yaxin Liu, Ziming Li, and Songlin Hu. Trojan-SQL: SQL injection against natural language interface to database. In Houda Bouamor, Juan Pino, and Kalika Bali, editors, *Proceedings of the 2023 Conference on Empirical Methods in Natural Language Processing*, pages 4344–4359, Singapore, December 2023. Association for Computational Linguistics.
32. Yusen Zhang, Xiangyu Dong, Shuaichen Chang, Tao Yu, Peng Shi, and Rui Zhang. Did you ask a good question? a cross-domain question intention classification benchmark for text-to-sql. *arXiv preprint arXiv:2010.12634*, 2020.

MIX
Papier aus verantwortungsvollen Quellen
Paper from responsible sources
FSC® C105338

If you have any concerns about our products,
you can contact us on
ProductSafety@springernature.com

In case Publisher is established outside the EU,
the EU authorized representative is:
Springer Nature Customer Service Center GmbH
Europaplatz 3, 69115 Heidelberg, Germany

Printed by Libri Plureos GmbH
in Hamburg, Germany